T0284810

LIES MY LIBERAL TEACHER TOLD ME

ALSO BY WILFRED REILLY

Taboo: 10 Facts You Can't Talk About

Hate Crime Hoax: How the Left Is Selling a Fake Race War

The $50,000,000 Question: An Engagingly Empirical Examination of the Relationship Between "Privilege" and Pride

LIES MY LIBERAL TEACHER TOLD ME

**Debunking the False Narratives
Defining America's School Curricula**

WILFRED REILLY

BROADSIDE BOOKS

LIES MY LIBERAL TEACHER TOLD ME. Copyright © 2024 by Wilfred Reilly. All rights reserved. Printed in the United States of America. No part of this book may be used or reproduced in any manner whatsoever without written permission except in the case of brief quotations embodied in critical articles and reviews. For information, address HarperCollins Publishers, 195 Broadway, New York, NY 10007.

HarperCollins books may be purchased for educational, business, or sales promotional use. For information, please email the Special Markets Department at SPsales@harpercollins.com.

Broadside Books™ and the Broadside logo are trademarks of HarperCollins Publishers.

FIRST EDITION

Designed by Michele Cameron

Library of Congress Cataloging-in-Publication Data
Names: Reilly, Wilfred, author.
Title: Lies my liberal teacher told me / Wilfred Reilly.
Description: First edition. | New York, NY : Broadside, [2024] | Includes
     bibliographical references and index.
Identifiers: LCCN 2023056273 (print) | LCCN 2023056274 (ebook) |
     ISBN 9780063265974 | ISBN 9780063265981 (digital)
Subjects: LCSH: United States—History—Study and teaching—
     Political aspects.
Classification: LCC E175.8 .R45 2024 (print) | LCC E175.8 (ebook) |
DDC 973.07—dc23/eng/20240117
LC record available at https://lccn.loc.gov/2023056273
LC ebook record available at https://lccn.loc.gov/2023056274

24 25 26 27 28 LBC 5 4 3 2 1

To Jean Marie Ward, and SNOO

It ain't what you don't know that gets you in trouble, youngster—it's what you know for sure that just ain't so.

—attributed to Mark Twain

CONTENTS

CONTENTS

INTRODUCTION

We often, bizarrely, hear the claim that American history is taught mostly from the political right—and that it presents our nation as bucolic.

In fact, many of the best-selling social science books of the past few decades focus on the idea that the "real" history of the United States was a virtually unending bloodbath. A short list of influential texts of this kind would have to include Marxist Howard Zinn's *A People's History of the United States*, Dee Brown's *Bury My Heart at Wounded Knee: An Indian History of the American West*, the *New York Times*–originating recent bestseller *The 1619 Project*, and . . . well . . . James W. Loewen's 1995 book *Lies My Teacher Told Me*. This entire body of work draws from and ties into the modern American obsession with racism.

A worthy topic of study, to be sure. But at some point the obvious needs to be said. The argument that the American intellectual class loves the country too much, and consistently slants its work product to the right, is insane. In reality, the contemporary U.S. national media and academic professorate lean roughly 93 percent to the *left*, and this has been the case for some time.[1] Within the secondary schools, two popular curricula currently in use come from the 1619 Project and Dr. Zinn himself.

If the old myth beloved of the Manifest Destiny fan club was that America and the West could do no wrong, the new hotness is that every wrong is uniquely Western and American. To read many leftist scholars, you'd come away thinking non-Western slavery was basically a fun vacation.

The opposite is true. The primary thing that was *unique* about slavery in the early modern West was that the nations of contemporary Europe and North America set out to end the practice globally, and largely did so.[2] British oceangoing fleets blockaded slaving ports around the world, sinking at least 1,600 slave ships and freeing 150,000 slaves—in what was explicitly an attempt to minimize or end the so-called peculiar institution.[3] Notably, in sizable nations of color where trod only briefly the Western galosh, slavery *still* often endures. The practice exists rather openly in Mauritania, and slavery/chattel serfdom was only banned in Saudi Arabia in the 1960s.[4]

The same historical myopia afflicts representations of European colonialism. Historical European colonialism (although, oddly, not Ottoman, Mongol, Arab Muslim, or Moorish colonialism) is today almost invariably described as an unmitigated evil. Meanwhile, the facts are more complicated. There is little if any evidence that states that were never colonized—think Liberia, Ethiopia, and Thailand—are on average better off today than those that were (India, Nigeria, Indonesia, Kenya, etc.).

I am clearly not arguing that these bloody wars of conquest were free of hypocrisy and what we would today consider injustice. But this brings us to a key point, which serves as something of a central theme for this book. Modern American morality is an aberration. If we don't understand that, then history will be nothing but one long shock to our naive systems.

The past is a foreign country, as the saying goes, with its own laws and customs. We'd be wise to familiarize ourselves with those rules before we go adventuring. The reality is that international law defending things like human rights and individual liberty and opposing wars of aggression is a distinctly modern concept. The right to conquest was only banned by an international body after World War Two. (And if we're honest, "neutral" international bodies often spend most of their time obscuring how seldom non-Western countries actually follow said international law today.)

In addition to applying our standards to the past, leftist teachers often try to argue that messy reality *should* have rather been more like impossibly pure alternative. But history isn't a choice between a bad present and a perfect hypothetical—all actions must be compared to their real-world alternatives and not to what might occur in Utopia. This isn't convenient for a leftist view of history. In their minds, all non-white peoples lived as noble savages in enlightened Gardens of Eden, before being corrupted by contact with grubby foreign invaders.

In reality, almost all areas of the world that were conquered by the West were previously under the thumb—or the boot-heel—of brutal and unelected "Native rulers," often external conquerors themselves. The previous ruling power across most of British India was the Turko-Mongol Moghul Empire, which imposed the state religion of Sunni Islam on the Indian subcontinent (if lightly) and taxed peasants at roughly half the value of their annual crop.[5] The choice for most Nigerians was between the redcoated rule of the Britishers and the Black Muslim Sokoto Caliphate— then the second-largest slave power in the world.[6]

There is, of course, a caveat here: something to add on to any truly accurate discussion of the American and human past. The fact that "everybody did X" virtually throughout history—that the great Native nations were easily as brutal to captives and women as their white opponents, slavery was a global practice since before Sargon of Akkad, whipping at the post was legal in the United States (for whites as well as beautiful POC) until 1972, etc.—does not mean that the things everyone did were *good*, or even okay.

For most ordinary people living through history, war for conquest was normal but brutal, whichever end of the gun you happened to be on. What most people cared about was what society looked like when the gun smoke cleared. For such people, Western societies were often the best bad option. That doesn't mean that Western conquerors were always "right" to conquer, or that they weren't often hypocrites even by their own loose standards. However, although normal isn't the same as good (when it comes to history or any other topic), it's important to be aware of norms because they determine the scale and tenor of our judgment of the past.

Per the moral standards virtually all of us profess to believe in today, enslaving your enemies is bad, even though it happened under colonizers in every shade of the human rainbow.* Breaking treaties that were based upon your sworn word, to pick just one sin common across the races and ages, is *bad*. But. The fact that almost literally no one alive prior to—say, again—the 1950s in the West shared modern dorm-room morality is critical to know, for many reasons. First, Westerners should temper their hysterical guilt about the past. The bad things that "we" did were in most cases done by all humans with the power to do them—the Arab Muslims, the horse-lord Mongols, the "Black" Moors, the Ottomans, the Aztecs—during eras when they were legally and ethically accepted as norms.

Second, we shouldn't be embarrassed of good things just because they're done by the "wrong" people. The unique contribution of the West to the Rest, as in the cases of the maritime slave trade or central African cannibalism, was very often ending the practices that today we all find repellent, or pretend to. This point is not only obviously accurate and sweeping in scope but also relevant specifically to our debates today about "compensations" for the past, such as slavery reparations—any serious plan for which would logically have to target the hood-rich Arab states, rising BRICS powers of Africa, and anyone else (bourgeois Scandinavian descendants of Vikings?) linked to the multicentury global trade in women and men.

Throughout this book I'll tackle the question of why liberal teachers teach common historical myths. But I'll also ask why they've been so vulnerable to ideological capture and the blinders of fashionable fallacies in the first place. How did we get here? Isn't studying history supposed to prevent repeating it? Apparently not.

Understanding the brutal reality of human nature and history has huge implications for the future. Most notably, we should recognize that all of the great heroes of *this* era are flawed human beings, who will be judged as such down the road by our descen-

---

* Although, to be fair, the Chinese Uighur Muslims who made your smartphone might silently chuckle to hear that said.

dants. Martin Luther King, for example, was in today's terms an obvious plagiarist, unrepentant sexist, and extreme homophobe.

Does that mean we should tear down his statues, along with those of similar men of the near-past (Kennedy? Patton?), because we have achieved ethical perfection today? Of course not. King, while imperfect, was rather obviously one of the greatest men in our nation's long history. And, no doubt, he would—as our own children almost certainly will—have had some tart comments of his own about the current United States' penchant for OnlyFans and commercialized abortion and drone warfare.

History's true lesson to us is a simpler and wiser one than "break all the icons." Perfection is impossible (and the pursuit of it often indeed the enemy of the good), close approaches to it are rare, and any guilt about things that one has not personally done is the profoundest sort of folly. Let us avoid folly, and instead engage the past, learn from it—and keep moving forward.

LIES MY LIBERAL TEACHER TOLD ME

LIE #1

"Brutal 'True' Slavery Was Virtually Unique to America and the West"

Modern histories tend to rely heavily on the new ideological pieties of left-wing activists. First among these is the belief that we live in a totally corrupt and oppressive society . . . in fact, in the world's *most* oppressive and corrupt society.

The very first popular lie on deck may be the most widely accepted—at least, within the modern Western world—and the most facially and obviously wrong of the lot. It draws from this activist-led, blinkered view of America's history, a sort of all-negative "American exceptionalism." Slavery is frequently described as the United States' "original sin" in major media articles and academic courses,[1] and it is even alleged to have been uniquely evil as practiced within the United States.[2]

One major American textbook resource, *The Unfinished Nation*, describes enslaved people in African and other slave systems as having been kept unfree only for a "fixed term" and as retaining major rights, "including the right to marry."[3] Allegedly, their children generally did not "inherit their parents' condition of bondage," unlike the children of slaves in the United States. Another text (*Traditions and Encounters*), while providing a fairly nuanced view overall, appears to describe the Western-dominated slave trade as the largest and most brutal in history, calling even the full sweep of Arab/Islamic slavery "smaller than the Atlantic slave trade of modern times."[4]

The 1619 Project's Nikole Hannah-Jones, who has also posited that the Revolutionary War was fought primarily to protect the peculiar institution and that "almost everything . . . unique" about the States grew out of slavery,[5] argues bluntly: "America's brutal system of slavery [was] unlike anything that had existed in the world before. Enslaved people were . . . property that could be mortgaged, traded, bought, sold, used as collateral, given as a gift, and disposed of violently."[6]

This take has become increasingly prominent within the modern American educational environment. "1619" has a formal curriculum.[7] Contained within this view are a number of unexamined assumptions about historical attitudes. Modern Americans tend to project our positive values back into the past while thinking that our sins are uniquely bad. What we don't understand is that contemporary Western beliefs about human dignity, inalienable rights, a right to freedom, etc., are the exception, not the norm. If they seem like the norm today, that is largely because we have remade much of the world in our image.

In reality, as conservative éminence grise Thomas Sowell says in the "Slavery" chapter of his book *Black Rednecks and White Liberals* (2005), it is probably fair to say that most Westerners think of historical slavery almost entirely in the context of Western white oppression of Blacks during what is technically known as the Atlantic Slave Trade. Almost nothing could be further from empirical truth: American slavery was not unprecedented, it was not uniquely brutal, and it did not invent any new oppressive systems. It was terrible, but talking about it as if it came out of nowhere means we understand less about history and about global norms. Slavery was ubiquitous throughout the ancient and historical world—often the step of human "development" after simply killing and eating one's defeated foemen.

Contrary to modern romantic notions that our earliest human

beliefs were those of love and innocence, quite literally the oldest human legal codes consist in large part of rules governing the care, feeding, and beating of slaves and other "human property." In an article for the prestigious *Chicago-Kent Law Review* (and in other venues),[8] Dr. Raymond Westbrook of Johns Hopkins University revealed how pervasive slavery was in truly ancient times, i.e., during the period between 2,500 BC, "when the earliest legal documents concerning slavery were found," and the conquest of much of the Middle East by Alexander the Great in the fourth century BC.

In his article, Westbrook blandly notes that slavery was a focus of all three major varieties of ancient law that he examines: "law codes, royal edicts, and documents of practice." His sources include virtually all the better-known legal documents—and legally inscribed rocks and boulders—from his era of study, among them the Code of Ur-Nammu from the primeval human city of Ur, the Code of Lipit-Ishtar "from Isin in . . . Mesopotamia," the Laws of Eshnunna from the eponymous Mesopotamian city, the famous Code of Hammurabi, the compiled "Hittite laws" from the Anatolian region, the Middle Assyrian Laws (or "MAL") from Ashur, and the Covenant Code and Deuteronomic Code from the Old Testament of the Bible.

Across every significant empire of the Bronze Age and Iron Age world, "namely Egypt, Babylonia, Assyria, Mitanni, and Hatti," slavery was extremely common and recognized in statute.

One reason for the ubiquity of slavery was that it provided an alternative to a marginally more brutal practice: the slaughter of prisoners of war. All of these ancient peoples recognized multiple legal sources of human chattel, the most prominent of which was war. As Westbrook bluntly states, "foreigners captured in war were booty" per virtually all ancient law and "could be dealt with as the captor saw fit." More than two millennia before today's Geneva Conventions, members of defeated armies or raiding forces could expect to be treated brutally—with their potential fates including not only enslavement but plain massacre, physical and sexual abuse before being ransomed back to their own society, and relocation onto unknown areas of the victor's demesne as serf labor.

Potentially dangerous male military prisoners were often enslaved, but they might instead simply be killed or blinded "as a security measure," while female captives who were "more suited for private domestic service" (as the author discreetly puts it) were almost invariably kept around. Neither group seems to have generally been in short supply: in Sumer there was at one point so much slave raiding between the people of the various city-states and the highland tribes from the surrounding hill country that the ideographic symbols for "slave/slave woman" and "man/woman from the mountains" were identical. One of the very first written human words, then, was "slave."

Slaves could also be taken domestically: Sumerian and ancient Babylonian law discuss "contracts of sale into slavery for debt," and not a few weary travelers and unpopular relatives—as discussed in the tale of Joseph and his brothers in the Bible—seem simply to have been knocked over the head and sold at regional markets. "The safest course was to sell the kidnap victim abroad," Westbrook dryly notes.

Contra a bizarre trend toward describing the historical enslavement of non-Blacks as somehow mild or "not really" slavery, chattel slavery in the ancient world was brutal for people of all races. The legal codes mentioned so far prescribe barbaric penalties for escaped or rebellious slaves, including "blinding" and "branding." While this varied across societies, slavery was also often hereditary and generational. Westbrook notes that, in multiple Babylonian documents describing the sale of slaves, it is mentioned that an enslaved person was "'house born' (*wilid bitim*)" or "born on the roof." He suspects that those terms refer to children conceived between a master and his slaves or between two slaves, all of whom would have been the legal property of the master. Similarly, Neo-Sumerian court records prominently include the case of an individual who claimed to be a free citizen "but was proved to have been born in [a] late master's house as the son of a slave" and was thus given as property to the sons of the dead man.

Popular memory of ancient Greece paints a dignified picture of austere philosophical principles and pure white statues. But actual ancient Greek statues were garishly painted, and the "freedom-loving" Greeks were no better than their regional predecessors when it came to slavery. In fact, they operated one of the more famous slave systems in world history.[9] No less a thinker than Aristotle wrote up a famous defense of chattel slavery and—as a current critic notes—"believed that being enslaved was just and even beneficial for many people."[10]

One piece discussing this, on a popular if short-form philosophy blog, opens by discussing context: in ancient Greek city-states like Athens, Corinth, and Sparta, "slaves were not citizens, and they considerably out-numbered male citizens." Here, too, "slavery was hereditary" and voluntary manumission—the good-faith freeing of slaves by an owner or master—almost never took place. Slaves were considered expensive property, like a fine vase or a jug of aged fish sauce. The legendary Greek wrote as a man of this world.

His arguments in defense of slavery begin with the baseline idea that the laws and norms within a society should reflect the natural state of affairs for human beings. So a city or state can justly engage in chattel slavery if there exist "some people who are . . . naturally suited to be slaves." Aristotle argues that such human beings not only exist but are common: at one point he contends that anyone lacking the full "capacity for rational deliberation" is a "natural slave." On another occasion he claims that the very bodies of slaves and free citizens are usually different, with slaves looking strong and well suited for brute labor and free people dangerous with weapons but "unsuited for that kind of work." Unsurprisingly, these attitudes grew out of the political realities of Aristotle's time: slaves in historical Athens were often burly captured barbarians or Persians and the like, unable to reason well in Greek. In practice, the philosopher is saying that essentially all non-Greek peoples are natural slaves, a convenient alignment of philosophical deduction with personal prejudice.

While we obviously cannot know how many Greeks accepted Aristotle's exact arguments, a great deal of reliable information survives concerning the size of the historical Greek slave population and the treatment of slaves during the pre-Roman city-state era in Greece. Most sources note that slavery was "universally accepted" and almost never challenged *as an institution* in the Hellenic world. Most Greeks grew to adulthood with enslaved people around them, brought them along on business or military trips, and not infrequently formed "a kind of friendship with them." Those masters who felt that slaveholders were generally too cruel—and there were some—would generally attempt to treat their own slaves "humanely and kindly" rather than trying to topple the institution itself. Dr. Robert Garland, in a lecture for the Great Courses, accurately notes that "even the greatest thinkers could not imagine a world free of slavery . . . owning a car is the modern-day equivalent of owning a slave."[11]

And automobile-based societies tend to have a lot of cars. Like virtually everything else, the exact number of slaves in ancient Greece is disputed within academia. However, there is no doubt it was empirically quite large. Historian and researcher Paul Cartledge, who has produced one of the more reliable estimates by "comparing data from modern slave societies like Brazil, the Caribbean, and the Antebellum South," pegs the total Greek slave population at between 80,000 and 100,000 people at any given time. Since the entire rolling population of classical ancient Greece between 450 and 320 BC was on the order of 2.5 million people, this would mean that roughly "one in four of the people" in at least larger Greek cities like Athens were unfree men and women.

Like Mesopotamian slavery, Greek slavery was harsh. As we have already noted, it was hereditary in nature—and this was in fact one of the most common features of chattel slavery worldwide. And while not all masters were invariably brutal to their slaves at all times, any master could simply decide to become so at any point.

As Garland notes, ancient Greek slaves had essentially no "human or civil rights." They could be subjected to torture for a variety of reasons outlined in Greek law, beaten at will, abused into "confessing to their own guilt or incriminat[ing] someone else" when their owners became involved in lawsuits, and often "forced to have sexual relationships without consent." Garland states simply, "They were just properties, like a table or a chair. The only difference was that they were living things." Such was the reality of slavery, worldwide and across all nations and races.

Such was certainly the reality of slavery in *la Rome antique*. As was so often true, the ancient Romans were morally no better or worse than their Greek predecessors when it came to slavery but operated on a larger scale. In a fascinatingly technical essay titled "Demography, Geography and the Sources of Roman Slaves,"[12] William Harris of Columbia says that Roman slaves—again, generally held in hereditary bondage—came from a whole variety of sources.

Among these were: "(1) children born to slave mothers within the Empire, (2) persons enslaved in provincial or frontier wars, (3) persons imported across the frontiers, (4) the 'self-enslaved,'* and (5) infants abandoned at places within the Empire." He estimates the Roman slave population at between approximately 16 percent and 20 percent of the entire Imperial Roman population of roughly 60 million people "on the eve of the Antonine plague"—meaning that between 9.6 million and 12 million individuals within Roman lands were slaves.

Although he largely disagrees with this thesis, Dr. Harris notes that many academics believe "the fertility of the existing slave population itself" was the largest single wellspring of Roman slaves, "at least five or six times as important as any other source." If true, this in essence means the Romans did exactly what the worst Southern slave masters did: maintain largely unwilling breeding populations of human beings in order to source unlimited free labor from them.

---

* This category would include, for example, debtors.

And even the skeptical Harris notes openly that the Romans appear to have understood an entire twisted science of what we might call human husbandry or stockbreeding. At one point he quotes Xenophon saying—through the heroic character Ischomachus—that "good slaves generally become more loyal when they have children, but when the bad ones form sexual relationships they become more likely to misbehave." Slave families were allowed or shattered in accordance with this principle, per all contemporary accounts, with submissive "good slaves" more likely to be allowed to reproduce.

Unsurprisingly, in this context, Roman slaves were treated as or more harshly than Greek ones. Harris states openly that there is a "long and tiresome tradition" among academics of minimizing the brutality of classical slavery (often while emphasizing the abuses of white-on-Black New World slavery: he cites Toni Morrison's *Beloved* in passing), but that such "takes" are simply inaccurate. Beyond Greece, "even the extremely unpleasant world" of the Caribbean of the 1700s was probably nowhere near as brutal as the slavery of the pre-Christian Roman Empire, which allowed for open torture and literal gladiatorial combat against lions and tigers. In the antebellum United States and the non-mainland British possessions, there were "slave codes aimed at limiting the exploitation of slave labor," while no close analogue existed in Rome. Simply put, Harris concludes, Roman views of enslaved persons and their health were "generally harder than those of Caribbean and North American slave owners."

Part of the reason scholars minimize these realities is the contemporary belief that oppressed people and oppressors are totally distinct classes of people and have always been so. The only reason we're able to keep this fiction in place is, ironically, because of our history's Eurocentric focus. Claims like those made in *The 1619 Project* are only possible if we focus on Western history to the exclusion of the vast swath of non-Western brutality.

Even should we leave Rome, Greece, and Babylon aside as examples of the horrors of historical slavery—although I see no particular reason to do so—we find that the more familiar African slave trade also stretched back over millennia, involving conflicts and emancipations that have often been forgotten for centuries in the West. Roughly 1,200 years ago, for example, the Zanj wars were fought (largely) between Arabs and slaves from civilized regions of West Africa and devastated much of modern-day Iraq. Broadly speaking, the Zanj rebels were members of Black African tribes who had been captured in Africa following military defeats or raids by Arab slave traders and who were subsequently forced to labor for Arab masters in blistering southern Iraq.

Even by Mississippi standards, a plantation in the Iraqi south—no longer home to the Garden of Eden—was a miserable place to work shirtless in the summer. Zanj workers were frequently given Sisyphean tasks like removing and replacing all the over-salinated topsoil on large farms; others worked in 110-to-120-degree conditions to drain the salt marshes near the modern city of Basra.[13] Contemporary sources, along with historical Arab ones, state the obvious: "Their conditions were extremely bad. Their labour [sic] was hard and exacting, and they received only a bare and inadequate keep consisting—according to the Arabic sources—of flour, semolina, and dates."[14] Under a variety of charismatic and soon-dead leaders, the captured African warriors tried to rebel against these "appalling conditions" at least twice (via organized raids from AD 688 to 690, and a more organized rebellion under "the Lion of the Zanj" in 694) before the conflict generally called the Zanj War,[15] but were broken and shoved back into the salt marshes on both occasions.*

The Zanj War caused destruction on a truly epic, modern scale. Contemporary estimates of the death toll during the fourteen-year conflict generally range between 500,000 and 2.5 million permanent casualties. While describing this figure as probably "exaggerated," the Western writer Silvestre de Sacy notes that: "Fakhr-eddin reports the same facts . . . it is claimed that 2,500,000 men perished

---

* As these dates indicate, Zanj slavery—like virtually all other large-scale systems of human chattel slavery—was long-lasting and generally hereditary.

in the war." The Arab writer Al-Masūdī provides the lower-end figure of half a million casualties (noting that 300,000 men were likely killed just in the single Battle of Basra).[16] There seems general agreement that the war devastated much of the countryside through which it was fought: "Its consequences must long have continued to be felt, and it can hardly be doubted that the cities and regions of the lower Tigris never entirely recovered from the injuries which they at that time suffered," reads one summary.[17]

Remarkably, the story of this massive and bloody war, which lasted more than fourteen years and killed perhaps a million human beings (before being almost forgotten today), is little more than a footnote to the full tale of the millennium-long Arab slave trade. As one academic writer quoted in an article for Germany's Deutsche Welle notes,[18] the Arab trade in enslaved Africans "can be traced back to antiquity." The trade became widespread in the AD 600s as Islamic power grew in the Middle East and North Africa, "seven centuries before Europeans explored [Africa] and ten centuries before West Africans were sold across the Atlantic to America," and it endured until the modern era.

By almost every metric, the Arab slave trade was larger in scale than the white-dominated Atlantic slave trade. The well-regarded Senegalese scholar Tidiane N'Diaye has argued that at least 17 million Africans were sold into Arab slavery, with 8 million or so shipped from Eastern Africa to the Islamic world "via the Trans-Saharan route to Morocco or Egypt," and 9 million more "deported to regions on the Red Sea or the Indian Ocean"—then both largely Arab lakes.[*]

And while it is difficult and a bit tasteless to compare these things, the Arab trade was by all accounts as brutal or more so than its Western counterpart. The best academic research on point has concluded that "about three out of four slaves died" before

---

[*] A "low-end" alternative estimate of the scope of the Arab slave trade is provided by *Traditions & Encounters* (see endnotes); the authors peg it as having involved up to 10 million Africans alone between AD 750 and 1500.

ever reaching their destination and being sold into bondage, from
causes including starvation, sickness, and plain "exhaustion after
long journeys." It was also longer-lasting than Western slavery,
with slavery not being (formally) banned in the fairly typical Arab
port of Zanzibar until 1873 and not abolished across Muslim East
Africa until 1909.

Some Arab and Afro-Asiatic slave traders—almost all of whom,
obviously, would have been Black or Muslim "people of color"—
achieved legendary status during their eras and are remembered
today. Probably most notable among these merchants of life was
Hamad ibn Muhammad ibn Jum'ah ibn Rajab ibn Muhammad
ibn Sa'īd al Murjabī—better known as Tippu Tip. A Black man
himself, in any normal sense of that term, Tip was also the most
powerful and widely known slave trader in Africa for most of the
period between his birth in 1832 and death in 1905, supplying
much of the world with Black slaves.[19]

Born in Zanzibar to parents of Arab and Bantu heritage, and
later nicknamed after the "tip-u-tip-u-tip" sound that his guns
made during a war against the Chungu tribe, Tip began raiding
into the African interior as a young man—by the 1850s at latest.[20]
Living a full and adventurous life if not a good one, from that point
forward, he became one of Africa's most notable historical figures.
The famous trader met both Dr. Livingstone and Henry Stanley,[21]
building up a private army that included thousands of men and
drew frequent allegations of cannibalism,[22] and at one point conquering the entire eastern Congo region in his own name and that
of the sultan of Zanzibar.

Tip had no particular problem doing business with, fighting, or
indeed selling Europeans as well as Blacks: no bigot, he. Following
an agreement between his own Sultan—Barghash bin Said of
Zanzibar—and the mad European king Leopold of Belgium, he
served briefly as governor of the Stanley Falls subdistrict in Belgium's
Congo Free State, and he was involved in the bloody Congo-Arab
War, where Europeans and Arabs fought primarily by means of
African proxy forces. When he finally retired, he wrote a darkly

hilarious autobiography: one of the first prominent African examples of that genre and apparently the first ever written in Swahili.[23]
And, he retired as a very rich man: by 1895, Tip had already come
to control seven large plantation farms and thousands of slaves, in
addition to his force of fighting men. He died in 1905 in the "Stone
Town" core of Zanzibar—old, famous, very rich, evil, and beloved.[24]

The "Tippu Tip" story of powerful whites and Blacks working
together to sell less powerful people of all shades would have struck
almost no one as unusual for the large majority of the history of
the slave trade. There was in fact—for centuries—a regional slave
trade focused entirely on the sale of white battle captives to Arab
and Black Muslim masters: the Barbary slave trade. Ohio State's
Robert Davis estimates that Muslim "Barbary" raiders from the
North African coast enslaved "about 850,000 captives over the century from 1580 to 1680," and "easily" as many as 1.25 million between 1530 and 1780.[25]

Interestingly, these figures probably represent significant
*under*estimates of the white slave population in the Near East.
Davis analyzes primarily the impact of slave raiding from modern Algeria, Libya, and Tunisia, and his numbers apparently do
not include Europeans seized in the Mediterranean or Black Seas
by other Muslim naval powers. Using imperial Turkish customs
records, another source—the *Cambridge World History of Slavery*—
estimates that between two and three million mostly European
slaves were shipped into the Ottoman Empire from the Black Sea
region alone between the mid-1400s and the start of the eighteenth
century.[26] In this context, it is hard to avoid agreeing with Davis
that—for whatever reason—many historians today "minimize the
impact of Barbary slaving . . . [and] the scope of corsair piracy."[27]

Barbary slavers were famously ruthless and daring—launching
military-scale raids on European cities on more than one occasion.
In 1544, the legendary Caucasian Muslim Hayreddin Barbarossa
("the Red Beard") captured both the sizable island town of Ischia
and the city of Lipari, enslaving approximately 1,500 Christian Europeans in the first strike and between 2,000 and 3,000 in the

second.[28] Just seven years later, in 1551, another Muslim raider—Dragut or "Turgut Reis"—conquered the island of Gozo and sold the entire population as slaves: shipping 5,000 to 6,000 Europeans into the Ottoman Empire as chattels.[29]

During just the years 1609 to 1616, "no fewer than 466" British merchant vessels were boarded and taken over by Barbary pirates during maritime battles or slashing longshore raids, with almost all captured sailormen and passengers sold as slaves.[30] Even the United States, half a world away, suffered at the hands of these slavers of color: the phrase "to the shores of Tripoli" in the Marine Corps Hymn refers to a punitive mission launched by President Jefferson following repeated and brutal North African attacks on Yankee shipping.[31]

Amazingly—to someone raised on modern curricula—totals from the Barbary era represent only a small percentage of those white Europeans enslaved by Muslim or African oppressors throughout history. Even leaving racially diverse Rome and her hordes of unfree people and the million-plus western European victims of Barbary raiders aside, the very word "slave" derives from "Slav"—the ethnic demonym for proud but historically "backward" whites occupying eastern Europe, millions of whom were sold into bondage over the centuries by Muslims and others.[32] Across the sweep of time, from Athens to Istanbul, it is far from impossible that more whites than Blacks have been enslaved.

Even inside the future United States in, say, the year 1619, the picture of human bondage was more complex than is generally recognized. Obviously, most if not all American chattel slaves were Black. However, as books like *White Cargo* have outlined in painful detail, white indentured servants—"slaves of war" from Ireland and the like—were often no more excited about their new country, or willing to work for free absent physical persuasion, than the captured Africans they labored alongside.[33] Perhaps more to the point, many North American slave-*masters* were also Black: free Blacks were permitted by law to own Black slaves and indeed white indentures. Many did so: the first slave owner in the area that would become the United States was in fact probably African American.

Anthony Johnson, a former Angolan who went on to become a well-off Black pioneer and family head in the United States, was captured by Portuguese fighters in Africa and sold in indenture to a white farmer named Bennett following his voyage to Virginia.[34] Notably, Johnson was sold as an indenturee because Virginia did not allow legal chattel slavery at this time and would not for decades to come. Over the next ten years or so, he survived a major Indian raid, married a Black woman named Mary who arrived a few boats later, and paid off his indenture contract—after which he was given a fifty-acre homestead by the colonial authorities as a potentially productive future citizen.[35]

As a farmer, Johnson rapidly acquired un-free workers of his own. By the early 1650s, he had purchased the indenture-service contracts of five bond-servants and "import[ed] [these] servants into the colony, for which he was granted 250 acres of land in Northampton County." Over the years, Johnson seems to have commanded a multiracial mix of white and Black bondsmen— importantly including one man named John Casor. In the year 1653, Casor came to the attention of the justice system, after he approached local leader Captain Samuel Goldsmith and declared that he was being falsely imprisoned: held illegally by Johnson despite the expiration of his indenture term some seven years earlier.

Johnson contested this claim, bringing a lawsuit (*Johnson v. Parker*, 1654) directed at a neighbor of Johnson's named Robert Parker, who had given Casor work and a place to stay while the matter was worked out. The courts initially found for Parker and Casor on the grounds that Virginia did not have slave laws and indenture contracts could not be binding past their expiration date. However, Johnson then *appealed* the case, and in 1655 the court not only "ordered Casor returned to Johnson" but also levied the judgment "that Casor was Johnson's servant for life, that is, his slave."

The unhappy Casor was returned to his former master. This case, to a very significant extent, laid the foundation for all chattel slavery in the future USA. It was the first time there'd been a judicial determination in the Thirteen Colonies that a person who had committed no crime could be enslaved for life, and John Casor is thus considered to have been the first person consigned to chattel slavery by the colonial justice system.[36] The first true American slave owner, very probably, was a Black man with African roots.*

Importantly, slave ownership was not a vice confined to Old World peoples (of whatever color). In addition to the staggering and almost impressive Aztec and Maya atrocities discussed elsewhere in this book, Native North American and Mesoamerican tribes almost all enslaved captured Native opponents—and later came to extend the same courtesy to white battle captives and purchased African Americans. While some of these individuals were treated almost as replacement members of the tribe, others were tortured to death after a few months or years of brutal captivity. Further, plain chattel slavery of a variety more recognizable to Westerners existed across today's Alaska, most of Canada, and the Pacific Northwest states, practiced by powerful tribes like the warlike Haida.[37]

When captured Africans began to arrive in North America, many tribes—notably the "Five Civilized Tribes" of the American Southeast—transitioned rapidly from intra-Indigenous to Black slavery. The United States' preeminent Native slaveholders were probably the members of the powerful Cherokee (Keetoowah) Nation, who increased their slave population from 600 in 1809 to 1,600 in 1835 and roughly 4,000 by 1860–61.[38] While these numbers might strike a casual observer as low, it is worth recalling that the population of the United States was below 5.5 million people in the census year of 1800[39] and that the same-year figures for the entire Cherokee population were respectively 12,400 (1809), 16,400 (1835) and 21,000 (1860). It seems fair to describe the Cherokee Nation as

---

* He was hardly alone for long. As several excellent books—notably Larry Koger's *Black Slaveowners: Free Black Slave Masters in South Carolina, 1790–1860*—have demonstrated, free Blacks and *gens de color* owned slaves almost proportionally in multiple Southern states during the antebellum era. As Koger documents, there were hundreds of Black slave owners in South Carolina alone.

having been at least as much of a slave state as the white-led Confederacy: 19 percent of all persons living in Cherokee territory by
1860 were enslaved Blacks,* and approximately 10 percent of all
families there "held others in slavery."

Even the official Constitution of the Cherokee Nation, ratified
in 1827, mentions Black slavery several times and imposed harsh
restrictions on enslaved people. According to scholar Tony Seybert,
"the 1827 Cherokee Constitution disallowed [among other things]
the ownership of property by the enslaved" or their multiracial children, "the buying of goods from enslaved people," and allowing
slaves to consume alcohol (masters were fined heavily when this
happened). It also forbade all marriages between Black slaves and
whites or Natives, and barred even free Black residents of Cherokee
lands from voting in any local or national election. While Seybert
points out that the Cherokee document did not include specific
clauses dealing with the punishment of slave revolts, and argues
more broadly that Native masters were kinder than white ones
in some respects, there seems no doubt that these Native North
Americans understood human bondage quite well.

And the Cherokee were hardly alone. The other mighty Civilized
Tribes exploited the slave system to nearly the same extent, with
the Choctaw and their Chickasaw allies alone "hold[ing] over 5,000
Blacks in slavery by 1860." This plain historical fact of common,
brutal Native American slaveholding is so undisputed—among
serious people—that some writers have argued it "complicates"
the standard narratives around anti-Native atrocities like the Trail
of Tears. "When you think of the Trail," says *Smithsonian* magazine's Ryan P. Smith, in a reported piece on a symposium at the
National Museum of the American Indian, you probably envision
"a long procession of suffering Cherokee Indians forced westward
by a villainous Andrew Jackson."[40] The symposium, which focused

---

* This figure assumes that enslaved Black residents of Cherokee territory were
counted as part of the general population of 21,000 there. If they were not, 16
percent of all residents were Black slaves.

on "intersectional African-American and Native American history," posited that this imagined vision was too simplistic. A historically literate observer of the same imaginary tableau might guess that the Indian removal federal policy "was not simply the vindictive scheme of Andrew Jackson, but rather a popularly endorsed, congressionally sanctioned campaign spanning the administrations of nine separate presidents."

What you most likely do *not* imagine, the Smithsonian summarized, "are Cherokee slaveholders . . . [and] the numerous African-American slaves, Cherokee-owned, who made the brutal march themselves, or else were shipped en masse to what is now Oklahoma . . . by their wealthy Indian masters." However, that ugly latter image would have depicted one of the most obvious and striking realities of the Trail: Civilized Tribes Natives owned tens of thousands of slaves, and most of them were frog-marched to the Middle West by their owners. Comanche author and museum curator Paul Chaat Smith, quoted in the *Smithsonian* piece, points out that "the . . . tribes were deeply committed to slavery, established their own racialized Black codes, immediately reestablished slavery when they arrived in Indian territory, rebuilt their nations with slave labor, and enthusiastically sided with the Confederacy in the Civil War."

That last line is worth repeating, for the 1619-educated innocents of today: at least part of the reason the U.S. government was so ruthless with the great Southeastern Native nations during this 1850s–1860s era of history was that many of them spoke openly in support of the Southern cause—*and fought with the Confederacy when the Civil War began.* Given the earlier removal campaigns, the Natives of the Five Civilized Tribes somewhat understandably hated the U.S. government, so any revolt against it would have struck many of them as good. But they also probably aligned with the Confederacy's pro-slavery goals. And while the highly intelligent chiefs of these tribes had few illusions about the Confederacy, all sources so far indicate that they saw this much smaller and less cohesive potential nation as easier to manipulate and work within.

Human behavior of this kind is often driven by complex amoral motives, a point that the experts cited in the *Smithsonian* piece make over and over again. They note that Native slaveholding was not generally accompanied by complex rationalizations or agonies of guilt: Native masters owned slaves for the same reasons white ones did: because they could, and they thought they would gain a practical advantage from doing so.

Notably, whites, Natives, and the many free Black slaveholders all saw slaves as symbols of financial and personal achievement: "The more slaves you owned, the more serious a businessperson you were . . . and the more serious a businessperson you were, the fitter you were to join the ranks of 'civilized' society." Slaves also, obviously, could be made to work fairly hard for free. As several of the authors discussing ancient Greece noted earlier in this chapter, their purchase was seen essentially as an investment—on the same order as buying an ox team, or one of the odd new mechanical tractors just coming to the market. Cherokee slave buyers were not somehow confused or misled: "They were willful and determined oppressors of blacks they owned, enthusiastic participants in a global economy driven by cotton."

Following this point, the *Smithsonian* piece goes on to make an absolutely essential observation about history and historical analysis, summarizing Paul Chaat Smith and Harvard professor Tyra Miles's argument: "American history is explained poorly by modern morality but effectively by simple economics and power dynamics." This thesis, while obviously true, is rarely stated so bluntly, and often seems nearly taboo to express in public. However, as Paul Chaat Smith points out, it is indisputable that human beings have been imperfect and incentive-driven in every era of history and that the generally accepted "moral" rules in the past were very different from those today—making it not merely silly but bizarre to judge rationally behaving historical figures by the standards of today.

"Andrew Jackson had a terrible Indian policy *and* radically expanded American democracy," he points out. Similarly, the great Cherokee chief John Ross "was a skillful leader . . . but also a man who deeply believed in and practiced the enslavement of black people." For almost all of history, an understanding of rather brutal rules of engagement ("*Vae victis*") governed the behavior of virtually all human beings alive on earth—and Arabs, West Africans, East Africans, Asians (whom we have yet even to discuss in depth), and Native Americans were no more an exception to this than were white Europeans.

If this is true—and it is—a valid question to ask is: Then what made the modern Western world unique when it came to slavery? The simple if unpopular answer is: Ending the practice *of* slavery. It was not keeping captured enemies or plantation serfs in bondage that made the West stand out historically—those practices were universal—but rather letting them go.

With all due respect to the brave slave rebels of Haiti or the occasional philosopher within the long Chinese and Indian intellectual traditions, "emancipation"—the widespread belief that people who are not themselves enslaved should vigorously oppose the entire institution of slavery—seems to have been a distinctively and almost uniquely Western idea. Whether it reflected relatively early European industrialization or a rare but genuine escape from human amorality, the freeing of most of the slave population of the earth was a Western (and Christian) triumph. Historian Philip D. Morgan writes in a collection of essays from the Organization of American Historians:

> Unlike other previous forms of slavery, the New World version did not decline over a long period but came to a rather abrupt end. The age of emancipation lasted a little over one hundred years: beginning in 1776 with the first antislavery society in Philadelphia, through the monumental Haitian Revolution of 1792, and ending with Brazilian emancipation in 1888. An institution that had been accepted for thousands of years disappeared in about a century.[41]

While U.S. history is today often described as an essentially unending sequence of white abuses of Blacks, a rock-ribbed American abolitionist movement dates back literally to the founding of the country. As I myself once noted for the online intellectual magazine Quillette, by the late 1770s, Black American veterans of the Revolutionary War—and more than a few of their white former bunkmates—began a petition-writing campaign that targeted Northern state legislatures and demanded an end to slavery. This and similar techniques were essentially successful: by 1795, ten U.S. states and soon-to-be-state territories, including Connecticut, the Indiana Territory, Maine, Massachusetts, New Hampshire, New York, all of the Northwest Territory, Pennsylvania, Rhode Island, and Vermont, were free land by law. Combined, these contained well over 50 percent of the free population of the United States.

And what I and others have called the antislavery upswell continued from there. In 1794, Congress formally barred all American ships from participating in the Atlantic slave trade. Just fourteen years later, in 1808, the same body passed the Act Prohibiting Importation of Slaves, which made it illegal for any ship from any country to bring enslaved people into the United States for sale. Finally, following some fascinating incremental steps and a big war, slavery was formally declared illegal throughout the United States in 1865.

It is well worth remembering the price we paid to reach that point: the shockingly bloody American Civil War—where men and boys not infrequently charged dug-in cannon manned by their brothers—killed 360,222 lads in Union blue, and another 258,000 or so in Confederate *Feldgrau*.[42] Roughly one in every ten American men of fighting age died during the war: 22.6 percent of Southern white men in their twenties were killed. In some Southern states, the majority of buildings over two stories high were burned; one Union soldier died for every nine to ten slaves who were set free. The war also boosted the national debt of the United States from less than $70,000,000 to $2.77 billion—an increase of many tens of billions in 2022 dollars.[43] As I noted for Quillette: "If the USA owed a bill for slavery, we have quite arguably already paid it in blood."

While a bit less drastic, the history of the abolitionist movement across the early modern Western world reads similarly. Following the 1787 establishment of the Society for the Purpose of Effecting the Abolition of the Slave Trade, Britain moved along with the United States to outlaw international slave trading in 1807 to 1808 and then heroically deployed the British Navy around the world to sink slave ships and blockade notorious trading hubs.[44] Not long after, slavery was eliminated across the British Empire (notably excepting India) by the Slavery Abolition Act of 1833.

On the continent, France abolished the practice of slavery throughout the global French Empire in 1794, briefly brought it back under Napoleon in 1802, but then permanently re-abolished it throughout the colonial system in 1848—and sent slaver-hunting French warships to patrol the World Ocean alongside England's.[45] Between France's abolition of the practice in 1794 (or Haiti's in 1804, if you prefer) and Brazil's in 1888, every major Western nation legally barred slavery.

Many other nations did not. While it is considered wildly politically incorrect to point this out, in powerful Muslim and Black African countries where the writ of the West never ran, chattel slavery quite often still exists today. A recent report from the International Labour Organization recently found that, "as of 2016," more than 40 million people currently "perform involuntary servitude of some kind" in situations that they cannot leave.[46] In other words, they are slaves. Per one widely read commentary on the report: "Today, there could be more people enslaved than at any time in human history. Chattel bondage still happens today . . . particularly in Africa."

The details provided by the ILO and the scholars analyzing its data are striking. Per one standard estimate, "between 529,000 and 869,000" human beings—most of them Black Africans—are currently "bought, owned, sold, and traded by Arab and Black . . . masters" within just five countries in Africa. Global sources estimate that there are currently 700,000 to 1 million desperate Black African migrants living in Libya alone, and that roughly 50,000 of them have been forced into physical or sexual slavery by Arab Libyans.

In Nigeria, where essentially all political and tribal violence is Black-on-Black, constant conflict between the sizable Muslim and Christian populations has led to "the growth of terrorist violence in which the taking of . . . slaves has become a source of compensation." Despite what some might call the best efforts of the media, some of this barbarity has attracted global public attention. An actual public slave auction was held in Libya and videotaped by undercover CNN reporters in 2017,[47] and the hashtag #BringBackOurGirls trended worldwide after Boko Haram fighters and slave traders kidnapped 276 Christian schoolchildren in spring of 2014.[48]

Even a few open slave societies continue to exist today, per the ILO and website sources like www.iAbolish.org. In the Islamic republic of Mauritania, "the very structure of society reinforces slavery." A racialized caste system still exists, where—in roughly this order—Berbers, lighter-skinned Arabs known as *beydanes*, and Islamized free Blacks called *haratin* completely dominate a group of Black chattel slaves referred to as *abid* or *abeed*.* The slave population is sizable: the U.S. State Department has estimated it at "just" 30,000 to 90,000 people,[49] but deep-cover research by CNN in 2011 placed the real number at between four and seven times State's highest estimate,[50] with the network's reporters and analysts estimating that "10% to 20% of the [Mauritanian] population lives in slavery."

Mauritanian slaves live very much as slaves always have: their yoke is not a light one. Perhaps because of the backlash to this practice in Libya or Algeria, few if any open markets exist, but all slaves

---

* This, like "Slav," is an old Arabic word used to denote a slave—in this case, generally a Black one. Essentially, the label for one of the country's major racial and class groups means "those slaves." Given the Western propensity for dramatic guilt, it also seems worth noting that Arab slave masters gave the world the most widely used terms for both white and Black slaves.

are held as chattels and most are born out of forced intercourse, "the master raping black slave women or ordering necessary episodes of sexual activity ['breeding']." Slaves are often used as a crude form of currency, serving "as substitutes for money in the settling of gambling debts," being privately traded between masters in exchange for other people or goods like rice, and often being available for short-term rental for whatever purpose. Like unfree people everywhen, they have no say in any of this, and can be (and often are) beaten or killed for attempting to escape their state of bondage.

Interestingly, sources almost invariably describe Mauritania as one of the countries in the world *furthest* from the West, an "endless sea of sand dunes" where the cuisine, dominant religion, and daily patterns of life show little if any European influence. And that may be the problem. When analyzed by serious people, across the sweep of history, slavery is revealed to have been not a "Western" practice but rather a universal one largely ended by Western arms. Where those arms reached never, or only briefly, it often continues to this day. As a previous writer once said,[51] in this context, it remains hard to give past Western colonial adventures three cheers—but we can perhaps manage two.

Hip. Hip. And forward.

LIE #2

"The 'Red Scare' Was a Moral Panic That Caught No Commies"

Perhaps the ultimate near-consensus left-wing belief is that the United States is a "McCarthyite" society prone to "Red Scares." The belief props up the narrative the political left uses to pooh-pooh any concerns about socialism these days, but itself is founded on a misleading understanding of history. Per the now standard media and academic storyline, the Red Scare was simply a case of rube politicians abusively harassing innocent teachers and actors, whom they falsely accused of being Communist agents or assets, throughout much of the 1950s and 1960s—and such insane behavior could begin again at any time.

Once again, of course, truth is very different from narrative. In the mid-1990s the U.S. government declassified the Venona cables, intercepted Soviet missives detailing post–World War Two Soviet espionage activities within the United States, which means we now know that most of the more prominent persons accused of spying for the Russkis during the Cold War were in fact spying for the Russkis during the Cold War.

Not that you're likely to see these revelations reflected in left-wing syllabi. The Los Angeles group Asian Americans Advancing Justice ("Episode 3, Lesson 2: McCarthyism and Racial Profiling")[1] put out a piece of K–12 educational content that sums up the main-stream take on Tail Gunner Joe and his historical era: "During the 1950s, the United States was gripped by McCarthyism, a period of accusations against individuals and groups for treason without just evidence."

A sentence or two down, the American security state is accused of "abus[ing] the First Amendment rights" of U.S. citizens, "profiling" people without just cause, and—with odd specificity—targeting Chinese American citizens in particular during the Korean War.

This historical crusade is directly and intentionally paralleled with alleged American sins during the modern era: McCarthy-era political profiling is compared to "modern racial profiling of Chinese" scientists, and students are instructed to "research and report back on current day issues of McCarthy-esque profiling." One of the first three discussion questions following the lesson asks what the McCarthy era can tell scholars about how any group of people in power "use profiling to target their own people, in the name of national security."

The lesson presents historical communism in a neutral or positive light. The definition given of communism/Marxism is: "a system . . . based on the idea of collective ownership of all goods and services in society, [which] are distributed to the population based on need."

Major classroom textbooks often take a similarly hostile view of McCarthyism. *America, Past and Present* opens a discussion of the McCarthy and anti-Communist era by presenting the Red Scare as paranoia, saying that the "fear of Communism abroad" was also turned against home front citizens not by "Democrats" but by "politicians willing to exploit the public's deep-seated anxiety." The textbook lists a number of historical events leading to the Red Scare, but it has a strong angle: "The Truman Administration, por-traying the men in the Kremlin as inspired revolutionaries bent on world conquest, frightened the American people [who] viewed the Soviet Union as the successor to Nazi Germany"; "the Justice

Department further heightened fears of subversion [by charging] eleven officials of the Communist party with advocating the violent overthrow of the government"; "events abroad intensified the sense of danger. The communist triumph in China . . . came as a shock"; "all the ingredients were at hand for a new outburst of hysteria." The *real* story, the book hints, is the emotional reaction to these events, not the events themselves.[2]

No wonder, then, that Senator McCarthy, the textbook claims, "failed to unearth a single confirmed Communist in government," despite keeping the entire Truman presidential administration "in turmoil."

The textbook strongly implies that this was because few if any such Communists existed: "The charges that there were Communists in the State Department—repeated on different occasions with the numbers changed . . . was never substantiated." The text goes on to approvingly cite a Senate subcommittee's description of McCarthy's actions as "the most nefarious campaign of half-truth and untruth in the history of the Republic" and as having "helped impose a political and cultural conformity that froze dissent" for a decade.[3]

Another textbook, *The Unfinished Nation*, gives a more nuanced take, from my reading. That text asks, "Why did the American people develop a fear of internal Communist subversion?"[4] and proposes: "The simplest argument . . . is that the postwar Red Scare expressed real and legitimate concerns about Communist subversion in the United States." However, while admitting that this position does "attract scholarly support," author Alan Brinkley continues by stating that most academic reads on the period have been much less "charitable." As early as the mid-1950s, "historians and social scientists began to portray the anti-Communist fervor of their time as an expression of deep social maladjustment." Then, as now, scholars contended that there was "no logical connection between the modest power of actual communists in the United States and the hysterical form . . . anti-Communism was assuming." Again, the book says, "McCarthy never produced conclusive evidence that any federal employee was a communist."

Coverage of the McCarthy era, and often of the Cold War entire, targeted at American adults tends to be entertainingly similar. A widely circulated piece on the period in the admittedly liberal *Progressive* magazine was titled "Reckless Cruelty: The Joe McCarthy Story," and opens: "In the tradition of . . . Darth Vader, *Harry Potter's* Lord Voldemort, and *Batman's* Joker, Joe McCarthy is a villain you love to hate."[5] The piece goes on to describe the then junior senator from Wisconsin with more comic book–worthy language: "an embodiment of evil," "the face of rabid anti-Communism—and what an ugly mug it was," the fellow who "put the badger in" the name of the Badger State (Wisconsin), and so forth.

More important than this colorful language—the *Progressive* is a serious publication, if one a bit to the left of Fidel Castro politically—is the magazine's serious study of McCarthy's career. Per author Ed Rampell's analysis, McCarthy was a man who skillfully exploited baseless "Reds-under-the-bed hysteria" to rise from back-benching obscurity to chairmanship of the U.S. Senate's Permanent Subcommittee on Investigations (the main American tool, along with the House Un-American Activities Committee [HUAC] for U.S. investigation of Communist infiltration). In that role, Rampell writes, McCarthy "wildly" alleged Communist espionage was targeting high levels of the United States government. He employed "Torquemada-like tactics" to bring claims against alleged spies before finally suffering an Icarus-like fall from grace when military officers called his bluff during the 1954 Army-McCarthy hearings.

One could go on quoting these sort of accounts for some time. Another typical take on the Badger State Bolshie Basher, titled "A Stunning Panorama of Evil," comes from the *Texas Observer* newspaper, reviewing a new book on the old pol. In his analysis of Ted Morgan's 704-page *Reds: McCarthyism in Twentieth-Century America*, reporter Robert Sherrill opens by mocking the entire idea of the Red Scare. In an era where the word "Communist" is rarely mentioned during serious conversations, he argues, young *Observer* readers might find it hard even to believe the "bizarre anti-Communist hysteria that gripped the nation" during the Cold War, driven by the real but absurd fear that "a horde of home-grown reds . . . were diligently seeking to overthrow our government by violence."

This was, of course—Sherrill says—never the case. McCarthy and those like him were pathological liars, constructing whole careers out of "endless" falsehoods while pandering to "the most ignorant, superstitious, meanest segment" of heartland America. If anything, the stoutly liberal and anti–anti-Communist Morgan is accused of giving too much credit to the absurd idea that domestic communism was a threat to the United States in the 1950s. Morgan, by Sherrill's account, "over-emphasizes the danger" from state-side spies and other pro-Communist actors, while simultaneously not speaking enough about the damage done by "the anti-Communist witch hunt" to "thousands of persons whose 'crime' was being liberal." At one point Sherill and the *Observer* state flatly that "the whole Red Scare business, from beginning to end, stands condemned by history as a colossal fraud."

Finally, Hollywood certainly supports the preferred academic and journalistic version of the historical narrative. Films lionize Tinseltown dwellers accused of being Communist spies or sympathizers during the Cold War. Most prominently, *Trumbo*— which drew several Academy Award nominations—focused on a screenwriter whose former membership in the Communist Party drew criticism from pro-American celebrities like Hedda Hopper and John Wayne and led to his becoming un-hirable under his own name during the Hollywood blacklist era of the 1950s and early 1960. Dalton Trumbo is the unabashed hero of the piece, which presents his financial difficulties in wrenching detail: he closes it by speaking about how the Blacklist "victimized" everyone in what seems on the surface to be a conciliatory speech.

There's just one problem with all of this tear-jerking about "civil rights violations:" Dalton Trumbo *was* a Communist,[6] and so—with the probable exception of most of those on Tail Gunner Joe's first bad-judgment "list of names"—were most of those accused of espionage or other pro-Soviet activity during this period. Hollywood is repeating the same mistake as the activist lessons, textbooks, and articles that dismiss the Red Scare as a moral panic.

But how did everyone get it so wrong? In part, it's because the U.S. government concealed the truth. In the 2007 book *Blacklisted by History: The Untold Story of Senator Joe McCarthy and His Fight Against America's Enemies,* renowned conservative historian M. Stanton Evans argues that much of the strong and immediate backlash to McCarthy's allegations occurred because the government wasn't about to admit how real McCarthy's worries were about infiltration. U.S. officials from both parties "weren't eager to have [the *reality* of] Communist penetration on their watch, and their failure to do much about it," broken down in front of the general public.[7]

While many people, including most of the authors presented above, seem to genuinely believe most McCarthy/HUAC targets were "mere innocent victims of [a] mid-century reign of terror," Evans persuasively contends that—to the contrary—most of the accused actually were bad actors within government departments "infested with Soviet agents and sympathizers."[8] For example, McCarthy target John Stewart Service of the State Department is widely seen as "a top-level martyr driven out of the Department by McCarthy's accusations." However, having "obtained 1,200 pages of Service's dispatches," Evans shows Service was an old Red China hand who had close and personal ties with multiple Soviet agents— and who briefly *lived* with two alleged agents in the Chinese city of Chungking during World War Two.

Similarly, sympathetic Black, middle-class code clerk Annie Lee Moss—whose questioning was for decades held up by McCarthy critics as a case of mistaken identity and was highlighted by Edward R. Murrow in a TV broadcast credited with taking down McCarthy for good—was very arguably a Communist Party member "with 'party membership book number 37269.'"[9] Professor Andrea Friedman, a "historian of gender and sexuality" at George Washington University in St. Louis, wrote complimentarily of Moss, "Never the helpless and passive victim that she was portrayed [as], Moss was a community activist, a woman ambitious for herself and her family, and," she added, "most likely a member, briefly, of the Communist party."[10]

Debates about each and every one of these individual cases could go on "in the weeds" for some time, to the delight of no one but the professional wonk community. However, as Evans and interviewers of his such as Robert Novak have suggested, there is a way to resolve them. Very often, Evans argues, "these McCarthy cases were right there in the Soviet cables." In other words, data recently obtained from no-longer-Soviet Russia demonstrates that specific individuals long thought to be martyrs of a kind were in fact "Communists, Soviet agents, or assets of the KGB—just as McCarthy had suggested."

Why is this a problem? Isn't it still persecution of Americans for their private thoughts? Something we don't fully appreciate today is that being a Communist at the time didn't just mean holding a mildly unfashionable opinion. As film critic Godfrey Cheshire notes in a review of *Trumbo*, the film is deceitful when "it invites us to the [sic] see the Communist Party USA as just another political party rather than as the domestic instrument of a hostile and ultra-murderous foreign tyranny."[11]

In truth, as historian Ron Capshaw writes, the film's "Trumbo-the-free-speech-avatar" is highly inconsistent with "Trumbo the actual person."

> [Trumbo's] daughter Nikola has said that being a communist in that period had "nothing to do with Russia" but was instead about the "rights of workers." If so, Trumbo spent a great deal of "wasted" time defending Joseph Stalin. It is easy to confirm his zigs and zags in accord with the policy changes out of Moscow throughout much of his adult life.
>
> When Stalin allied with Hitler in 1939, and announced that comrades should not support Great Britain's military response to the

Third Reich because it was an "imperialist war," Trumbo followed suit. He wrote many vociferous attacks on the British....

To help the non-interventionist cause, Trumbo even defended the Third Reich. In response to Hitler's crackdown on France, the famous civil libertarian disputed reports of Nazi brutality coming out of France, declaring that "To the vanquished all conquerors are inhuman."[12]

So as you can see, despite leftist myths to the contrary, McCarthy's target wasn't eccentric but harmless political dissidents whose greatest crime was supporting, say, better healthcare for the working class.

Contrary to the claims in textbooks, there *was* real proof behind McCarthy's crusades. The vital if passing reference by Evans and Novak to "the cables" or "the Russian/Soviet cables" brings up one oft-forgotten critical point here: *we now know who most of the Soviet spies were.* The Soviet Union is no more, and the United States maintained fairly good relations with the primary successor state of Russia, a member of the G8, from the mid-1990s up until the 2021 onset of the Russia-Ukraine War. During this period, in late 1995, almost all of the 3,000 secret Soviet messages captured and decrypted by the top secret U.S. Venona project between 1943 and 1980 were declassified and released to the general public and the global community of scholars.

The results were rather remarkable. They showed conclusively that a very large number of the prominent Yanks and Brits accused of Soviet espionage during the Cold War were in fact Russian spies. Venona messages confirmed that at various times Soviet spies worked for the atomic Manhattan Project, in the U.S. Office of Strategic Services (OSS), for the State and Treasury Departments, and in the White House. The declassified cables added a great deal of significant data to the famous case of Julius and Ethel Rosenberg—making it clear the pair was guilty. Julius was the "leader of a productive ring of Soviet spies," and loving wife

Ethel was at least "an accessory to her husband's activity, having knowledge of it and assisting him."[13]

Venona also vindicated Whittaker Chambers, author of the controversial anti-Communist classic *Witness*, conclusively demonstrating the guilt of famously accused spies Alger Hiss and Harry Dexter White.[14] As the Daniel Patrick Moynihan–led Commission on Government Secrecy confirmed, thanks to Venona, "The complicity of Alger Hiss of the State Department seems settled. As does that of Harry Dexter White of the Treasury Department."[15] In his fascinating 1998 book *Secrecy*, the scrappy senator discussed the case again, saying simply: "Hiss was indeed a Soviet agent, and appears to have been regarded by Moscow as its most important."[16]

And so on. John Earl Haynes and Harvey Klehr, authors of the technically laden *Venona: Decoding Soviet Espionage in America*,[17] have argued that the Venona transcripts specifically identify more than 340 Americans who worked at some point for Soviet intelligence—although less than half of these individuals have so far been matched to confirmed actual-name identities. The OSS, the predecessor agency to the Central Intelligence Agency (CIA) of today, appears to have been a particular hotbed of skullduggery—for obvious reasons—playing host to at least fifteen confirmed Soviet spies over the years.

Among the more prominent confirmed agents to appear in any decoded Venona list of Russki operatives were Maurice Halperin, Lieutenant Colonel Duncan Lee, Donald Wheeler, and Jane Foster. Elsewhere, the Board of Economic Warfare, Office of the Coordinator of Inter-American Affairs, Office of War Information, and War Production Board all housed at least a half dozen Russian moles apiece. It is worth noting that at least some of these estimates regarding spy numbers match historical claims by Senator McCarthy and by HUAC rather exactly, and more than a few of the now confirmed Russian assets—such as Lieutenant Colonel Lee—were in fact previous HUAC accusees.

A truly remarkable line-up of prominent Americans were mentioned by name in the Venona cables,[18] with some highlights including Theodore Bayer, president of lefty Russky Golos (Russian Voice) Publishing; journalist Cedric Belfrage; Earl Browder, general secretary of the U.S. Communist Party; Morris Cohen, Communist Party of the United States of America member and employee of physicist Ted Hall; Department of Justice staffer Judith Coplon; FDR adviser and World Banker Lauchlin Currie; William Dawson, our ambassador to Uruguay; labor organizer Eugene Dennis; Laurence Duggan, head of the State Department's South American desk; Linn Farish, senior U.S. liaison with Marshal Tito in Yugoslavia; Harold Glasser of the Treasury Department; disgraced physicist Ted Hall himself; Maurice Halperin (code-named "Hare" by the Russians); economist Charles Kramer; Richard Lauterbach of *Time* magazine; United Laboratories owner William Malisoff; Robert G. Minor, OSS Belgrade; Frank Oppenheimer; Vladimir Aleksandrovich Pozner, U.S. War Department; Kenneth Richardson of World Wide Electronics; Samuel Jacob Rodman, UN Relief and Rehabilitation Administration; Julius and Ethel Rosenberg; Nathan Gregory Silvermaster, top War Production Board economist; Helen Silvermaster, American League for Peace and Democracy; investigative journalist I. F. Stone; and Harry Dexter White.

Some scholars have pointed out, accurately enough, that not everyone named in the cables is a currently confirmed Russian agent or asset. President Franklin Roosevelt himself makes some unavoidable appearances under the code name "Capitan," as does Winston Churchill ("Boar" or "the wild boar"). However, the large majority of prominent ordinary Americans frequently discussed by a Russian espionage agency clearly were spies.

The influence exerted by some of these proven spies on what became the modern Western order was remarkable—Harry Dexter White, for example, was the chief architect of both the International Monetary Fund and what would become the World Bank. It is no exaggeration to say that Russian espionage during the 1950s and 1960s, far from being some kind of paranoid fairy tale, was a real problem that reached the very highest levels of U.S. and Allied governments. On more than a few occasions (i.e., Alger Hiss at

Yalta),[19] Russian agents sat by the American president's side and gave him advice.

While horrifying, this is at some level not surprising. Russians and other Eastern Europeans have a long tradition of *maskirovka*—skillful camouflage designed to confuse and manipulate an opponent—and subtle infiltration of systems has long been a strategy for Communists of all backgrounds. The original coat of arms of Britain's Fabian Society, founded just a year after the death of Marx as one of the first openly Communist organizations in the West, literally depicts a wolf in sheep's clothing. The group is often credited with originating the policy of "permeation" of business, education, civil society, and politics by Marxists—encouraging members to befriend "figures such as Cabinet ministers, senior . . . officials, industrialists, university Deans, and church leaders." A famous old Fabian Society pamphlet includes this advice: "For the right moment you must wait, as [Roman General Quintus] Fabius did . . . but when the time comes you must strike hard, as Fabius did, or your waiting will be in vain."[20]

In the mid-twentieth-century United States, the main organization doing the "waiting" and lurking was the Communist Party of the United States of America, or CCPUSA. Founded in 1919, the CCPUSA never became a major player in American politics but had a "significant" influence on national discourse, attempting with reasonable success to infiltrate "workers' and student movements, the church, and the government." Outlining the activities of the CCP to the House Un-American Activities Committee during the height of the Cold War, anti-Communist thinker and former radical Fred Schwarz described American Marxists as playing an influential stewardship role: "Communism is the theory of the disciplined few controlling and directing the rest. One person in a sensitive role can control and manipulate thousands of others." As we have seen above, exactly this often happened during the 1950s and 1960s.

An obvious through line so far is: Communist infiltration of the United States, abetted by geopolitical foes like Russia and Red China, was never a made-up bogeyman but rather was—and arguably is—a real threat to American national interests. In a passage worth quoting as one block, the right-leaning website the Other Half of History provides a solid summary of our material thus far:[21]

> Within the United States, a virtual army of Communist spies and sympathizers labored to promote the interests of mass murderers like Stalin and Mao. Soviet spies provided Stalin's government with the secrets of the atom bomb. Soviet agents in the State Department shaped American policy in ways that facilitated Communist conquest in . . . Hungary and China. During WWII, Communists in the federal government's Office of War Information even pressured Hollywood to make movies portraying the Soviet Union in a positive light.
>
> But don't expect to hear those things in a college history class.

The last two sentences merit attention. If all of this evidence of real spies has emerged, why isn't it taught in schools? Considering Communist demographics may provide an answer. Let's look at the people responsible for writing the "first rough draft of history." In his 2015 *Journal of Slavic Military Studies* article "Spies in the News,"[22] Ohio University's Alexander G. Lovelace points out that, "broken down by occupation," more American journalists worked secretly for Soviet intelligence than was true for literally any other profession "except engineering." Nor were these writers mere messenger boys. Journalists of the era were often given extensive access to key military sources and other top-level sources, and "journalist spies collected a large amount of secret diplomatic and military information."

As early as 1941, a now declassified report from a Soviet intelligence operative listed no fewer than twenty-two prominent American journalists as actual "agents" inside the United States. From that point forward—throughout World War Two and deep into the Cold War—"the number of journalist spies" in the United States only increased, and the amount of information they gathered increased. Lovelace notes that some of these operatives, such as Robert S. Allen of the *Christian Science Monitor*, essentially worked for money, while many others—for example, the *Call's* John L. Spivak—were "motivated by ideology." However, both groups of reporter assets possessed the essential Gray Man's skill, being able to easily mingle with very different groups of influential people and "ask probing questions." They used it well and often.

In a truly remarkable example of the prevalence of Communist propagandists within newsrooms and film studios during the period following World War Two, the *New York Times's* top Cuba correspondent was seriously described in 2001 as "[Fidel] Castro's publicist."[23] Per Eric Fettmann of the crosstown *New York Post*, the Cuban dictator would "never have come to power were it not for Herbert Matthews," the primary Cuba reporter for the *Times* from the early 1950s to mid-1960s. Quoting former *New York Times* executive editor Max Frankel and clearly agreeing with him, Fettmann describes Matthews as the fellow who essentially "invented Fidel Castro for the American people."

Most notably, Matthews argued for years that Castro was *not* a Red—despite almost certainly knowing otherwise, after most non-Communist supporters of the Cuban revolution had been killed or imprisoned by their Marxist former allies. As a result of actions like this, the dictator and the reporter became genuine friends: when Frankel himself was granted a single interview with Castro, he was greeted warmly and told by the Cuban leader that "any friend of Herbert's was also his friend." Unsurprisingly, Matthews himself was allegedly at least a socialist: before ever taking on his Cuban assignment, he had served as a de facto propagandist for the Soviet-backed side during the Spanish Civil War and been supported as a Pulitzer Prize candidate by the Communist publication *New Masses*.

During the period when he wrote and the era immediately before, remarkably, Matthews would not have been the most prominent supporter of global communism even among *Times* men. That honor would have to go to Walter Duranty, the famous "journalist" who "functioned as a blatant apologist for Joseph Stalin," writing a Pulitzer Prize–winning series of intentionally false articles that minimized the horrors of the Holodomor terror famine and of the Soviet show trials. And as Fettmann dryly notes, both men had plenty of company at the Newspaper of Record. During the mid-twentieth century, there were so many Communists on the *New York Times* staff that "they were organized in a cell that published its own monthly news-letter." Down the street, *New York Herald Tribune's* foreign desk editor Joseph Barnes and prominent CBS News reporter Winston Burdett were both actual Soviet spies.

Nor, among the U.S. intelligentsia, were these Communist-sympathizing journalists close to alone. Recent research indicates that American intellectuals—likely including both moviemakers and professors—were dramatically overrepresented among Communist "fifth columnists" inside the United States during the Cold War. As Trumbo more than hinted, there was substantial CCPUSA representation inside Cold War Hollywood: the famous question "Are you now, or have you ever been, a member of the Communist Party?" was no mere fascist snare. As a 2000 article in *Reason* magazine pointed out,[24] CCPUSA "cultural commissar" V. J. Jerome established a Hollywood chapter of the party as early as 1935, and this "secretive unit" enjoyed decades of success organizing some of the major unions in the film and production business, raising money from "pinko" supporters, and recruiting hundreds if not thousands of active members. Prominent industry-affiliated groups like the Hollywood Anti-Nazi League were almost entirely front groups for American communism.

Influence on this scale impacted the very content of American pop culture. *Reason* magazine writer Kenneth Billingsley points out that CCPUSA functionaries controlled the Screen Writers Guild and Story Analysts Guild for periods of years at a time and were "sometimes able to prevent the production of movies they opposed." In an article in hard-left publication the *Worker*, which Billingsley cites in some detail, Dalton Trumbo himself took credit for blocking a whole range of books from being made into films, including Arthur Koestler's *Darkness at Noon*, James T. Farrell's *Bernard Clare*, and the anti-Communist works *The Yogi and the Commissar* and *I Chose Freedom*.

And, albeit to a lesser extent, such malign influence continued for decades after the Cold War. Remarkably, the Hollywood of the 1980s and 1990s—which still leaned hard to the left and employed more than a few warhorses from the era before—produced essentially no movies addressing "the actual history of communism, the agony of the millions whose lives were poisoned by it, or the international deceit that obscured communist reality." With the exception of a few action flicks like *Red Dawn*, the defining conflict of the twentieth century was "missing from American cinema."

And a brief pause for thought indicates that this is *still* the case. As the article points out, one would hunt pretty much in vain for a post-2010 cinematic depiction of the bloody Khmer Rouge regime, the rise and fall of Fidel Castro, the Marxist and Maoist revolutions in postcolonial Africa, the toppling of the Berlin Wall, and so forth. Given our death duel with Russia well into the 1990s, and current sparring with China, an obvious analogy is drawn: "It is as though, since 1945, Hollywood had produced little or nothing about the victory of the allies and the crimes of National Socialism." (Unsurprisingly, Eastern European filmmakers are more faithful in chronicling communism's horrors, as in Polish director Agnieszka Holland's 2019 film *Mr. Jones*, a narrative dramatizing Welsh journalist Gareth Jones's exposé of the Holodomor in the early 1930s, or German director Florian Henckel von Donnersmarck's 2006 film *The Lives of Others*, about a Stasi surveillance officer in East Berlin.)

Interestingly, another piece of "muddled mythology" that *Trumbo* recycled into the mainstream was the commonly held belief that Joseph McCarthy was responsible for the Hollywood blacklist system. In fact, Godfrey Cheshire writes:

HUAC never blacklisted anyone. Hollywood's studio chiefs set up the blacklist after the 1947 hearings; for over a decade, it was a practice that most people in the industry either supported or didn't openly resist. Trumbo himself, while allowing that he did indeed hold the 1947 Congress and some subsequent ones in contempt, was adamant in insisting that the U.S. government and its vicious right-wingers weren't to blame for the blacklist—Hollywood was.

Cheshire also points out the film lacks a true understanding of the fact that communism in this era was no friend to liberalism:

[M]issing is any sense of the utter contempt that Trumbo and his communist cohorts felt for liberals, who, in fact, they often regarded with more enmity than they did right-wingers. But that makes sense, of course. The communists were hoping for a revolution to overthrow American democracy. A takeover by fascists would only hasten that result, they thought; successful liberalism could only impede it.[25]

If we've lost sight of both the self-inflicted censorship and the real communists in Hollywood, we've also forgotten the historic prevalence of communist sympathies in academia.

Communist infiltration was hardly confined to the media and the arts. In fact, it was focused with particular intensity and success on the sector of American secondary and higher education. In 1954, Louis F. Budenz—former Communist agent and American labor activist—in fact wrote a white paper titled *The Techniques of Communism*.[26] In chapter ten, "Invading Education," Budenz opens: "In undermining a nation such as the United States, the infiltration of the educational process is of prime importance," and goes on to state his thesis—that he will prove "Communists have accordingly made the invasion of schools and colleges one of the major considerations in their psychological warfare."

Budenz knows his Commie history, noting that Joseph Stalin described cultural and educational institutions as essential targets during his 1924 Sverdlov University lectures, which focused on outlining a strategy for global Communist revolution. By May of 1937, enough Party members had sought jobs as teachers or expressed an interest in the educational issue that a special issue of the *Communist*, titled "The Schools and the People's Front," was published. Among many pieces of advice given to Communist educators, two stand out: "Marxist-Leninist analysis must be injected into every class" and "all teacher comrades must be given thorough education" in proper Marxist doctrine.

The subtlety and intrigue of all this is notable. At one point, for example, Budenz notes that anyone arguing that CCP members and other Marxists should be allowed to teach in the American educational system "as long as they do not teach Communism openly" would immediately reveal herself as being unaware of how Communist infiltration would actually operate. In reality, a Communist academic or teacher would "very rarely, if ever" openly teach what would universally be seen as enemy doctrine by Americans of this era. However, "there are hundreds of indirect ways of reaching the same end."

Instructors might focus on scathing but facially nonpartisan critiques of American inequality, for example, or quote Ivy League or other ivory-tower experts "who invariably take a pro-Soviet position." Closing one memorable paragraph of his speech, he argues that it would be easy to draw up "an entire syllabus" that would lead a median-IQ university student to support, or at very least sympathize with, global socialism without including a single explicitly pro-Stalin citation. A point very relevant today, some might think!

All this talk of Marxist infiltration of the educational system is not merely theoretical: like McCarthy, Budenz names names. Citing the 1951 HUAC report *The Communist "Peace" Offensive: The Attempt to Disarm and Defeat America* in his own white paper, he points out that University of Chicago prof and former Virgin Islands governor Robert Morss Lovett was credibly charged with being a member of "at least eighty-five" organizations that operated as Communist front groups. While this was obviously not typical, other credibly accused academic Communists identified at some point by HUAC included Dr. Harry F. Ward (Union Theological Seminary), Walter Rautenstrach (Columbia University—one of the United States' leading engineers), Henry Pratt Fairchild (NYU), Robert S. Lynd (Columbia), Frederick L. Schuman (Williams), and Dr. Colston E. Warne (Amherst College).

All told, drawing on the HUAC document and another dead-serious and essentially forgotten source, Professor J. B. Matthews's "Communism and the Colleges,"[27] Budenz estimates that "the Communist Party has enlisted the support of at least thirty-five hundred professors." Some of these men and women were actual spies for the Soviet Union or another power, many were card-carrying members of the CCPUSA, and more than a few others were simply ideological fellow travelers, or what Matthews calls "the unwitting dupes of subversion." However, all of them had at least some documented tie to the American or global Communist movements following "careful examination of the records." This figure for Communist agents and assets within one field of enter-prise, notably, is higher than any ever provided by Senator McCar-thy for the United States overall.

Budenz's and Matthews's estimates may be—almost surely are—on the high side. But a sober review of data-based arguments at this level brings up an obvious question: Why have most people never even heard this take on the "Red Scare"—or for that matter the plain fact that major and universally beloved figures like Martin Luther King and W. E. B. Du Bois at very least flirted with commu-nism?[28] One obvious explanation would seem to be that very many of those charged with bringing knowledge to the U.S. population are, even today, themselves Marxists or Marxist sympathizers.

This is not some right-wing scare claim. Academia, famously, leans almost entirely to the political left. Per a piece titled "The Prevalence of Marxism in Academia," posted to the Econlib web archive in 2015—although based on somewhat older data—a remarkable 17.6 percent of American social scientists *currently* identify as Marxists.[29] To put this figure in context, even the con-servative *Washington Times* notes that 1 percent or less of all Amer-icans describe Marxism as their "primary worldview."[30] In addition to the open Reds, 24 percent of social science professors describe themselves as political radicals, and another 20.6 percent describe themselves as "activists."

Things are better over in, for example, business (5.3 percent radical, 3.2 percent activist, 1.9 percent Marxist). However, in the humanities fields, 19 percent of academics identify as radicals, 26.2 percent identify as activists, and 5 percent identify as Marxists. Accepting each of these categories as distinct, which seems to reflect the formatting of the original questions, about 63 percent of all faculty members in the softer sciences and 50 percent of those in the human studies fields are active political leftists. This gels well with other recent data, such as the finding that Democrats outnumber Pachyderms by ratios that range from 4–5:1 (economics) to 33.5:1 across the academic fields that make up these sectors.

And without getting into the endless current dogfight over how real "*cultural* Marxism" is or isn't, the results detailing the prevalence of Marxism on campus probably underreport left-wing extremism there, given the growing popularity of far-left thinkers who are not traditional Communists. Marx himself (a "dead white male") seems to be falling a bit out of fashion among radical faculty, who nonetheless remain almost universally hostile to the conservative politics and American traditions.

As philosophy professor Matthew Sharpe has pointed out, Marx "ceded the laurel as the most written-about thinker in academic Humanities" way back in 1987—now thirty-five years ago.[31] However, he has not exactly been replaced at the top by Tom Jefferson. While Nietzsche did skate past Marx, others among the most cited and discussed thinkers of today include Antonio Gramsci (480 articles in the modern era), the thinkers of the Frankfurt School (about 200), and Herbert Marcuse (220 major articles)—all of whom are generally seen as founding fathers of cultural Marxism.

Most notably, postmodernist and post-structuralist thinkers such as Judith Butler "are today more prominent than Marxist scholars." While sometimes referred to as "conservative" in philosophical terms—which Sharpe notes—all of these writers are obviously extreme political leftists. Butler has been the driving force behind the gender revolution of today. Given this, a metric measuring levels of Marxism or conventional political radicalism alone may well underestimate the level of mono-culture in the American academy of 2022.

While this is not the focus of this chapter, the one-sided political bias of the "discursive" class today is fairly remarkable, extending well beyond the ivory tower and the hallowed grove into more worldly sectors like nongovernmental organization (NGO) fund-raising. In 2016, for example, conservative publication the *Federalist* ran an article titled "How Black Lives Matter is Bringing Back Traditional Marxism."[*32] Author Thurston Powers argues, supported by data, that powerful BLM organizations like the Black Lives Matter Global Network Foundation not only lean far left but in fact are largely turning away from the sort of "intersectional theory" just discussed and back to a frankly Communist focus on "the traditional class struggle"—albeit with Blacks sometimes subbed in for poor people as the oppressed revolutionary cadre needing liberation.

The actual BLM policy platform is very open about all of this. In addition to some perfunctory suggestions for the field of policing, the platform explicitly calls for "collective ownership of resources, banks, and businesses," a more progressive national income tax, "a guaranteed minimum income," and government jobs for all who want them. In a passage that Powers notes seems to be a rather direct paraphrase of *The Communist Manifesto*, the anonymous BLM authors call for "an end to the exploitative privatization of natural resources—including land and water. We seek democratic control over how resources are preserved, used, and distributed." Wealthy "trained Marxists" indeed, the major Black Lives Matter organizations have so far drummed up roughly $11 billion in donations and grant funding and amassed a great deal of political power on the strength of sentiments like these.[33]

---

* None of this *faux*-Commie Judith Butler crap for BLM!

While few major outlets publicly venture to the same extremes as Patrisse Cullors and her crew, almost the same degree of bias toward one side of the political aisle characterizes the modern U.S. mass media. As the Daily Wire recently summarized several dense reams of data: when it comes to political bias, a new study shows that "just about everything you would assume about journalists covering the financial industry is true."[34] According to DW's primary source, a 2018 survey of journalists conducted by professors from Arizona State and Texas A&M, 17.63 percent of the writers and reporters who responded to a recent empirical questionnaire described themselves as "very liberal," while 40.84 percent described themselves as liberal but only "somewhat."

In contrast, exactly 0.46 percent of the journalists surveyed labeled themselves "very conservative," while another 3.94 percent went with "somewhat conservative." All in, assuming a representative sample, about 4.4 percent of journalists lean right, while roughly 58.5 percent called themselves left of center: a ratio of 13 to 1—although an additional 37.12 percent did identify as moderates. It should be noted that this study focused on *financial* journalists, who are generally considered to be mossbacked former businesspeople, and by far the most conservative of all reporters.

This was hardly a one-off, atypical result. More broadly, per a famous Pew Research Center survey of media contributors, exactly 7 percent of national journalists lean right: the other 93 percent(!) identify as liberals or (mostly left-leaning) moderates.[35] Even among local reporters, only 12 percent describe themselves as conservatives, while roughly twice as many (23 percent) identify as liberal. In contrast, conservatism is far more popular than liberalism among the American population: only 20 percent of Americans arc liberals, while 33 percent are conservatives, 41 percent are moderates, and 6 percent have no opinion, or "don't know." In proportional terms, conservatives are roughly 500 percent as common among members of the general public as they are among members of the national media.

This bias, despite occasional frantic denials of it by the mass media,[36] is rather clearly reflected in press coverage. The written endorsements provided by the major newspapers before the 2016 presidential election provide a good example of a general pattern. That year, according to data compiled by the American Presidency Project at the University of California, Santa Barbara,[37] fifty-seven of the nation's one hundred largest, most significant newspapers (total circulation 13,095,067) endorsed scandal-plagued Democratic nominee Hillary Clinton. In contrast, two newspapers (circulation 315,666) endorsed Republican Donald Trump. Four papers (738,750) endorsed long-shot Libertarian candidate Gary Johnson, three (3,243,140) endorsed "Not Trump" or anyone but the Donald, five (440,976) endorsed "none of the above," and twenty-six (6,102,180) did not endorse a candidate.

In the end, the bombastic GOP nominee—who beat Clinton by 77 electoral votes[38]—lost the media battle to her by fifty-five newspapers representing 12,779,401 more regular readers. This ratio was by no means as atypical as casual observers of politics might think. In the immediately previous 2012 election, involving two highly "respectable" candidates—popular senator Barack Obama and Mitt Romney, the former governor of Massachusetts and CEO of Bain Capital—forty of the same fifty-seven (70 percent) pro-Clinton newspapers endorsed Senator Obama, while only fourteen (25 percent) endorsed Mr. Romney.*

This sort of thing has consequences. Following more than a decade of media partisanship on the left and sometimes the right, combined with extreme over-sensationalization of events like the COVID pandemic—which the average American believes to have killed 9 to 10 percent of the national population by late 2020[39]—trust in journalists and indeed "experts" overall has dropped to near record lows. According to a set of recent polls from Gallup,[40] just 7 percent of American adults say they have "a great deal of trust"

---

* Three other papers "did not endorse in 2012" or split their endorsement during that year. Both of the, er, two pro-Trump papers did endorse Mr. Romney.

in U.S. mainstream media—defined as reporting of contemporary news by "newspapers, television, and radio." Another 29 percent have "a fair amount of trust," and these figures combined (36 percent) fall just 4 percentage points above the all-time low mark of 32 percent set during the Trump-Clinton race in 2016.

Notably and unsurprisingly, trust in the media is even lower among conservatives than among Americans overall, with Gallup recording combined "great deal" and "fair amount" confidence rates of 68 percent for self-identified Democrats, 31 percent for Independents, and just 11 percent for Republicans. The trust gap between Republicans and Democrats is currently 57 percentage points, which—insanely—seems to be fairly typical: well inside "the 54 to 63 point range" that has existed between the two groups of partisans for at least the past five years. In a truly remarkable data-based finding, Republican levels of belief in "the accuracy and fairness of the news media" have in fact not risen far above 50 percent during the past *twenty*-five years.

People who believe with reason that they are being lied to become understandably reluctant to trust the words that they hear. And, when those doing the talking within a given field genuinely *are* biased or dishonest actors, this instinct proves to be a good one. This is a useful rule to keep top of mind when it comes to one of the great lies of history: the denial of Communist infiltration within the United States . . . by academics or writers who may well be Marxists themselves.

LIE #3

"Native Americans Were 'Peaceful People Who Spent All Day Dancing'"

Modern historians often bewail the fact that the historical understandings of Native Americans have frequently been negative and one-sided, representing them as a mass of faceless and malignant enemies to white protagonists. They're the extras who ride out to shoot at John Wayne. But since the 1960s, another myth has supplanted that false picture—one just as misleading, recycling the myth of the "noble savage."

The new lie almost every modern American schoolchild's teacher has told him, her, or xir—at least since the late-1960s publication of Vine Deloria Jr.'s *Custer Died for Your Sins: An Indian Manifesto* and the 1972 drop of Dee Brown's *Bury My Heart at Wounded Knee: An Indian History of the American West*—is that Native Americans were peaceful Gaea-worshipping people, killed via intentional genocide by ruthless and land-hungry white settlers. Again, reality proves to be considerably more complex.

The U.S. government's official "Native American Contributions" series of lessons provides such a perfect synopsis of what has become the standard worldview that it is worth quoting at some length.[1] Lesson number one opens: "Native Americans have contributed many things to the American way of life today . . . [what]

you use or do now, many Native Americans have been using or doing for many, many years."* One of the most important of these things, apparently, was stewardship over the planet.

While "people of today have just begun" to think about this, Indigenous Americans always had a profound love and respect for the natural world: "There was a love of every form of life. The Native Americans did not kill anything they could not use. They never killed an animal or fish for the sport of it." Higher forms of ecology were apparently also practiced. Across all or almost all tribes, "Native Americans lived in harmony with nature and did not abuse the natural world. Native Americans were ecologists long before [the word was] ever used." While such powerful peoples as the Anishinaabe did not even have a word for "conservation" (or "mercy"), this was hardly because such high concepts were unknown. Instead, peaceful husbandry of natural resources was such an accepted way of life that "it did not have to have a special word."

And so on. After noting accurately enough that many of the foods eaten in the modern world—corns, beans, tomatoes, pumpkins, peppers, sunflowers, squash, and most nuts—were first developed by skilled Native American plant breeders, "Native American Contributions" goes on to argue that the idea for the U.S. government was "adopted" or stolen directly from Native Americans. Per the anonymous author, "Benjamin Franklin said that the idea of the federal government, in which certain powers are given to a central government and all others are reserved for the states, was borrowed from the system . . . used by the Iroquoian League of Nations." This historical myth, which has snowballed in a game of historical "telephone" from one scholar to another—and was officially promoted by the U.S. Senate in 1988—originates in a rather backhanded compliment by Franklin

* This quote-heavy technique will be common throughout this book, as one of my goals is specifically providing evidence both of the "lies" I respond to in very mainstream forums and of rebuttal arguments to them.

for the league. There's little evidence that he turned that onetime admiration into inspiration for a grander plan.[2]

Despite a few potentially embarrassing slips from the narrative—one of the Native American words that "became part of the English language" around this time was "cannibal"—"Native American Contributions" proceeds fairly smoothly on from there to the outline of a supposed shared Amerindian value system, which is argued to have existed fairly universally in the Western Hemisphere prior to 1492. Some of the more notable components of this alleged epistemology are Respect for Fellow Man ("no prejudice"), "no major wars (no Indian nation destroyed another; there were thousands of years of peace before 1492)," "no poor and no rich," and "no jails . . . taxes, borders, or boundaries" limiting the migration or even potential of people(s) in any way.

Many mainstream takes on the topic, at least those targeted at students, sound like this. Another example, the primary entry for "Native Americans Prior to 1492" on History Central, takes a similar tack, praising each region of precontact North America in turn. On the Northwest Coast of what would become the United States, "the Native Americans . . . had no need to farm."[3] Food and other resources all but fell from the sky: "The land was full of animals, the sea was full of fish. . . . Wood was plentiful." Peaceful communal projects were the norm: one of the cultural innovations of Northwest Coast peoples like the Haida was large and well-built canoes that "could hold 50 people." And what were such well-made big boats used for? The authors don't say, although I will later on in this chapter.

The narrative exists in actual textbooks, too. After some discussion of the more traditionally "civilized" accomplishments of the Incas, Mayans, Mound Builders, and Aztecs, *The American Pageant* by David M. Kennedy and Lizabeth Cohen leaps into hyperbole, describing other Amerindians thusly: "Unlike the Europeans, who would soon arrive with the presumption that humans had dominion over the Earth, and with technologies to alter the very face of the land, the Native Americans had neither the desire nor the means to manipulate nature aggressively." While the book concedes that tribes did sometimes set large forest fires to improve their ability to hunt deer, the authors insist Indians overall "revered the physical world and endowed nature with spiritual properties."[4]

With a green heart, apparently, comes a green thumb. Another common contention of the texts—with these words from *The Unfinished Nation: A Concise History of the American People*—is that the settled Native American tribes were such skilled cultivators that cultural exchanges with them "were at least as important" for the Old World as for the New.[5] After correctly noting that Natives introduced Europeans to crops like corn, squash, most beans, tomatoes, and potatoes, author Alan Brinkley goes on to argue that they also taught them major "new agricultural techniques" and that encounters with them were objectively "more beneficial" for Westerners than Indians. Given that large domestic animals, metal tools, and the wheel essentially did not exist in North or South America before 1492, this seems at very least debatable—but it is not debated.

Anyone reading through this sort of stuff might be forgiven for thinking that, as the title of a modern blockbuster movie argued, Columbus and the Westerners who followed him rather literally conquered Paradise.[6] However, the realities of history have a way of being brutally insensitive to flowery narratives from any side of the modern political aisle, and most of the Spaniards and others who originally encountered the mighty Native nations saw their lands as far closer to hell than heaven. Instead of being paradisical utopias free of the sins of European civilization, Native societies were just as likely as their Old World equivalents to be plagued by oppression, unjust hierarchies, environmental abuse and waste, and political dissension. In other words, Native Americans were just as human as the rest of us.

Mesoamerican peoples like the Aztecs, in particular, shocked even jaded European mercenaries—many of whom had fought their African and West Asian counterparts back in the Old World—with their level of brutality.

A major recent article in *Science* by Lizzie Wade titled "Feeding the Gods: Hundreds of Skulls Reveal Massive Scale of Human Sacrifice in Aztec Capital" serves as a reminder of how shockingly bloody Aztec society was before any Westerners got here.[7] The piece centers on the recent rediscovery by a team of archaeologists of the giant towers of human skulls that used to be a feature of the Aztec/Mexica capital of Tenochtitlan. As Wade notes, multiple different literate Spanish conquistadors wrote about the *tzompantli* skull towers— which seems a difficult architectural touch to ignore—estimating that the main skull rack alone held 130,000 human crania. However, for many years, scholars viewed the claim as conquistador propaganda, believing the skull towers to be a fable that "exaggerate[d] the horrors of human sacrifice to demonize the Mexica culture."

Now we know the truth. At the conclusion of a project beginning in 2015, scholars at Mexico's excellent National Institute of Anthropology and History discovered the remains of the towers in Ciudad de Mexico, under a house from the Colonial period and (ironically) just a half block from the National Cathedral. The *tzompantli* was as big as advertised: "an imposing rectangular structure, 35 meters long and 12 to 14 meters wide, slightly larger than a basketball court." It was also about 5 meters—15 feet—high, indeed capable of containing the remains of hundreds of thousands of ex-enemies.

And this was no perverse one-off example of atrocity. Multiple-person human sacrifice was a feature of Mexican Indian culture for hundreds of years. Per Vera Tiesler, a bioarchaeologist in the Yucatán region of Mexico, a half-dozen polished and drilled skulls (the holes suggesting a *tzompantli*) were discovered in the *Mayan*— not Aztec—city of Chichén Itzá. These date to "some 700 years" before Tenochtitlan even existed and were found more than six hundred miles away. What scholars are finding is at least some evidence of New World human sacrifice stretching over most of a millennium, with the custom reaching its apex during the Aztec Empire. According to Tiesler: "The Mexica certainly brought this to an extreme. . . . Tenochtitlan was the maximum expression [of the *tzompantli* tradition]."

Instead of the progressive Eden imagined by modern scholars, this was a society full of far harsher "power dynamics" than those we see today. As I noted in the first chapter, slavery was often a way to deal with prisoners of war. Another way would be human sacrifice. All of this was specifically done to intimidate or, as a modern leftist might put it, to show power. Aztec sacrificial victims were generally battle captives—like those brought back from the long-running series of wars "with their archenemy, the nearby republic of Tlaxcala"—or *Hunger Games*–style tributes extorted from previously defeated subject populations living within the Aztec Empire. The brutal killing of these individuals and subsequent display of their heads or skulls in public forums was among other things a way to keep the helots in line. "The killing of captives is a strong political statement," Wade quotes John Verano, a bioarchaeologist at Tulane University, "It's a way to demonstrate power and political influence . . . it's a way to control your own population."

In addition to killing probably millions of people, the Aztecs also *ate* a ton of them, a practice sure to shock modern sensibilities. There is essentially universal agreement among scholars that many Mesoamerican peoples engaged in ritual and dietary cannibalism alongside regular human sacrifice.[8] Older sources are close to unanimous in confirming this. In his *The True History of the Conquest of Mexico*, Spanish soldier and writer Bernal Díaz del Castillo writes of seeing caged war captives ready to be eaten in the Mexica city of Cholula, of noticing large cooking pots in the temples of Tenochtitlan where human meat was prepared for the meals of Aztec holy men and pilgrims, and even of being threatened with consumption himself during battle against Cholulan and Aztec warriors.

As the encyclopedias note, Diaz's testimony is supported by many other Spanish and even Mesoamerican sources. Diego Muñoz Camargo, who wrote *The History of Tlaxcala*, mentions almost in passing that some (not most) Meso-American cities contained "public butcher's shops of human flesh, as if it were cow or sheep."[9] Juan Bautista de Pomar, author of *Relación de Texcoco*, describes the process of sacrifice and cannibalism in methodical terms, stating that the slain bodies of military captives would generally be given to the specific fighter who took them prisoner—who would then boil or roast the body and offer pieces of meat as gifts to allies and personal friends.* In his *Historia general de las cosas de Nuevo España*, Bernardino de Sahagún—himself a Mesoamerican ethnographer who hardly hated the Native peoples of the region—included an image of a captured Aztec being cooked by enemies as a representative image.

Cannibalism was prevalent enough to have a significant impact on the overall Aztec diet, although there is serious debate about how large this was. The renowned Hispanic archaeologist Bernard Ortiz de Montellano has argued that the historical Aztec diet was basically adequate in protein and cannibalism "would not have contributed greatly."[10] However, even he concedes that "large numbers of sacrifices" took place during multiple large annual festivals of celebration and Thanksgiving, and "many captives were sacrificed and eaten." At one point, he uses a rather sophisticated series of mathematical proofs to conclude that Aztec cannibalism could have satisfied 6.5 percent of all protein needs inside at least the city of Tenochtitlan if the whole bodies of captives were eaten, and well over 2 percent if only selected "extremities" were chosen for consumption.

At the other extreme of this debate, Marvin Harris—author of the aptly titled *Cannibals and Kings: The Origins of Cultures*—has argued that the Aztec diet *was* lacking in key proteins simply not provided by beans and squash, and the flesh of sacrifice victims made up an important part of the Aztec military and upper-class diet. To Harris, all those gaudily feathered columns of Aztec prisoners seen on temple stele represented walking meat, heading into Mexica cities for much the same reasons cattle today travel to Chicago and Fort Worth. To quote him: "All edible parts [of human

---

* To be fair, Pomar also notes that some of these individuals considered human meat to be "of no value" and would not eat it.

sacrifices] were used in a fashion strictly comparable to the consumption of the flesh of domesticated animals."[11]

Grim stuff. And cannibalism—which was likely also far more prevalent in recent-past Europe, Asia, and West Africa than we like to admit, reading between the "Won't you stay for dinner?" lines of many a fairy tale—appears to have existed above the Rio Grande as well as below it. Multiple scholarly accounts describe cannibalism within the sophisticated and often quite humane Iroquois Confederacy, with an interesting piece titled "Iroquois Cannibalism: Fact Not Fiction" pointing out: "Archaeologists, working on Iroquoian . . . sites, report that evidence of cannibalism appears in the archaeological record in sites dating about AD 1300 and continues into historic times." In Ontario, Canada, and the northeastern United States, they quote other researchers as finding that "the practice survived into the historic period but appears to have reached a peak around the mid-16th century. . . . [A]n *overwhelming* mass of evidence exists . . ."[12]

Much of that evidence consists of contemporary accounts. In the *Jesuit Relations*, a document prepared by Christian missionaries, a priest describes the not-atypical death of a man: "Because I had baptized him, they carried all his limbs—one by one—into the cabin where I abode—skinning, in my presence, and eating his feet and hands." On a larger scale, Governor Jacques-René de Brisay Denonville of New France (today's Quebec, Newfoundland, etc.) summarized the actions of his Iroquois allies after a 1687 battle against Seneca and Europeans as follows: "The savages . . . cut the dead into quarters, as in slaughter-houses, in order to put them in the pot. The greater number were opened while still warm that their blood might be drank."

Some of this might be dismissed as calumny from foreign warriors and divines, hailing from a civilization not then notably less "savage." However, the greater part of it is almost certainly just true. The Iroquois Great Law of Peace itself includes an awkward section dealing with cannibalism and the defeat of a "Cannibal" faction of tribal society led by the mad Onondaga medicine man

Adodaroh by the more peaceful Cultivators, titled "The Cannibal Converts."[13]

Even where cannibalism was uncommon, Native life prior to Western conquest was far from Edenic.

In his excellent article "Predatory Warfare, Social Status, and the North Pacific Slave Trade," Professor Donald Mitchell of the University of Victoria argues that a key feature of life for Haida tribal members and members of other Pacific Northwest tribes was continual "predatory warfare": "warfare for the acquisition of slaves and the maintenance or enhancement of high social status." After looking through what appears to be all of approximately 725 of the primary sources on point, Dr. Mitchell notes that there were essentially no peaceful human groups in the region. "Preying on other groups for plunder and captives" was a reality of life for tribes and chiefdoms ranging from the Eyak and Yakutat in the north of Alaska to the more familiar Chinook living by the continental USA's Columbia River.[14]

Let us, briefly, return to the Pacific Coast of North America and see what those large canoes praised by History Central were used for! As it turns out, in addition to occasionally engaging in ritual man-eating, powerful Pacific Northwest tribes like the Haida and the Kwakiutl were among the greatest warrior-pirates in history—using hand-carved boats the length of Byzantine warships to effortlessly raid hundreds of miles down the left coast of North America. As with the Aztec fondness for long pig, and the well-documented similar tastes found among such tribes as Texas's Tonkawa and Karankawa, the driver for this constant piracy seems to have been situational necessity.

In an economy with no coined or paper money, and apparently no reasonably standardized units of "wampum" or metals, slaves were one of the few universally accepted forms of currency and universally recognized indicators of wealth. Like "fine canoes, long strands of dentalia, blankets, or coppers"—the latter two presumably obtained from white traders themselves known for piracy, and imperfectly available—slaves figured in virtually all "economic transactions and ceremonial occasions." Thus, while Northwest Coast battles were no doubt sometimes fought to avenge a beloved kinsman or obtain new lands—humans gonna human—the prime motive for violent raiding throughout most or all of this area was "to gain captives for enslavement" and later sale. ("Warfare between the tribes usually took the form of brief raids and skirmishes," downplays *America, Past and Present*. "Most conflicts involved only a few warriors intent on stealing horses or 'counting coup'—touching an enemy's body with the hand or a special stick."[15])

Slaves—unsurprisingly, given all this—had a fairly standardized value throughout the Pacific Northwest region. Per Mitchell, a single healthy slave was valued at 150 to 200 woven cloth blankets by the Haida, 100 blankets by the Kwakiutl, 200 blankets by the Tsishaat, 100 to 200 blankets by the Makah, 80 or more blankets by the Halkomelem, and up to 100 blankets (although, oddly, sometimes as few as 20) by the Chinook. Where elk skins were used in barter instead, Tsimshian tribal members would pay 15, and Stikine warriors and women 18 to 20. One of the few real outliers on the chart is the northerly Yakutat, who preferred to trade in exotic sea otter skins and would only pay two of them for an unfortunate *Homo sapiens*. Overall, however, slaves were readily exchangeable at similar rates across an area spanning perhaps one-eighth of a continent: "marching money" if not usually "marching meat."

One through line visible across the articles on this topic is that, because of the centrality of warfare and slave-raiding to tribal life, the Pacific Coast tribes and in particular the Haida were genuinely no slouches when it came to naval weapons technology. Anthropologist Diamond Jenness[16] describes Haida war canoes as being up to 100 feet long, "each hollowed out of a single cedar tree and manned by fifty or sixty warriors." Most were equipped for sea warfare, employing ropes of cedar bark tied around heavy rings of polished stone as a crude but effective proxy for artillery, "hurled to smash enemy canoes." A more mystical form of armament was, presumably, provided by wizards: each canoe generally carried a senior shaman or medicine man in the bow, trained "to catch and destroy the souls of enemies before an impending battle."

Long before the arrival of Europeans, the Haida were feared up and down the North American West Coast as "Indian Vikings." The by-no-means-weak Tsimshian people were at one point so plagued by Haida raids that they developed a signal-fire system capable of alerting every village in their Skeena River area when a Haida raider reached the mainland. Even after whites arrived, the Haida proved no slouches in their element, winning several maritime conflicts and "successfully captur[ing] more than half a dozen" Western ships—including the good-sized vessels *Eleanora* and *Susan Sturgis*. Some raider chiefs adopted Western technology to their own ends ("Swivel guns were added to many Haida war canoes"), and at least one forced a cannon-armed British merchantman to stop bombarding his village by effectively firing back, with cannons and ammunition apparently taken from a captured U.S. schooner.

The aptitude of the Haida and similar peoples for military technology often extended to the fortification of any land *touching* water. As the Canadian Museum of History points out, forts and entire fortified towns were part of "the defensive strategy of all Northwest Coast groups for at least 2,000 years." Typical defenses at Haida forts, probably the best of the lot, included log palisades, trapdoors, and hidden entrances, "rolling top-log defenses," and actual fighting platforms equipped with boulders and other weapons to use against attackers. The famous British naval officer Captain James Cook christened one such fortification "Hippah Island" because it reminded him of the best of the Maori forts he had seen while campaigning in New Zealand. For centuries both before and after the white man came, the U.S. and Canadian Pacific Coast was the setting for constant, sophisticated, brutal warfare.

Reading between the lines of those scholarly resources dealing with Native tribal mobility indicates that much the same was probably true almost everywhere.

Another vital pillar of the leftist case against European conquest is Natives' alleged eternal inhabitance in their lands. While modern Americans tend to think of Amerindian groups as having occupied much the same lands since time immemorial—"For so long as the grass has grown," and so forth—modern research increasingly indicates that many major tribes moved into the territories they held when they first encountered Westerners during recorded history or not long before, often conquering them from previously resident populations. The Anishinaabe/Ojibway provide a typical example.[17]

According to Ojibway tribal legend, much of it confirmed by archaeologists, the tribe originally resided in the northern region of what is today American New England. However, around the year AD 900, "this nation was visited by the Seven Spirits"—and a few consecutive years of bad hunting and harvests—and told to migrate west "to a place where food grew on the water." The entire tribal population duly did so, "start[ing] their migration," fighting a number of battles along the way, and arriving in the uplands of Minnesota and Michigan around 1500 to 1600. There they found wild rice growing and decided to settle, no doubt to the consternation of the peoples then living there. Invading Europeans often conceptualized America as a vast blank slate, uninhabited and virgin. We shouldn't make the same mistake and pretend that pre-Colonial Native migration took place in a vacuum.

When the Ojibway arrived in the uplands, they discovered peoples there already. One of those peoples was the great tribe we mostly know today as the Sioux. Per the invaluable *Encyclopedia Britannica*,[18] prior to the early seventeenth century, almost the entire population of at least Santee Sioux lived near the shores of Lake Superior, "where they gathered wild rice and other foods, hunted deer and buffalo, and speared fish from canoes." When Anishinaabe tribal members arrived to contest the rice paddies, "constant warfare with these Ojibway to their east" drove the Santee Sioux down into more temperate southern Minnesota, where they displaced the Teton and Yankton (also generally considered Sioux tribes).

These migrations created a domino effect of displacement and warfare. Displaced by the Santee fleeing the Ojibway, the Teton and Yankton tribes fled to the Great Plains of the U.S. interior, where they took advantage of just-arriving horses to abandon agriculture altogether and become mounted buffalo hunters—and constant raiders of the "Mandan, Arikara, Hidatsa, and Pawnee." Even the cross-tribal name of "Sioux" dates to this period of intense intra-Native warfare and was originally an Ojibway military insult. The term is a condensation of *nadouessioux* (rattlesnakes) and originally simply meant "enemy."

Interestingly, "Apache" has the exact same meaning, for the same reason.[19] The ancestral Apache were not, as it happens, from the "eternal and sacred" lands that are held by the modern tribe, either. So far as anyone can tell, these most famous of Southwestern Indians did not reach the Southwest until "at least 1100 CE,"[20] and probably a bit later—which might sound like a long time ago until you realize the earliest residents of the area were the Cochise culture, and they arrived in 7000 BC.[21] They apparently came quite a distance, led by many champions: linguists point out that Apachean languages are "clearly a sub-group of the Athabaskan language family," and—with the sole exception of the Navajo—every other Athabaskan-speaking tribe is located near the Arctic Circle in northwestern Canada.

Upon arrival, the Apache wasted little time settling into their new home. Per an encyclopedia account, "before [Western] colonization" began, Apache arms had managed to conquer "east-central and southeastern Arizona, southeastern Colorado, southwestern and eastern New Mexico, and western Texas and (in Mexico) northern Chihuahua and Sonora states." The Apache held most of this land until the 1700s—"Plains Apache farmers were living along the Dismal River [near Kansas] as recently as 1700"—when they in turn began to experience substantial pressure from horse-and-gun-equipped raiders from the Comanche tribe. However, they managed to retain much of the core of the Apacheria even during that series of wars. At some point during all of this, the Apache ("enemy") label itself was bestowed on members of the tribe by warriors of the Zuni, still another opponent group.

Reviewing actual history of this kind, more than a few scholars have concluded that—to quote the headline of a 2014 piece from Science 2.0 that summarizes recent academic findings—"The most violent era in American history was before Europeans arrived." While noting specifically that "there is a mythology about the native Americans . . . they were all peaceful and in harmony with nature," the authors point out considerable evidence that the exact reverse was often the case: arguably the most violent per-capita era in American history involved the Native tribes of the American Southwest. (Though notably, in "the northern Rio Grande region of what is now New Mexico, people had far less violence while experiencing similar [population] growth and, ostensibly, population pressures."[22] Native culture was no more monolithic than European. Just ask the Swiss.)

The Science 2.0 article relies heavily on a piece from the academic journal *American Antiquity*, which found that an astonishing 90 percent of all human remains from the relevant time period in the Mesa Verde region display "trauma from blows to either their heads or parts of their arms." This surge in violence would explain a persistent mystery: the radical and "mysterious depopulation of the northern Southwest, from a population of about 40,000 people in the mid-1200s to none 30 years later."[23]

What happened? According to Washington State University archaeologist Tim Kohler and his colleagues, a long "time of troubles" began when people in the Chaco culture—dominant between the Rio Grande and southern Colorado—attempted to spread into the more northerly Mesa Verde area after roughly the year 1130. The migration of the Chaco people(s) was motivated by desperation caused by environmental pressures ("a severe drought") and possibly by pressure from other tribes in their original home region: their völkerwanderung resulted in population loss throughout the Chaco region and then a surge in violence in central Mesa Verde that "peaked" around 1160. Constant back-and-forth warfare apparently made much of the area unlivable—it is difficult to plant corn when heavily armed warriors might at any point come running out of the woods—and, by "slightly more than a century later," most of the Mesa Verde population was gone as well, in the mystery depopulation.

This tragedy is all the more ironic because it took place after "a cultural boom that has no parallel in North American prehistory," Hampton Sides wrote in a history of the wars for the American Southwest. The Chacoans' tremendous technical skills, coupled with beneficent and unusually wet weather, led to a remarkable civilizational rise and fall over a century.

> Rapidly, the Chaco Anasazi began to centralize their government, intensify their agriculture, and concentrate their population ... They built razor-straight highways ... they erected "lighthouses" in which they burned signal fires that broadcast messages over hundreds of miles.... [However, they] overfarmed, overhunted, and overlogged. In only a few generations their deforested land became eroded, the topsoil depleted, the drainages choked with salt and silt....
> This environmental upheaval led, predictably enough, to a social upheaval.[24]

We can see here a societal arc not dissimilar to European civilizations that grew massive, decayed into decadence and environmental abuse, and split into violent civil war.

Obviously, Native violence of this kind did not cease when the first Westerners—often Spaniards, Scotsmen, Irishmen, captured Black West Africans, and others hailing from different long traditions of *razzia*—entered the picture. Here we should moderate the simple picture of peaceful Natives attacked by unprecedented violence from European conquerors to a more realistic portrait of the ruthless, mutually savage, highly disorganized, semi-racial wars that defined the earliest conflicts between Old Worlders and Natives in the future United States. A Ron Rosenbaum piece titled "The Shocking Savagery of America's Early History" does a good job of summing up the true dynamic of "first contact" violence. Interviewing esteemed historian Bernard Bailyn, Rosenbaum draws out a recitation of small anecdotes that come together to form a coherent larger picture.

Both Western and Native actors had complex motivations, says Bailyn. The Natives—and very arguably the whites, at least at first—"were not genocidal on the whole" in any standard sense of this word. Indian leaders generally wanted settlers, who would have been English in the region of North America under discussion, to exist accessibly at the fringes of Native society "so that they would have the benefit of their treasure, their goods, even their advanced weapons. They wanted that, but under their control."

The problem with this arrangement is that it virtually guaranteed constant provocations and border breakings by members of *both* warlike cultures, with young Native men at fault as often as young white ones—a reality of shared fault that is often intentionally minimized today. Asked to provide a typical "vignette" from the Native side of the ledger, Bailyn notes the murder of four Dutch traders. One of the luckless men was "eaten, after having been well-roasted," while two more were burnt alive for little or no reason. The Native bravos responsible "carried a leg and an arm home to be divided amongst their families."

However, the whites of 1622 were also "savages" by our standards: Pilgrim leader Miles Standish once outraged his Indigenous neighbors by cutting the head off a dead chief after a victorious encounter, bringing it back to Plymouth, and "displaying it on the blockhouse together with a flag made of . . . cloth soaked in the victim's blood."

Happy Thanksgiving!* Much the same sort of conflict, defined by mutual raiding and breaking of treaties, would go on to define U.S. history until almost the year 1900. For example, the Grattan Fight, the incident that almost single-handedly touched off the bloody First Sioux War, which started off in a surprisingly mun-

---

* The original article also makes this joke.

dane dispute over stolen livestock that quickly evolved into a violent debacle thanks to the pigheadedness, arrogance, and panic of a group of young men.

It all began when a detachment of U.S. Army soldiers entered a Sioux camp to arrest warrior High Forehead, who was suspected of stealing a white farmer's cow in breach of the then-current treaty. By doing so, notably, the soldiers were themselves also in breach of the treaty, which mandated that such incidents be resolved by a U.S. government Indian agent.[25]

Sioux chief Conquering Bear refused to hand over High Forehead, instead proposing to compensate the settler with a better-quality cow or a horse. The settler, however, specifically demanded monetary reparations of twenty-five dollars. In this, he was supported by Second Lieutenant John Grattan, late of West Point, who did not much like Indians and was bored, inexperienced, and raring for adventure. He badgered his commanding officer into letting him go arrest the thief and went along with loaded cannon. This, as it turns out, was to be the young officer's only encounter with the Native peoples of the Americas.

As white and Native fighting men milled about, arguing over livestock, a nervous U.S. soldier fired his gun. He shot at least one Sioux, obviously prompting the many Sioux warriors in the encampment to begin returning fire with their saddle bows and rifles. In the ensuing violence, Chief Conquering Bear was killed and Grattan's entire twenty-nine-man command was essentially wiped out—losing "more than one officer, one civilian employee, twenty-nine enlisted men, twelve mules and their harness, and one horse." A single doughty U.S. trooper survived the initial battle but died later of his injuries. This avoidable incident led directly to the first of the great Sioux Wars, in which thousands of both Americans and Native Americans were killed.[26]

Such incidents were tragically common. Mistrust and nuance lost in cultural translation—egged on by bad actors—can and often did lead to tragedy. The Whitman Massacre, which also caused a large-scale war, provides another example. The Massacre, or "Tragedy at Waiilatpu," resulted from one Dr. Whitman's inability to cure an epidemic of measles, which was afflicting a Native tribe already struggling with "opposition to American expansion, the . . . inflexibility [of Christian missionaries], the demise of the fur trade, the language barrier" with incoming whites, and more.[27] During the mid-1840s, tensions arose over a variety of issues between Marcus Whitman—an American missionary to then lightly settled Washington Territory—and the powerful local Cayuse tribe. First of these was the use by Whitman and his wife, Narcissa, of modern agricultural poisons.[28]

During the winter of 1846, the Whitmans apparently placed large pieces of poisoned meat near their home and near Marcus Whitman's Christian mission, to kill area predators like wolves and coyotes. Several members of the Cayuse tribe found and ate the poisoned meat, becoming very sick but not dying. A local chief, Tiloukaikt, visited the Waiilatpu site of Whitman's mission not long after this and stated that he would have killed Whitman if any of the sick men had died. I get the impression that the incident led to a view of the missionary as an irascible and potentially dangerous medicine man among the local Indigenous population. All of this became relevant near the end of the same year, when a severe measles epidemic struck the Waiilatpu area.

Putting old grudges aside, the Whitmans attempted to treat Cayuse tribal members during the disease outbreak. However, many Native patients died during what was fairly close to a "virgin field" epidemic, and "it was hard for the Indians to understand why so many of their number died, both children and adults, when only one white child at Waiilatpu was taken. They knew nothing of immunity."[29] At least some Cayuse came to believe that Whitman was trying to poison them rather than cure them—perhaps by using medicines laced with strychnine.[30]

In this, they were encouraged by one Joe Lewis, a mixed-race white and Iroquois man who unsurprisingly disliked white Americans after his own experiences with racial bias in the eastern United States and personally wanted to "ransack" the Whitman

Mission. When rousing anger against the Whitmans, Lewis and others took advantage of a long-standing tradition among Native American tribes in the Columbia Plateau region: the absolute right of the "relatives of a deceased person"[31] to kill a *te-wat*, or medicine man, who unsuccessfully attempted to treat their family member.*

Agitation based on this stout form of anti-malpractice policy came to a head on November 29, 1847, when a large band of armed Cayuse warriors attacked the Whitman Mission. Whitman himself was hatcheted to death during a struggle, and his young wife killed by a barrage of rifle and musket shots. The Native fighters then attacked essentially everyone else then present at the mission, killing eleven more people (Crocket Bewley, Isaac Gilliland, Jacob Hoffman, Nathan Kimball, Walter Marsh, Andrew Rodgers, brothers Francis and John Sager, Amos Sales, L. W. Saunders, and James Young) and dragging fifty-four missionaries and their spouses away as captives.

Following the usual inventive tortures, several prisoners died: the rest were ransomed back by their community on or shortly after December 26, 1847, for "twelve common guns, six hundred loads of ammunition, twelve flints, thirty-seven pounds of tobacco, sixty-two three point blankets, [and] sixty-three common shirts." *This* incident began the Cayuse War, which lasted for five bloody years and largely destroyed the tribe.[32]

While most white-Native wars frankly followed this same pattern, some tribes were uniquely brutal. The Comanche of Texas and Oklahoma "were reputed to be the most diabolical in their cruelties to captives," Hampton Sides writes. "Comanches liked to take their victims to a remote stretch of the plains and stake their bodies to the ground. Then the Comanches would slit open their

---

* The Cayuse Indians apparently took this traditional right particularly seriously. The traveler Archibald McKinlay, quoted in the source just given—Clifford M. Drury's *Marcus and Narcissa Whitman and the Opening of Old Oregon*—notes that the tribe "shot seven of their own medicine men by the fort during my five years' stay there, and probably over three times that number altogether." *Te-wat* was no job for the lily-livered, apparently.

bellies and poke their organs with spears, making a slow study of it, delighting in the bloodcurdling screams, sometimes slicing a bit of a victim's liver and eating it right in front of him."[33]

Authors like S. C. Gwynne, who penned *Empire of the Summer Moon*, note that many whites were taken prisoner in a similar fashion during the Western Indian Wars.

About the Comanche specifically, Gwynne says: "No tribe in the history of the Spanish, French, Texan, and American occupations of this land ever caused so much havoc and death. None was even a close second." The plan of action behind Comanche raids was, he argues, "straightforward": "All the men were killed, and any men who were captured alive were tortured [to death]; the captive women were gang raped. Babies were invariably killed."

Gwynne and Sides are quick to point out—quite properly—that the white and Mexican opponents of the Comanche were often also brutal to noncombatants. Even as Sides describes a truly epic battle between the iconic Kit Carson leading 400 men and a force of 3,000 Comanches and Kiowas—Carson cannily survived the defeat with judicious use of howitzers—Sides follows up this story with the description of Colonel John Chivington, the "Fighting Parson," leading his men to massacre at Sand Creek, in Colorado Territory, "150 Cheyenne, mostly women and children . . . in cold blood that day, in a massacre that is now widely regarded as the worst atrocity committed in all the Indian wars."[34]

Many times over the years the Europeans failed to live up to their promises or, as in many a case, the federal government concocted top-down plans to force formerly free populations to live in the way they assumed was most efficient. That went about as well as you'd expect.

Still, with atrocities like those committed by the Comanche, it's easy to see why the warfare between the groups became so brutal. The taboo obvious must be said: it is frankly not surprising that most Western settlers, probably including all of those ever to see the aftermath of a Comanche raid, wanted to wipe out the "Lords of the Plains" in their entirety rather than make friends with them.

Many Comanche likely felt the same in reverse: they were being so brutal in order to chase the odd-looking strangers off of their ancient ancestral hunting grounds (which they themselves conquered from the Apache in the "late eighteenth century"). They also, like their early opponents the Mexicans, had no concept of "all-out war or unconditional surrender or treaties that endured beyond a season—these were European concepts," Sides writes. "The attacks and reprisals were simply part of the grim metronome of life, swinging with the same logic of a feud."[35]

It is both "presentist" and more than a bit patronizing to paint complex historical conflicts of this kind as simple matters of good and evil. White settlers were not invariably the "bad guys," and one of the most powerful and aggressive of all Native tribes was not a mere hapless set of victims of oppression.

Despite romantic leftist images of Natives as innocents uncontaminated by thoughts of greed or dishonest gain, the reality is that Natives were also prone to starting wars over mercenary concerns. Larger conflicts involving whites and Natives were very, very often no easier to summarize in terms like "good" and "evil." Take, for example, the Beaver Wars, which lasted between 1609 and 1701 and almost certainly resulted in tens of thousands of deaths.[36] The Beaver Wars began when the powerful Native nations of the Iroquois Confederacy sought to achieve monopoly control of the North American fur trade with European merchants. The Iroquois, who were supplied with weapons and sometimes with fighting men by their English and Dutch allies, essentially attempted to conquer the region then known as the "Ohio Country" by defeating the resident Huron and a coalition of Algonquin-speaking tribes. The latter peoples, for their part, were supplied with weapons and matériel by the French, with whom they traded extensively.

While the wars are sometimes described as indecisive, "partial Iroquois victory" seems like a better description. During the years following 1650, according to one historical resource, "The Iroquois Confederacy drove out the Huron, Petun, Erie, and Sisquehannock Tribes who were allies with French fur traders and who had well-established communities and territories in the Ohio Country. The . . . Confederacy pushed these Tribes west, and destroyed [the] alliances of the Erie, Huron, and Shawnee. The Iroquois Confederacy gained control of the Ohio Country."[37] The alliance between the Iroquois and the English would also prove durable: the famous French and Indian War of 1754, during which the two populations fought together, witnessed a white European polity—France—being totally defeated and losing almost all of her North American lands.

It is worth noting, re: the prevalent "stewards of the woods" stereotype, that none of these warrior peoples—white or "red"—were environmentalists of any kind. Following the Wars and the Iroquois takeover of the best beavering lands, the North American beaver was largely eradicated in the Northeastern region of the country. The reduction in beaver numbers, in natural ecosystems where their dams played a major ecological role, was so sudden and substantial that large-scale environmental changes occurred in some areas, while others saw actual droughts. Even today, scholars remain divided on whether North American populations of the world's second-largest rodent merely took generations to recover, or never have.[38]

Somewhat remarkably, cyclical white-Native ultraviolence was still going on more than 250 years after the beginning of the Beaver Wars and 163 years after their end. In an interesting bit of historical trivia, one typical "later Plains wars" conflict—the Dakota War of 1862—involved the powerful Sioux tribe, whom the Iroquois had previously helped drive west onto the short-grass prairies of the Great Plains. Once again, the causes of the war and the behavior of all sides during it were complex and hardly reflect a perfect exercise of mutual morality.

The Dakota War, like most human wars, began over issues of land and money. On three previous occasions—in 1837, 1851, and 1858—the Dakota Sioux had ceded large areas of prime hunting land to the United States government by treaty. However, the powerful tribe was not simply giving land away under duress: the cessations took place in exchange for sizable cash annuities, the payment of some tribal and individual debts, an annual tribute of goods and provisions, and guaranteed ownership of two reservations bordering the Minnesota River and measuring roughly 1,400 square miles in area. The U.S. government apparently expected the Indians to use their money and new river-bottom land to become settled farmers rather than nomadic hunters, although accounts differ as to whether this was effectively communicated to the Dakota and whether the Dakota had any intention of keeping up their side of the deal if it was.[39]

At any rate, they did not do so: in what sounds almost like the punch line to a joke, the most famous of all High Plains warriors never amounted to much as sedentary wheat farmers—and, over the years, the tribe became more and more dependent on annual deliveries of annuities and tribute. Then, finally, in 1861, this somewhat stable system fell apart: a crop failure and subsequent harsh winter destroyed most of what grain the tribe had been growing, and all annuity payments were months late because of budgetary pressures caused by the American Civil War. During this time, Sioux leaders were also aware that many U.S. soldiers had left their previous postings to fight the rebellious South in the Civil War, and that the Army had failed to punish perpetrators of a recent massacre at Spirit Lake.[40] By June or July of 1862, the Dakota began to raid white settlements.

As usual, both the raiding and the white riposte to it were utterly brutal—"savage," if you will. Hostilities opened with the massacre of a settler family by four to six Native warriors in Acton, Minnesota, when, after an almost friendly shooting match, a group of young Dakota "reloaded their guns and fired on" an innocent group of white women and men and went on "to kill 15 year old Clara Wilson."[41] This action was followed by Dakota Sioux chief Little Crow's open declaration that he planned to drive all settlers out of the Minnesota River Valley.

In the following weeks, between August 18 and September 26, 1862, war-painted Dakota warriors attacked isolated settlers without provocation, killing 358 and causing thousands to flee the region.[42] The Dakota also took more than 250 captives, largely white and mixed-race women and girls.[43] In the absence of an effective government response during the Civil War, an army consisting largely of volunteer militia was assembled by Minnesota governor Alexander Ramsey and retired colonel Henry Hastings Sibley and sent off in pursuit of the Indians. After some misadventures and a few atrocities of their own, this force brought Little Crow's force to bay at the Battle of Wood Lake and defeated it[44]—with the seven soldiers and fifteen Dakota killed in the battle serving to punctuate the roughly seven hundred total lives lost during the war.[45]

The short but brutal conflict had a number of consequences. Disgusted by the atrocities committed by Little Crow's fighters, a Minnesota military-judicial commission sentenced some 303 Dakota men to death by hanging following the conclusion of the war. After reviewing the death sentences, President Abraham Lincoln reprieved all but 38 of the men. However, their mass hanging still stands as the largest single execution in American history: it is often presented, without context, by activists as a prime example of Western brutality against Natives.[46] The war also led to the dissolution of the United States' treaties with the Dakota Sioux, and in fact of the eastern Dakota reservation itself (surviving Dakota were sent to new lands in southern Dakota Territory)—another action frequently treated as a dishonest act of American calumny.

The last scars of 1862's battles seem to have only just healed, in fact. In 2021, the Minnesota Historical Society and the legislature of Minnesota announced the transfer of more than one hundred acres of land back to the Sioux nation and the official Lower Sioux Indian Community, with this transfer to include the historic site of the Dakota War's major battle and the land where the Lower Sioux Indian Agency once sat.[47] The tribe and the historical society now jointly administer the site, and there has been talk of building a shrine there to all who fell in defense of their respective nations. Peace, perhaps, has finally been achieved.

The complex war-for-four-hundred-years reality of white-versus-Native conflict has caused more than a few modern scholars to reevaluate the popular *Bury My Heart at Wounded Knee* claim that white settlers committed organized genocide against Native Americans. In a fairly typical recent article in *History Is Now* magazine, frankly enough titled "Did Settlers Commit Genocide in America?,"[48] the authors take the general position that the answer is: "No." Citing previous scholars and writers from Daniel L. Smith to Michael Medved, they contend that "the word genocide does not truly apply to the treatment of Native Americans by British colonists or, later, American Settlers."

Obviously, only a fool would deny that the brutal warfare chronicled throughout this chapter was common between the two populations. As the right-leaning Medved frankly admits: "The 400 year history of American contact with the Indians includes many examples of white cruelty and viciousness . . ." However, as we have seen, it is as easy to make the same point in reverse: Native American chieftains and warriors "regularly dealt with the European newcomers with monstrous brutality and indeed savagery." In a nuanced and important passage, he notes: "In fact . . . it is obvious that the blood-thirsty excesses of one group provoked blood-thirsty excesses from the other, in a cycle that lasted with scant interruption for several hundred years." Further, the majority of even this sanguinary warfare was not conventionally genocidal: the 1862 Dakota War was not fought with the goal of wiping out the Dakota tribe.

While claims of this kind can be contested, a less debatable point is simply that warfare against Westerners was simply never the primary cause of death for North American and Mesoamerican Indigenous peoples. The true mass killer of Natives, as well as millions of whites, during the premodern era was the unseen horror of disease. Quoting *Guns, Germs, and Steel* author Jared Diamond, the *History Is Now* team notes that "throughout the Americas, diseases introduced [by] Europeans spread from tribe to tribe far in advance of the Europeans themselves, killing an estimated 95 percent of the pre-Columbian Native population."

European warriors never even *got* to fight some of the most advanced and well-armed Native societies, such as the famous Mississippian chiefdoms that built the giant mounds near Cahokia, Illinois, and elsewhere: these were wiped out by fast-spreading disease before any Western explorers ever saw them, leaving behind only empty ruins and vast Golgothas full of bones to greet late-arriving expeditions. Across these fascinating and advanced cultures, and many others, "the main killers were Old World germs"—the product of the dense and stock-breeding human populations in Europe and Asia—"to which Indians had never been exposed" and against which they had no built-up resistance. The largely unintentional annihilation of Native American populations by these microbes was clearly an enormous tragedy, but, argue these authors and others, "in no sense does it represent a crime."

While this is not the focus of this chapter, it must also be noted that the settlement of the American continent was by no means accomplished entirely by Anglo-Saxon whites, who displaced "POC" Native Americans. Black Americans, or Mexicans and Mexican Americans of Castilian descent, are no more "from this continent" than Irishmen are, and authors like Sarah Laskow and Anna-Lisa Cox have recently begun to document the "homesteading" efforts of thousands of *minority* pioneers in the historical Northwest Territory—the massive area including most of modern Illinois, Michigan, Ohio, and Wisconsin.[49] During the process of putting together a genuinely fascinating database, Cox has so far assembled evidence of at least 338 Northwest Territory settlements, established between 1800 and 1860, that consisted of one or more Black-owned farms according to "census records, deeds, and other documents."

No evidence exists that these Black pioneers clashed with Native American Indians any more—or any less—than their white peers, but Cox argues that they certainly knew what they were doing out there on the cutting edge, "colonizing the newest portion of the nation, laying claim to citizenship in powerful ways." Even farther West, Blacks and Hispanics were—if anything—*over*represented among cowboys and Indian fighters, in tough male professions where bravery and aggression usually counted for more than skin color did. William DeLong, author of the short piece "The Forgotten Black Cowboys of the Wild West"[50] and much else, argues that Hollywood has "white-washed the West" and that, in reality, as many as 25 percent of all cowboys in the Western states during the 1870s and 1880s were of African descent.

Often freed slaves, these Black 'pokes headed West for the same reason many broken, desperate, and searching white men did: "to find their fortunes among cattle ranches and rows of crops," springing up where once dwelt the Red man. Many of these men had previously tended cows and managed fields, surprisingly often while armed, for white masters on their plantations or large farms, and settled with relative ease into the newly open lands of the Great Plains states and beyond. While this may be an exaggeration, DeLong at one point says flatly: "The American West was settled by a large portion of freed slaves." Some such pioneers inspired legends that live on today: U.S. marshal Bass Reeves of Oklahoma served as a frontier lawman for twenty-seven years, arrested or killed around 3,000 accused criminals, rode with a Native American former warrior as a sidekick, and is believed to have provided the original character model for cinema's Lone Ranger.

For that matter, arguably the most legendary and brutal Indian-fighting regiments in the history of the U.S. military, the "Buffalo Soldiers" of the Ninth and Tenth Cavalry, were virtually all Black. Technically speaking, the Buffalo Soldiers were created by the 1866 passage of the Army Organization Act, which authorized the creation of six all-"Negro" units tasked with protecting settlers across the expanding Western front and—in particular—with "control[ling] the Native Americans of the Plains."[51] Noting this latter duty, History.com points out the darkly ironic: "The Black soldiers, facing their own forms of discrimination from the U.S. government, were tasked with removing another minority group in that government's name."

They did so very well, if that word can be used in this context.

The Ninth Cavalry played a critical role in American success during the brutal Red River War—fought against the Comanche, Arapahoe, Kiowa, and Cheyenne—and the Ninth and Tenth Cavalry together defeated hundreds of well-prepared Native warriors during the Battle of Beaver Creek, not long after. By about 1880 the two regiments and their occasional white partners had almost completely "minimized Indian resistance" in their original state of Texas. The Ninth was sent to Indian Territory to tamp down white-Native conflict in what would become the state of Oklahoma, while the Tenth fought through the 1890s in the final borderlands campaigns against the Apache before relocating to Montana to break the last of the free Cree tribes.

By the late 1890s, "with the 'Indian problem' mostly settled," the Buffalo Soldiers traveled to Florida and were almost immediately deployed into the Spanish-American War, where they earned a reputation for heroism in the battles of El Caney, Las Quasimas, and San Juan Hill. Remarkably, during at least the latter stages of the Indian Wars, roughly 20 percent of *all* "U.S. Cavalry troops that participated" were Buffalo Soldiers. These essentially all-Black units participated in "at least 177" battles and other large-scale conflicts.

The face of Manifest Destiny, then, was never as white as historians (and racists!) would have us believe. Importantly, the Buffalo Soldiers were neither angels nor devils, but men—capable of great heroism and more than occasionally guilty of atrocity. The exact same was true of their white and Hispanic military counterparts and of their Native American opponents. The original inhabitants of North America were not the bloodthirsty naked savages of traditional U.S. mythology—but nor were they the peaceful Eloi that the newer storytellers of today prefer to falsely describe. They were just people: warriors who fought among themselves from time immemorial and who fought our own ancestors hard and well for four hundred years. Honor to their dead, and living, and to our own.

LIE #4

"Hippies Were the Good Guys, the Sexual Revolution Was Great for Women, and the Vietnam War Was Unpopular and Pointless"

Another commonplace social belief, at least in upper-middle-class circles—which is also reflected in more than a few academic lessons—is that the 1960s and early 1970s ("the Sixties") were the sun-kissed era of the Summer of Love, when shaggy-headed-and-crotched Flower Children represented the best of American pop culture, and the youth of a nation marched together against the abuses of a racist and corrupt government . . . before setting off to positively change society. The sexual revolution was great for Americans and human beings overall, especially women. The Vietnam War was pointless to evil, and justifiably unpopular. Again, however, reality diverges sharply from the narrative.

The hippies-were-the-good-guys narrative itself is unavoidable. To diverge from my usual chapter opener of quoting blocks of word salad from textbooks, a major article ran in (of all places) *Gentleman's Quarterly* under the header "The Hippies Were Right After All."[1] In the piece, author Devin Friedman declares: "The secret truth is that hippie culture won. That's right, you chia-seed motherfuckers. You

Transcendental Meditators. You alkaline-water drinkers. You Goop readers with your mushroom face masks and your vampire sprays. You don't believe me? How many yoga studios come up in Google Maps when you open it?" He goes on to argue that most hippie enthusiasms, from solar panels on the roof to "downward dogs" in the ashram or the bedroom, are now simply part of modern life.

Friedman, who opens his article by discussing the popularity of cannabis boutiques among stodgy older businessmen, clearly enjoys the absurdity of his topic and has no problem poking fun at the long-haired human components of his subject matter. However, he is kidding on the square: the core thesis of his article is that hippie culture remains common today because the hippies were correct about almost everything. As he puts it: "Hippie values are enduringly good. Preserve the environment, treat your body well and the people around you well-er, chill out, be tolerant . . . they're human values." The GQ piece, which includes a fascinating list of twelve things that the hippie movement allegedly "Made Cool" ("Brown Rice . . . Tofu . . . Love Free Sex . . . Orgies . . . The Dead") closes with the dead-serious claim that the prophesied Age of Aquarius is in fact taking place *right now*, "it is sponsored by Lululemon," and it will make this old world a better place.

More "serious" and standard-for-this-book sources make the same sort of claims all the time. In an article for History News Network, a commentary site hosted by George Washington University, which currently boasts 18,100 shares online, University of Washington history professor W. J. Rorabaugh argues that the hippies won the culture war.[2] His thesis, like Friedman's, is simple: as free love, tattered denim jeans, legal weed, tattoos and piercings, and single motherhood become essentially commonplace throughout middle-class America, "it is now clear that the hippies won the culture wars which were launched nearly fifty years ago."

Dr. Rorabaugh, again, seems to see this victory of the long-hairs as largely positive for society. To his credit, he certainly includes valid critiques of the 1960s-era movement and the associated sexual revolution ("Many hippie women came to see free love as a male sexual fantasy that did not meet women's needs . . ."). However—like most *bourgeois* city kids of his generation—he appears to perceive the hippie phenomenon as having oft been a good and honorable thing. To Rorabaugh, the three core principles of hip counterculture were "a search for authenticity, an insistence upon individualism, and a desire for community." The flower revolution was deeply spiritual: "Being true to one's self" meant rejecting the flawed mainstream culture of the period in pursuit of something deeper. Sometimes, he argues, "the past must be cast aside" so that citizens can perceive and plan for a better future: the 1960s was a period during which this happened in America.

American textbooks often employ similarly romanticized language to describe the era. A fairly typical passage, from 2016, describes hippies as idealistic young activists who "challenged the prevailing adult values in clothing, hairstyles, sexual conduct, work habits, and music." Comfortable trousers and strings of beads "took the place of business suits and wrist-watches . . . long hair, bare feet, and bralessness for women became the new uniform." At the macro-level, monogamous two-parent families and dull suburban subdivisions "gave way to communes for the 'flower children' of the 1960s."[3]

In addition to the impression that hippies constituted a majority or at least a sizable plurality of society, coverage of this kind almost invariably conveys an undertone of sympathy for even the most extreme elements of the counterculture. In the same source, the often-violent Students for a Democratic Society—the infamous SDS—is described as a "radical" organization but also as one that legitimately wanted to "rid American society of poverty, violence [!], and racism." For all their flaws, members are called serious people who pursued a new form of "salvation" via "the individual rather than the group." "Personal control of one's life and destiny," rather than the mere capitalist accumulation of power and filthy lucre, was "the hallmark of the New Left." And so on.

As we will later see, the modern-day romanticization of the hippies represents yet another example of modern scholars unable to admit the failure and unpopularity of left-leaning revolutions. Not only has the modern world rejected the hippie aesthetic, but history has proven the key elements of their project to be incorrect.

In step with our decades-later reverence for the hippie scene and the peace/sex movements, the mainstream "schoolbook" take on the Vietnam War today seems to be that it was an epic tragedy, unpopular at the time and now known to have been fought for amoral and illogical reasons. In 2018, Bloomberg's Max Hastings released his 857-page *Vietnam: An Epic Tragedy, 1945–1975*, the latest of a great many widely read and assigned books, in the tradition of David Halberstam's *The Best and the Brightest* (1972) and Andrew Hunt's *The Turning* (2001), to make these arguments. Per a lengthy review of the text in the *New York Times*, Mr. Hastings perceives Vietnam as "a conflict without good guys, an appalling conflagration" defined in large part by "the brutality, cynicism, and incompetence of the United States and its South Vietnamese ally." Overall American/allied military strategy during the war is compared, early on, to using "a flamethrower to weed a flower border"—and the takes get harsher from there.[4]

To be fair, Hastings also seems to despise the Viet Cong and the North Vietnamese Communists, whom he describes—per a close *New York Times* paraphrase—as "ruthless ideologues willing to spill any amount of blood to conquer the South." Ho Chi Minh, often treated almost as a hero by chanting American college students, is accurately called a "merciless despot" who directed "systemic cruelties" at the common people of Vietnam. Most other leading figures in North Vietnam are presented as still worse: Le Duan, who followed Ho Chi Minh as general secretary of the Communist Party of Vietnam, is summed up as having built "a mountain of his people's corpses" during and after the War.

However, at least as many of *Tragedy*'s criticisms target the good ol' USA. "Hastings shows," *Times* reviewer Mark Atwood Lawrence argues, that the powerful "American war machine devastated the society it intended to save . . . [doing] more to demoralize the South Vietnamese population than to defeat the Communists."

Inventively, Hastings himself claims directly that the overwhelming strength of American arms "hurt the war effort in the eyes of American and global publics," because many young people and other observers were willing to back the American side only if they perceived "proportionality between forces employed . . . casualties incurred, and the objective at stake."

At the level of grand strategy rather than tactics, Hastings accuses most American decision-makers—notably Henry Kissinger and President Richard Nixon—of significant "errors and misdeeds." At one point he contends that most members of the American leadership team were aware by roughly 1968 that the United States "could no longer achieve its objectives in Vietnam" but that domestic and international political concerns caused them to prolong the war until the "weak peace" of 1973—"at the cost of 21,000 American lives." And, for good measure, the author of *Tragedy* does not think much of the *South* Vietnamese. Setting aside some recent revisionist scholarship, he lambasts leaders like Nguyen Cao Ky as "corrupt autocrats reliant on the United States and uninterested in the welfare of their people." The general thrust of both text and review is clear: the war in Vietnam was an illogically begun and badly handled mistake—a tragedy indeed.

This read of Hastings, and indeed of the Vietnam War literature in toto, is not an "edgy" or unusual one. To the left of the *New York Times* (in a zone where dwelleth dragons), the Daily Beast also reviewed *Vietnam: An Epic Tragedy* in late 2018 and expanded their analysis into a twenty-two-page discussion of the entire Vietnam conflict. This article provides an even clearer summary of the contemporary, mainstream-at-least-within-academia take on the war. Lest anyone potentially be confused about what that take is, it opens: "The Vietnam War was the greatest disaster in the history of American foreign policy."[5]

This piece constantly touches on the actual and perceived legitimacy of the Vietnam War within the United States, in Vietnam, and further abroad—with Beast author James A. Warren arguing that Hastings's book proves the United States would not have won the war even "if the media had been 'on the team'" and U.S. military forces "had been given a free hand to fight the war." The (alleged) reason he gives for this is simplicity itself: the Communists were a better option for the Vietnamese people than the American–South Vietnamese alliance and were seen that way by ordinary Vietnamese. In a rather remarkable passage, Warren argues that "it was the Communists who best spoke to the aspirations of the ordinary Vietnamese people, and harnessed their energy. Their voice was the voice of Vietnamese patriotism, and Ho Chi Minh was its embodiment."

Looked at in this light, the United States lost the war in the jungles of Indochina because American leaders fundamentally misjudged the nature of the enemy and even of the war that they were fighting. Warren certainly argues that this is the case. Noting Hastings's point that, during 1964 and into 1965, Lyndon Johnson and several of his top advisers seemed confused about "the kind of war on which they were embarking," the Daily Beast scribe frankly leaps beyond his source and contends that Vietnam was not necessarily or "fundamentally" part of the international struggle between the West and communism at all.

Instead, he argues, the Vietnam War can best be understood as a multifaceted civil war between "communist . . . revolutionaries with impeccable nationalist credentials" and a Saigon-based South Vietnamese regime that was accurately seen as corrupt, incompetent, and backed by the warmongering United States. The conflict was inherently unjust and was unpopular at home and abroad for good reason: it pitted an invading U.S. military against Communist guerillas who likely had a more legitimate cause to fight for. In this take, common across the political left, the Americans were the bad guys in Vietnam, and many citizens realized this early on.

Whatever the facts, the hippie narrative of history seems to have stuck: the establishment was bad, the war was bad, and hippies were brave, benign defenders of the cause of peace, love, and universal human values.

As you may have realized by now, however, the reality of both the 1960s movement and the decade-long Vietnam conflict was a great deal more complex than simple narrative "takes" like that one. Far from their near veneration in modern elite media, the original reaction to hippies was *hatred* from most of their American contemporaries. One of the most popular songs of the era was the hippie-bashing outlaw country ballad "Okie from Muskogee" by Merle Haggard, which included the lines "We don't smoke marijuana in Muskogee / We don't take no trips on LSD" and "We never make no party out of lovin'," played frequently to rapturous audiences, and reached #1 on the *Billboard* Country charts.* Actual anti-hippie riots were far from uncommon, with the most notable of these—and now wholly and interestingly forgotten—being the May 1970 Hard Hat Riot in New York City.

The riot, which took place in the Financial District in Manhattan in May 1970, began when hundreds of construction workers and office employees attacked a large group of student and "general hippie" protesters demonstrating against the war in Vietnam and the recent National Guard shootings at Kent State University. Describing the wild scene, labor historian Philip S. Foner recounts: "Millions of television viewers saw . . . helmeted construction workers, armed with lead pipes and crowbars, range freely through the heart of New York's financial district."[6]

The workers were arrayed into rough battle formations: one chronicler describes them as "march[ing] to the cadences of 'All the way! USA!'" while dressed in matching overalls and carrying oversize American flags from their job sites. And they apparently had at least some sense of tactics: the real fighting began when "the workers, reinforced in the rear by some thousand vocal supporters from the Wall Street area," targeted and broke through "the easterly terminus of the police line" separating them from their hirsute targets.[7]

---

* Entertainingly, the same song—perhaps played ironically—also reached as high as #41 on the pop charts, and stayed on the *Billboard* Hot 100 for months.

As reinforcements for both sides arrived from around the huge, diverse city, the initial brawl turned into a medieval-style melee, with tens of thousands of men in the streets and New York's City Hall taken under siege for at least an hour. By the end of the day, at least one hundred people had been badly injured, six arrested, and at least seven active-duty police officers hauled off to the hospital.[8] This incident led to several other massive "sympathy" demonstrations and brawls, for a while inspiring almost "daily blue collar protests, culminating with as many as 150,000 workers flooding City Hall with a sea of American flags." Quoting *Time* magazine of the era, author David Paul Kuhn refers to it all as "Workers' Woodstock."[9]

A few weeks later, President Nixon indicated that he basically supported the hippie-stomping workers: he invited the leaders of the Hard Hat Riot and subsequent mass demonstrations to Washington, where he was photographed accepting a "personal" hard hat from these men.[10] The specific fellow who gave him the hat, Pete Brennan—then president of the Building and Construction Trades Council of Greater New York—would in fact go on to become U.S. Secretary of Labor under Nixon.[11]

All of this largely reflected U.S. public opinion. For a variety of reasons, including frequent public lewdness by anti-war activists and their treatment of Vietnam combat veterans, the anti-war and hippie movements were extraordinarily unpopular with most non-elite citizens—with positive ratings for them falling down into the single digits among some subcategories of at least white Americans.[12]

Such was the actual perception of the Aquarians, during their age.

Data far beyond that just discussed supports the same conclusions. Not only was there significant public distaste for left-wing protesters and agitators, but Americans also displayed majority or near-majority support for the United States' role in Vietnam until very late in the war. Most wars become more unpopular as they drag on, but serious analysis of cached results from pollsters like

Gallup shows that Americans held more positive year-by-year attitudes toward Vietnam than toward many contemporary conflicts, such as the Second Gulf War.[13]

In mid-1965, more than six months after Lyndon Johnson approved significant U.S. ground operations in Vietnam, "Gallup found just 24% of Americans saying it was a mistake to send troops, while 60% said it was not." Obviously, Vietnam was not "unpopular from the beginning," and this same pattern of public opinion continued for some time to come. In July of 1967, nearly three years after the boots-on-ground U.S. surge into Vietnam, a strong plurality of citizens (48 to 41 percent) "still supported the notion that it was not a mistake to send troops to Vietnam." Even by the end of 1967, only 3 percent more Americans said it had been a mistake to send troops to Vietnam (47 percent) than that it had not been (44 percent)—and *this* pattern then remained consistent for almost one year.

Per the Gallup data, it was not until August of 1968—almost four years into the war—that a slight majority of Americans (53 percent) said that it had been a mistake to put boots on the ground in Vietnam. *This* figure then remained relatively stable until the conflict ended: "The percentage of Americans who said it was a mistake averaged 55 percent in 1969 and 1970," and never got above 60 percent—a mark neared but not quite reached in 1971 and 1973. Widely cited polls recording approximately 70 percent opposition to the war generally date to many years after the conflict ended—three large ones took place between 1990 and 2000—and reflect literally decades of constant media revisionism since the last G.I. came home.

In reality, American attitudes toward Vietnam were quite normal if not—given the length of the war and the prevailing patterns of media coverage of it—more balmy than might have been expected. To provide a direct comparator: when Gulf War Two began in March of 2003, "only 23% of adults nationwide said it was a mistake to send troops to Iraq," a figure almost identical to that first recorded for Vietnam. However, as the first casualty reports—ours and the enemy's—began to filter back to the United States, this percentage increased drastically.

By the last few months of 2003, it had already "reached the 40% range," and by early June of 2004—"just one year and three months after the war began"—a clear majority of Americans were labeling the war a mistake. Per the graphics provided by Gallup's pollsters, this attitude persisted at least intermittently for the duration of the conflict. Just as hippies were far from universally loved, actual citizen attitudes toward the Vietnam War were far from unusually negative.

There were logical reasons underlying both of these dead-common perspectives. Simply put, people disliked hippies because most of them struck the average taxpayer as slovenly, money-bumming drug addicts. Pieces like Joan Didion's "Slouching Towards Bethlehem" in the *Saturday Evening Post* and Mark Harris's "The Flowering of the Hippies" in the *Atlantic* painted an amusing but disturbing picture of the hip scene in outposts like San Francisco's Haight-Ashbury district—one full of open-air drug markets, doped-up street kids on the nod in public, pimps preying on so much unprotected young flesh, and the occasional lunatic bow-man hunting stray cats for food.*

One piece in this vein, "The Death of the Hippies"[14]—the *Atlantic*'s 2015 requiem for its older article and a comprehensive summary of what finally happened to the San Francisco scene—opens by discussing the joy and hope that many at first associated with the famous Summer of Love. In the Haight, and even more notably along Telegraph Avenue in left-of-Castro neighboring Berkeley, pretty long-haired kids "crowded the sidewalks day and night," "talking, protesting, kissing, dancing, fighting, and taking lots and lots of drugs." For a short while, acid-boosted Southern

---

* Much of this, I will note, as a former Chicago raver, would seem as familiar to any 1990s party- or street-kid as to our 1960s equivalents. In the absence of civilization, barbarism flourishes.

California was a wonderful place to be, during a magnificent time to be alive.

But only for a short while. As recounted by the article's author, Jennie Rothenberg Gritz, and contributor Joe Samberg—both veterans of the youth counterculture—after less than a year, any basic civilizational restraints on the scene essentially disappeared. Printed signs arguing for the most basic limits on behavior (i.e., "No Heroin Dealers Here" in a neighborhood park)—many put up by long-term Black or working-class residents of the area—were almost universally torn down and thrown away. "Over time," says Samberg, "those . . . came down and more and more people started using hard drugs. All the [hippie] stuff about higher consciousness was just sort of dropped."

At around this same time, damaged and often sexually abused teenage kids—especially girls—started showing up in San Francisco and Berkeley in droves. One pack of Berkeley middle school girls became known as the Minnie Mob because they often hit the avenue in their Mickey Mouse–themed "tween" clothing. And these little kids apparently partied hard. One veteran of the Telegraph Avenue scene, describing the Mob or a similar group taking down two 1.75 liter bottles of Southern Comfort whiskey, said: "Those . . . bottles appeared and disappeared in what couldn't have been more than two minutes. Those kids were 13, maybe 14. But they just consumed anything that would come their way."

Where you find prey, you find predators (and you may find that the two categories often overlap to a disturbing degree). Almost immediately, pedophiles, dealers, and street hustlers began to follow the hip young seekers into the parks and squats of the Bay Area. Per Gritz and Samberg: "There were people who had these young kids very much in their thrall. . . . [T]hey told them 'Listen, you don't need to go to school. Everything you need to learn in life is right here on the street.'" Many runaways and Children of the Secret heeded the call of the wild, selling drugs at a lower level than their mentors, or simply exchanging their bodies for street food and a warm place to stay.

The "Scene" as it actually was didn't last very long. As Gritz notes, within a few years—and certainly by the time of the publication of her article—the bright-colored human beings hanging out on Telegraph Avenue "barely even pretend[ed] to be hippies anymore." Instead of the aspiring revolutionary poets or backroom chemists they had once been, most were simple dope fiends or winos. Samberg, quoted again, makes this point eloquently and explicitly, saying: "There's no growth for people if they're continuously on drugs. It started out with all this higher thinking—expanding your mind to become more conscious of what's really going on in the universe." But once the hard addictive drugs took over, "all of the big ideas disappeared."

So did Joe Samberg—disappear, that is, from the Scene—to do what may have been the most rebellious thing actually possible in the modern West, as this whole era drew to an end: marry his sweetheart, have several kids, and settle down to adult upper-middle-class life. Around the same time, many of his longtime friends left the hip world via a different path: they died. As the *Atlantic* article notes near its conclusion: "The movement itself is dead, and so are many of the people who used to frequent the Strip." Ken Kesey wept.

That was a few years before the end of the Sixties, when Woodstock gave way to the violence of Altamont Speedway Free Festival in 1969 (more on that shortly). The dark "Altamont" endgame of the hippie movement was not due merely to the fact that most people do rather badly under conditions of anarchy. Autopsies of the period—some literal—have also made it increasingly plain that quite a few certifiable lunatics took advantage of the general chaos to establish lairs and larders among the hard-to-track Flower Children and basically go hunting. To open with one rather minor example, we now know that the founder of Earth Day was a domestically abusive murderer who killed at least one woman.[15] To quote NBC News: "Ira Einhorn was on stage hosting the first Earth Day event at the Fairmount Park in Philadelphia on April 22, 1970. Seven years later, police raided his closet and found the . . . body of his girlfriend inside a trunk." Appropriately enough, she had been composted, using at-home techniques.

Earth Day, the holiday Einhorn played such a pivotal role in founding, of course continues today, being celebrated annually on April 22.

Einhorn was not unique but rather just one of many lunatics and predators living inside the hippie subculture and exploiting its lax norms. On a far larger scale, the legendary and insane Manson Family sprang directly from 1960s and early 1970s "hip" West Coast culture, another example of the way a charismatic predator could manage to gather a following among lawless young hedonists. At root, as the Historic Newspapers database still notes, the entire Manson Family was a hippie commune and near cult founded in the Joshua tree–dotted California desert near the end of the 1960s.[16]

Per researcher Tom Matthews, the Family included roughly one hundred followers, "all of whom lived uncommon lifestyles" and were slavishly loyal to their leader—criminal and failed surf musician Charlie Manson. These acolytes, many of them girls from upper-middle-class or wealthy backgrounds, "were drawn to the hippie culture and communal living of The Family" and radicalized by Manson's rantings about the coming fall of American society. Importantly, they also used a lot of dope: "habitual uses of hallucinogenic drugs" like LSD and yohimbe were expected, and most Family members were essentially tripping every day.

All of this became relevant when the Family left their lair—"a deserted ranch in the San Fernando Valley"—and started killing people. A rather unlikely, mostly female raiding party of Manson Family members carried out one of the most famous and dramatic murders in American history on August 9, 1969, striking deep into wealthy Beverly Hills to kill beloved and heavily pregnant Hollywood starlet Sharon Tate (wife of director and pedophile Roman Polanski). According to the first policemen to arrive on the scene, the house where Tate was murdered looked "like a battle-field." The young movie star, "clad only in a bikini," had been hanged with a nylon cord from the main beam of her home's ceiling. Another person, who turned out to be Tate's ex-lover Jay Sebring, had been executed in a similarly ritualistic fashion nearby, apparently after bravely defending Tate.

Wandering outside, police found still more bodies, in even worse shape. Pretty mid-twenties "American coffee heiress Abigail Folger" had been cut down while running, still clad only in a skimpy nightgown. A few feet away from her, on the same front lawn, lay "19-year-old Polish born Voyteck Frykowski." Another dead man, whose identity would remain unknown for some time, was found inside a car that had been parked in the driveway of Tate and Polanski's mansion.

Many elements of the ghastly crime scene directly and intentionally called to mind the revolutionary ethos of the era. The word "PIGS" was written in blood across Tate's front doorway. When Manson Family members were finally arrested and charged with the multiple homicide—an innocent household hand named William Garretson spent some time in jail first—they said openly that they had wanted to trigger a race and class war by killing rich people and police officers and teaching "niggers" how to do the same. Manson's dreamed-of conflict, which he called "Helter Skelter," never happened, but not for want of effort.

Another alliance of two violent groups is important to note on the road to Altamont. Not only were many hippies and activists criminals, in the technical legal sense of this term, but organized criminal outfits like the Hells Angels and Bandidos motorcycle gangs also quickly became very involved with hip and drug culture—entertainingly, sometimes serving as a sort of alternative police force for dealers and brawlers who could not easily call on the legitimate alternative. A surprisingly insightful piece from the CrimeReads police resource argues that outlaw bikers and serious hippies saw one another as "well liked acquaintances," sharing many of the same "favored pastimes" during at least the early to mid-1960s.[17] A big part of the relationship was a sense of shared opposition to square-world society, with both sides "seeking allies in the battle against middle-class, bourgeois mores."

In the Bay Area and along the West Coast, members of multiple different rebel subcultures had long seen themselves as "a kind of outlaw posse" made up of everyone contemptuous of mainstream norms—and much the same was true elsewhere in urban America. In this climate, gigantic and filthy members of 1-percenter motorcycle gangs were often treated almost as mascots and defenders of the rest of the scene, sharing girls and drugs with their new and more political buddies. As CrimeReads author Saul Austerlitz notes, gonzo journalist Hunter S. Thompson and psychedelic-bus riding Merry Prankster Ken Kesey famously introduced the Hells Angels to liquid LSD, which the bikers eventually took to selling and sometimes making on their own.

In the end, as was so common during the *real* 1960s, bloody violence between what were essentially two groups of outlaws disrupted the beautiful friendship. Politically, the blue-collar Hells Angels, many of whom were war veterans and professional mechanics, were far to the right of the Pranksters and the rest of the hip scene—something neither group was sober enough to notice for quite some time. However, the honeymoon ended (at least regionally) in late fall of 1965 when Oakland Hells Angels "broke through police lines and disrupted an anti-Vietnam War rally in Berkeley." The protesters, who included SDS types and other serious radicals, fought back hard but lost—with their erstwhile biker allies "tearing down their banners" and shouting, "Go back to Russia!" Then came a true turning point, which some see as the end of the hippie era, at the Altamont rock concert. Not long after the brawl at Berkeley, Angels providing "security" beat a gun-wielding African American music fan to death—leaving part of his brain exposed—during the concert, and the biker-longhair pact was essentially over.

So, many socially negative trends did not survive the Sixties. However, many did. As feminists (and quite a few homemakers) have noted, one especially unfortunate society-wide pattern to endure from Altamont until today has been the near-universal embrace of the darker side of the sexual revolution. As feminist writer Virginia Ironside points out for the *Daily Mail*,[18] "The sexual revolution of the swinging 60s—kick-started by the arrival of the pill—seems glamorous, exciting, and seductive when depicted in hit TV shows such as *Mad Men*. But . . . there was a bleaker side to such freedom."

As Ironside notes, the *girlfriends* of the Pranksters and Angels and Diggers we have been discussing so far found themselves in a series of completely unprecedented positions (no pun intended). These women were, and not always willingly, "trailblazers for . . . completely new attitude[s]" toward extramarital sex, oral and anal sex, sex at very young ages, and more—"And blazing trails is always horribly uncomfortable." This must especially have been the case following the generation of the 1940s and 1950s, when virtually any frank discussion of human sexuality was "completely taboo." In one remarkable passage, Ironside notes that, until just a decade before the Age of Aquarius hit full swing, major ladies' magazines like *Woman* were not allowed even to print words such as "bottom" or "wet" (i.e., "After a good soaking, the bottom of the garden is . . .").

From there to Woodstock, in—geologically speaking—the time it takes to pull down a zipper! Sounding a bit harassed even decades later, Ironside argues that, for many "scene" women of the era, the reality of free love was "an endless round of miserable promiscuity."

Most men—and I might suspect many women—of the period were terrible in bed but nonetheless all too insistent on exploring their newfound social freedoms as much as possible. In a sentence that sounds absurd but is rather familiar to anyone to survive the rave scene thirty years later, Ironside says flatly: "It often seemed easier and, believe it or not, more polite to sleep with a man than to chuck him out of your flat."

This state of affairs simply did not work, mentally, for a great many women. In a poignant reflection on *her* scene, Ironside admits that "many of us girls spent the entire 1960s in tears . . . however one tried to separate sex from love, we'd been brought up to associate the two." Thus, "every time we went to bed with someone, we'd hope it would lead to something more permanent—and each time it never did."

Further—as any veteran of Tinder or Grindr could attest today— another reason 1960s hipster "sex was so grim" was that physical intimacy had become so easy to get that romance and seduction nearly vanished. In an unintentionally hilarious passage, the *Mail*'s feminist author notes that working-class men temporarily became very attractive to upper-class office ladies because the art of actually talking to women never vanished entirely within their own "saloon society." However, all too often, these fellows proved no more interested in long-term commitment than the lawyers and dentists they could out-patter.

After many poignant observations of this kind, and a few about the many STDs/STIs that essentially did not exist before 1975 or so, Ironside closes her piece with what I frankly suspect is a good piece of advice for most women and indeed men: Have sex only with people you actually like. "After a decade of sleeping around . . . indiscriminately," she says, "girls of the 1960s eventually became fairly jaded about sex." The solution? At least for this author, recognize that "continual sex with different partners is . . . joyless, uncomfortable, and humiliating. One of the ingredients of a good sex life is, at the very least, a grain of affection between the two partners involved." When asked, hypothetically and at the very end of her article, whether she would opt to go back to the wild and clothing-optional 1960s if possible, the rad-fem veteran of the pleasure wars has a one-word answer: "Never!"

One especially creepy aspect of the sexual revolution that lingers today—or at least did until the peak of the #MeToo movement— was explicit sexualization of young, often underage girls. As I write these words, one of the hot-button issues in U.S. politics is the increasing prevalence of explicit education about sexual intercourse and even gender flexibility in American primary schools. For that matter, any listing of the top clothing and style brands targeting tween and early teen girls would have to include names like "Hard Candy," "Juicy," "Pink Cookie," "Horze," "Love Pink" from Victoria's Secret, the "Slippery When Wet" novelty line, and so forth. While crude banter between young males and females—of the "grass on the field" variety—has almost certainly always existed, we again have the cultural shifts of the hip era to thank for the widespread, direct targeting of sex at kids by mainstream institutions and entire musical genres.

Another well-known urban female author, Naomi Schaefer Riley, points out that "the days of free love weren't hippie and care-free" for many young American women.[19] From the beginning, modern pop and hip culture was targeted at men, and "sexualized underage girls" to a degree we often forget today. Very young groupies were a constant feature of the 1960s and 1970s music scene, and rockers and movie actors quite openly slept with people who were basically kids. As Schaefer Riley points out, in one of the most famous dalliances of the era: "David Bowie took [famous 'groupie'] Lori Maddox's virginity when she was 15; soon afterward she was bedded by Jimmy Page." In a written response to an entire modern-era article about Bowie's preference for young women and girls, *Harper's* editor and former scenester Rebecca Solnit summed up the zeitgeist of the time thusly:

> The dregs of the sexual revolution were what remained, and it was really sort of a counterrevolution (guys arguing that since sex was beautiful and everyone should have lots, everything goes and they could go at anyone; young women and girls with no way to say no and no one to help them stay out of harmful dudes' way). The culture was sort of snickeringly approving of the pursuit of underage girls.
>
> It was completely normalized. Like child marriage in some times and places. Which doesn't make it OK, but means that, unlike a man engaged in the pursuit of a minor today, there was virtually no discourse about why this might be wrong.

For decades after the 1960s ended—and we still see the residue of this attitude today, in bantering stories about pretty moms screwing high school athletes, or Jeffrey Epstein's private flights packed full of cheerleaders—a widespread social assumption, Riley writes, "was that some 'experimentation' was good for teenagers. . . . [T]his is what adolescence was supposed to be about." The conservative writer Midge Decter, attempting to sum up all of this in her classic *Liberal Parents, Radical Children*, famously said that the 1960s-born children of the American professional and managerial class were at once staggeringly spoiled and some of the "most neglected [kids] in the history of the world." Decter was likely not far wrong, if wrong at all.[20]

Entertainingly, there are still hippies and hard-core hipsters around in the United States today, and the same "Haight-Ashbury" problems arise whenever they gather together in numbers—often leading to the same attitudes toward them from "square" citizens. Perhaps most notably, the Rainbow Family of Living Light famously puts on annual outdoor public camping events that invariably tend to be characterized by a high level of chaos.

Just as historical dislike of hippies was widespread enough to lead to mass rioting and was based in large part on actual behavior, public support for the Vietnam War (or "conflict") also reflected actual geopolitical realities. As was discussed in chapter two of this very book, the threat of global communism during the Cold War era was not an invented or theoretical one. In the same way the domestic threat of Soviet agents has been erased from the public memory, so modern historians prefer to act like the Vietnam War was just an international Red Scare, provoked by . . . nothing much at all. A remarkable single paragraph on History.com's respected "Communism Timeline" makes strikingly clear how wrongheaded that view is.[21]

Per the authors:

[Between 1940 and 1979] Communism was established by force or otherwise in Estonia, Latvia, Lithuania, Yugoslavia, Poland, North Korea, Albania, Bulgaria, Romania, Czechoslovakia, East Germany, Hungary, China, Tibet, North Vietnam, Laos, Guinea, Cuba, Yemen, Kenya, Sudan, Congo, Burma, Angola, Benin, Cape Verde, Kampuchea, Madagascar[!], Mozambique, South Vietnam, Somalia, Seychelles, Afghanistan, Grenada, Nicaragua and others.

Not until the mid-1980s, which witnessed U.S. victories in Grenada and Afghanistan, did historical momentum begin to shift in favor of the "free world." In this context, the primary, widely understood reason for U.S. participation in a war in North and South Vietnam—literally two of the countries appearing on History's depressing list—was to prevent the fall of another major state to the Communists.

From Eisenhower's perspective, "the loss of Vietnam to Communist control would lead to similar Communist victories in neighboring countries in Southeast Asia," like Laos, Cambodia, and perhaps Thailand. This school of thought underlying American anti-Communist activity had a name: the domino theory.[22] During the Cold War, many senior Western military officers and policy analysts and professional political scientists believed a Communist military victory in one nation-state would lead to "Red" coups or takeovers in neighboring states, with "each falling like a perfectly aligned row of dominoes." This theory was often invoked specifically in the context of Vietnam, with the U.S. National Security Council discussing it in their 1952 report on what was then called Indochina, and President Eisenhower, the former general, describing the decisive French defeat at Dien Bien Phu as a classic example of a "falling domino" or "domino falling."

Objectively speaking, Eisenhower was correct: almost exactly this happened. Despite some frankly odd rearguard claims from academics in my field—for example, that "only Laos and Cambodia," out of the Laos/Cambodia/Thailand triad, fell to communism—the plain reality is that the former North Vietnam, the former South Vietnam, all of Laos, and Cambodia were Communist states within several years of the 1973 U.S. withdrawal from Vietnam. In Cambodia, the Communist takeover led directly to the horror of dictator Pol Pot's killing fields, where "an estimated 1.7 million people died at the hands of the extremist, Communist regime,"[23] and millions of other urbanites and intellectuals were forced into agricultural stoop labor and survived near-starvation only by eating (at very least) "frogs, snails, and insects."

Simply put, the 1960s "movement," now almost universally lauded, was widely hated in its own time, but that didn't stop it from doing damage. To return to one of the headlines that opened this chapter . . . the hippies did "win," but not in a way we should truly applaud. Their pro–free love, antiestablishment, anti-war, pro-drug ethos left a trail of destruction in its wake. The negative effect that it had on public attitudes toward the Vietnam War was a real, if minor, factor that contributed directly to the defeat of the domino theory strategy. And that defeat had exactly the devastating eventual effect on tens of millions of people that American leaders of the time predicted, as the dominoes fell in the rest of Southeast Asia. To some degree, however small, the Western hippies glee-fully chanting "Ho! Ho! Ho Chi Minh!!!" bear responsibility for the killing fields halfway across the world.

Once again: life is complex, and icons should be chosen with care.

LIE #5

"The Founders Counted Slaves as 'Three-Fifths of a Person' and 'the Only Victims of Lynchings' Were Black"

That American history has often been violent and terrible for Black Americans is uncontested. Sometimes, though, this truth has become so isolated and all-consuming that it warps any big picture view of the country's history. Centering this narrative means we often simultaneously think history is worse and better than it actually was because we assume the worst about ambiguous stories and ignore historical sins that don't fit the picture we've settled in our heads.

One universal upper-middle-class misbelief, a consequence of this myth-making and pervasive in American education, is that the United States at one point made a racist decision to count all Black Americans as "three-fifths of a human" and that we remain (irreparably?) tainted by this. This example is often used to lead off long classroom lists of Blacks-only stories about lynchings and race riots that serve—to simplify a difficult topic down to a few words—to make history seem even worse than it was. The reality of both the constitutional three-fifth compromise and later Black history, once again, is far more messy and complex than the accepted narrative will allow.

Let me tell the story of a typical misunderstanding of these is-sues. In May of 2021, prominent Republican Tennessee state repre-sentative Justin Lafferty was attacked by sources ranging from CNN[1] to "LGBTQ Nation" for his comments about the compromise, which he called a "bitter, bitter pill" but one that "actually limited" the elec-toral power of slaveholding Southern states. In response, writer Alex Bollinger—who titled his piece "Tennessee Republican Defends Counting Black People as 3/5 of Human Beings"—described Lafferty as saying that calling Black slaves inside the United States "60% of a human being" was "a good thing."[2] Those quotes were Bollinger's paraphrasing of Lafferty, not what he actually said, but Lafferty is quoted at some length in Bollinger's piece, saying among other things: "The Three-Fifths Compromise was a direct effort to en-sure that Southern states never got the population necessary to continue the practice of slavery everywhere in the country." How-ever, Bollinger tells readers, this is flatly false: "None of this is true."

He proceeds from there to make a series of arguments against the validity of the compromise. The first is direct: it increased rather than lessened the electoral power of whites living in slave-holding states by giving them "an extra 60% representation" com-pared to Northern whites or Blacks. He's technically right about that, but his other claims are broader and more moral in nature: the compromise was racist because it failed to bring about an end to U.S. slavery prior to the Civil War, sent the "horrific message" that all "Black people were not full human beings," and so forth.

These points are more difficult to defend, especially since Bollinger cites not experts but confused politicians. In support of these points, he sympathetically quotes Black members of the Tennessee legislature, notably Tennessee Black Caucus of State Legislators chair Antonio Parkinson, who sums up Lafferty's take: "It was horrible." A consistent theme for both men is that slavery is bad. "I don't care if it's policy or how you're counting heads," Parkinson emotes at one point, "there is nothing good about slav-ery." (Everyone in the piece is wrong. Bollinger and Parkinson are summarizing poorly, and Lafferty is *more* right but still doesn't quite understand the historical purpose of the compromise.)

Even in the context of a great deal of coverage of this kind— the first sentence about the three-fifths compromise on the education-focused website ConstitutionUS.com is "[This] is an infamous passage in the U.S. Constitution"—a recent article from the *Washington Post* manages to stand out. The widely read 2015 piece is headlined "We Used to Count Black Americans as 3/5 of a Person. For Reparations, Give Them 5/3 of a Vote."[3] Inside it, for what prints out to four single-spaced pages, author Theodore R. Johnson argues for doing exactly that.

Per Johnson, accurately enough, the compromise "set the Census value of a slave at 60 percent of the value of a free person," despite the fact that slaves could not vote—and Black Southerners were often prevented from doing so for decades after slavery. To compensate for this past, and to facilitate the handling of modern problems like "systemic racism," he contends, we should flip the old ratio and "let each African American voter now count as five thirds" of a man or woman.

While the *Post* man concedes that some might find this proposal out of sync with the treasured American idea of one man, one vote, he argues innovatively that "the precise legal meaning of that phrase is . . . unclear" and further that his five-thirds compromise would give Blacks "a larger political voice" that is desperately needed during the racial reckoning of today. To at least one journalist for a prestige publication, the historical three-fifths compromise was such a racist mistake that we need to make up for it by almost doubling the political power of African Americans today.

In reality, of course, much of this opprobrium borders on the nonsensical. To quote my lovely and talented 1776 Unites partner, Dr. Carol Swain:[4] "One of the most mis-understood clauses in the United States Constitution is found in Article 1, Section 2." Per the Constitution itself, the relevant language reads: "Representatives and direct Taxes shall be apportioned among the several States . . . by adding to the whole Number of free Persons, including those bound to Service for a Term of Years, and excluding Indians not taxed, three fifths of all other Persons."* As Swain concedes, the last portion of this—along with several of the other sections, if you read closely—does raise a clear ethical question: "How could the Founding Fathers, who endorsed the idea that all men are created equal, also endorse the idea that some men aren't?"

Here, however, Swain provides an answer that the various experts quoted so far have not: the three-fifths compromise was the most ethical position that would have been acceptable to both sides around the constitutional bargaining table in 1781. The founders essentially had to agree to it or the end result would have been either *no United States at all* or a country where the pro-slavery South was far *more* powerful than ended up being the case. Citing former Emory University president James Wagner, she argues that "the northern and southern states would never have agreed to form a single union" absent some sort of deal allowing slaves to count toward the census totals at least in percentage form. "No three-fifths compromise," Swain and Wagner claim, "no United States of America."

Both Swain and Wagner are insistent that the compromise was the anti-slavery position: it was drawn up by those opposed to slavery, rather than by those who supported it. Put differently: "It wasn't the racists of the South who wanted to count slave populations less than white populations; it was the abolitionists of the North." Interestingly, given the commonplace claim that a racist United States once treated Black human beings as "two-thirds of a man," it is worth noting that the ideal outcome for anti-racists would have been a decision to treat all Black slaves as *zero*-fifths of

---

* Notice that there is, in fact, a great deal going on here. White indentured servants (persons "bound to a term of service") *do* count as full humans, but one suspects that this took some negotiating. And, interestingly, although this is almost never mentioned, Native Americans count as zero "fifths of a human being" unless permanently resident in a white settlement. Women, of course, could not vote—and would not be able to for another approximately 140 years. History sucked, for almost everyone.

a person—reducing the legal population of the South as much as possible. At the time of the passage of the compromise, the only individuals advocating for treating African American slaves as "full men"—sometimes using that exact misleading language—were Southern slave owners!

While it was obviously an imperfect deal, the three-fifths compromise clearly had a positive impact on subsequent U.S. history. As Swain notes, the enslaved population of the American South had grown to more than 4 million persons by the time of the Civil War. Had all of these people each been counted as 100 percent of a voter by their masters—while being allowed to do zero percent of the voting—it is entirely possible that the congressional actions that led up to the War Between the States would never have happened, and slavery might "very well have lasted into the twentieth century." On the other hand, had the Northern states simply attempted to forbid their Southern peers to count slaves, "the slave states would never have agreed to join the Union: they would have formed their own country."

In this scenario, we would have had two distinct and well-armed states, "one free and one slave," existing as hostile neighbors from the very beginning of American democracy. One wonders what hay Britain, or France, or even Spanish-held Mexico, might have made of *that* situation. After a full and fair analysis, Swain's summary of the compromise is probably the correct one: "[It] was the solution to the most difficult challenge the framers faced: how to create a single country out of people so divided on a fundamental issue." In the end, in succeeding in answering this question: the three-fifths compromise did not "deny the humanity of Blacks" but rather "affirmed it."

Swain does not write alone in defending the three-fifths compromise. Even the Gray Lady of Record, the *New York Times*—albeit before the true racial reckoning—published a backhanded defense of the three-fifths compromise in the context of a handful of pieces debating the issue, titled "The Three-Fifths Compromise Was an Understandable Deal on Slavery."[5] Here, Sanford Levin-

son of the University of Texas College of Law, notes that James
Wagner—the same academic referenced by Dr. Swain—could be
said to have "committed a gaffe of monumental proportions" by
resolutely calling the three-fifths compromise "necessary to avoid
dissolution of the fragile United States into separate countries."
However, Levinson points out, the famous political and show business *definition* of a gaffe is someone slipping up and telling an
uncomfortable truth—and that is what happened here.

"Wagner was correct in his basic assertion," he is brave enough
to say, "and he is in good company." Citing past endorsers of the
three-fifths deal, including an offhand Barack Obama in 2010,
Levinson states flatly that the Constitution is full of compromises
that can accurately be called "lesser evils"—like the rule of senatorial
composition that gives Delaware and Rhode Island voting power
equal to that of Virginia or California. However, he says accurately,
"the greater evil" would have been for these never to have taken
place and thus for there to be "no Constitution at all." More specifically, he makes the point that the three-fifths compromise in
particular was an anti-slavery deal: Northern delegates "wanted . . .
to deny slaves their personhood completely" for political purposes,
and the ideal outcome for an anti-racist Black American would
have been for disenfranchised slaves to count not as "whole men"
but for as little as they did or even less. He is not wrong.

As is true of most compromises, no one came away from it
totally satisfied. The slave states would have preferred to count all
of their slaves for political representation, but they were made content with less representation because it also meant less taxation.
Abolitionists didn't want slaves to count toward representation at
all, but they judged that only the united colonies could possibly
overthrow British rule, and their concerns about the three-fifths
compromise were assuaged by the addition of clauses enabling
Congress "to tax slave imports and, after 1808, prohibit slave importation completely."

The slave states went home convinced the federal government
could never accomplish emancipation, while abolitionist James

Madison, acknowledging that it was a "dishonorable" compromise, argued that it was a victory that they had refused in their wording "to admit in the Constitution the idea that there could be property in men." This may seem like a small win, but it's worthwhile to consider that the abolitionist movement was still in its political infancy. At the beginning of the Revolution, slavery was legal in all of the American colonies (though not by its end). Abolitionist Benjamin Rush saw the lack of enshrined slavery in the Constitution as a triumph: "The 'cloud' of anti-slavery, 'which a few years ago was no larger than a man's hand, has descended in plentiful dews and at last cover'd every part of our land.'"

Abolitionists did not see the Constitution's compromises as roadblocks to their future plans for emancipation. Ultimately, slave states agreed with abolitionists that it was a compromise favoring abolitionists, which is why they eventually judged the Constitution such a burden and threat to their way of life that they would secede and write a new slavery-friendly constitution.

Rush's point of view is unlikely to be represented in modern curricula, which prefer to unthinkingly promote the slave states' initial view of the matter instead of the reality that it was a pragmatic and, in the long term, very effective political compromise.[6*]

The description of the three-fifths compromise in the mainstream liberal press is hardly unique. Very often, as was discussed in the chapter dealing with white-Native warfare, we find that ambiguous incidents or realities are presented as no-doubt-about-it American failures, while all-too-real imperfections or atrocities receive excessive focus if not plain exaggeration. Activists tend to see history as a series of simple binary choices. Any choice that involves compromise is unambiguously bad. It's a way of looking at

---

* The extreme correlation between far-left and Confederate views of the United States ("This is a white man's country!") is not discussed often enough. Remarkably, the title of what is probably scholar Ibram X. Kendi's most famous book, *Stamped from the Beginning: The Definitive History of Racist Ideas in America*, appears to have been taken verbatim from a speech by gray-states president Jefferson Davis.

history that disallows any possibility of partial victories and judges all decisions by the standards of modern America.

This sort of uncompromising puritanical spirit also animates a variation on this trope, which is the presentation of almost universal human evils as somehow being uniquely linked to American or Black American history. Our society is not just "sometimes unfortunately bad, like all the others": we alone are the *worst*. In order to create this historical tunnel vision, activists focus on specific historical evils outside of the broader context of their time. To give an example: at least from my own casual in-classroom surveys, a very widespread belief among American youngsters is that lynching/posse justice, whipping, and even hanging were exclusively American institutions that exclusively targeted African Americans.

Reading through the mainstream resources on the point, it is not hard to understand why this perception exists. The widely read National Association for the Advancement of Colored People (NAACP) report "History of Lynching in America" focuses almost entirely on white-on-Black Southern violence in the United States, opening:

> White mobs often used dubious criminal accusations to justify lynchings. A common claim used to lynch Black men was perceived sexual transgressions against white women. Charges of rape were routinely fabricated. These allegations were used to enforce segregation and advance stereotypes of Black men as violent, hypersexual aggressors.
>
> Hundreds of Black people were lynched based on accusations of other crimes, including murder, arson, robbery, and vagrancy.
>
> Many victims of lynchings were murdered without being accused of any crime. They were killed for violating social customs or racial expectations, such as speaking to white people with less respect than what white people believed they were owed.

Much of this is accurate enough, but the report soon ventures into novel and disputed territory, arguing that lynching is still fairly common today. The authors reference the case of Ahmaud Arbery, a Black man killed in a clash with several whites who followed him, believing him to be the suspect in a series of neighborhood robberies[7]—all of whom were sentenced to prison[8]—and describe him as a lynching victim despite no real evidence of any preexisting plan to kill Arbery. (Recall that the definition of a lynching is a planned extrajudicial killing, not a stupid citizen's arrest gone wrong.)

Similarly, despite the fact that George Floyd was killed specifically by a police officer rather than extrajudicially, the NAACP also argues that his death was a lynching: "The videotaped death of George Floyd was a modern day lynching. . . . Lynchings like these should not be part of American society today, just as they should not have been 100 years ago." But worry not: the organization concludes its report with a somber commitment to keep fighting "white supremacy," white-on-Black "violence," and lynching.

The "take" that lynching was and is exclusively white-on-Black and still occurs with some frequency is significantly more common than I would have expected before starting to write this book. In 2022, Vice President Kamala Harris declared during a major public speech that "lynching is not a relic of the past. Racial acts of terror still occur in our nation. And, when they do, we must all have the courage to name them and hold the perpetrators to account."[9]

Harris went on to define the most common victims of lynch mobs—in the past and presumably today—as minority activists working to build the Great Society: "teachers educating the next generation," "activists defending the sacred freedom to vote," and so forth. Rather remarkably, she gave this address just after her boss, President Biden, signed off on the Emmett Till Antilynching Act—an actual 2022 law designed to end the alleged problem of racial lynching by making such acts hate crimes at the federal level.*

While they frankly do not argue that lynchings are still common

---

* Murder is, of course, already illegal. The maximum penalty for it is death.

today—thank Athena for small mercies—the major U.S. textbooks universally, if unsurprisingly, describe lynching almost entirely in the context of anti-Black violence in the United States. Alongside a sepia-toned photograph of a Black man about to hang, *America, Past and Present* opens its discussion: "Perhaps no event better encompasses the cruel and barbaric nature of the racism and white supremacy that swept the South after Reconstruction than lynching . . . the protection of southern white womanhood became the rallying cry for many lynch mobs."[10] The book does note that lynchings were not entirely confined to the South but focuses on the fact that the majority occurred there, and on the region overall, throughout its discussion.[11]

The Unfinished Nation similarly describes lynching and "posse" justice in the context of the United States' postbellum "increase in white violence against Blacks," primarily as a practice designed to "inhibit Black agitation for equal rights" alongside the Jim Crow legal codes.[12] Again, the book does note some historical context: "Those who participated in lynchings often saw their actions as . . . law enforcement, and some victims of lynchings had in fact committed crimes." However, "lynchings were also a means by which whites controlled the black population, through terror and intimidation."

Reality, of course, paints a considerably more complex picture than "Whites used to lynch us, and still do, and hate is bad." First, to open with the obvious, there are almost no actual lynchings in the United States of America today. The official and hard-researched statistics on American lynchings, maintained by Tuskegee (a famous historically Black college) and the University of Missouri at Kansas City, stop in 1968—a year during in which no confirmed lynching took place.[13]

The most recent lynching actually on record, given the conventional definition of an intentional extrajudicial murder committed by a mob, occurred in 1964: there have been few if any true lynchings since that date. Further, these heinous murders began declining in frequency at the beginning of the modern era: no single year has witnessed more than ten lynchings or posse killings—nationwide and across all races and sexes—since 1936. In contrast, without intending an exact comparison, there were roughly 20,000 U.S. murders each of the past two years, the huge majority of them intraracial and more than half of them involving a Black victim.[14]

Although this has been almost entirely, and perhaps intentionally, forgotten today, historical lynching was also hardly an all-Black affair. All told, more Blacks (3,446) than whites (1,297) were lynched during the usual 1882–1968 period of analysis, and no serious scholar denies this or the role played by racism in this barbaric practice. However, more than 1,000 whites were killed by lynch mobs, apparently before the Hispanic or Native totals are added in—and *more* whites than Blacks were lynched in a remarkable twenty-three states, including: Arizona (31:0), California (41:2), Colorado (65:3), Idaho (20:0), Indiana (33:14), Iowa (17:2), Kansas (35:19), Maine (1:0), Michigan (7:1), Minnesota (5:4), Montana (82:2), Nebraska (52:5), Nevada (6:0), New Mexico (33:3), North Dakota (13:3), Oklahoma (82:40), Oregon (20:1), South Dakota (27:0), Utah (6:2), Vermont (1:0), Washington (25:1), Wisconsin (6:0), and Wyoming (30:5).

The two racial groups were "tied" in two other states, New Jersey (1:1) and New York (1:1), while other states, like Kentucky (63:142), Missouri (53:69), and West Virginia (20:28), massacred a diverse range of accused rapists and horse or cattle thieves.[15] Obviously, extreme racialized violence was centered in the Deep South, with Alabama, for example, killing 299 Blacks and only 48 whites during the period under discussion. However, disgusting though the idea is to almost all of us today, mob justice (or mob "justice") was very common and not always racial in nature in the wild postbellum and frontier era. It is worth recalling that the very term "posse," today remembered in the titles of now-classic cowboy movies and often used as a casual label for a group of friends, basically refers to a lynch mob—a group of essentially random taxpayers summoned together by a local official or plain old citizen to catch and execute an accused criminal offender.

Not only were lynchings of whites (and Hispanics) not historical outliers, what is probably the largest lynching in post-1882 American history involved almost entirely Caucasian victims. As Erin Blakemore describes the situation for History, on March 14, 1891, "a mob of tens of thousands of angry men" surrounded the New Orleans city jail, "shouting angry slurs and calling for blood." After eleven prisoners were literally dragged out of the building, they were "shot and mutilated in an act of brutal mob violence that took place in front of a cheering crowd . . . one of the largest lynchings in U.S. history." And Blakemore notes: "Though the New Orleans lynch mob was driven by bigotry, its targets weren't Black people."[16]

Instead, all were Italian immigrants. If a short history lesson can be allowed, between the late 1870s and the 1920s, tensions regularly flared up between Italians and "native" New Orleanians as large-scale Italian and Sicilian immigration brought well over 200,000 immigrants from the boot of Europe to the Southern port city, at one point "earning the French Quarter the nickname 'Little Palermo.'" Some of this hostility, on the native side, was due to plain ethnic bias, but a fair amount was related to real or strongly suspected criminal activity. Italians were "suspected of Mafia connections"—not always without cause, at this point in history—and the New Orleans Police Department devoted a good deal of time to keeping an eye on familial and commercial ties among Italian immigrants.

In 1891, tensions boiled over after well-liked police chief David Hennessey was publicly murdered by gunmen shortly after "earn[ing] the enmity" of the powerful Sicilian Matranga family by arresting and helping deport a well-known alleged criminal and ally of their faction in the city. When asked who was responsible for his death, Hennessey used what was almost literally his last breath to say, "Dagos," then as now a slur for Italian Americans. The reaction was predictable if extreme: policemen eager to avenge their dead boss man "rounded up hundreds of Italians"—almost certainly including many young men who had no connection to the city's criminal underworld at all—and "harshly questioned" them about the killing. Finally, nine males, all of Italian descent, were arrested and charged with murder in connection with the case.

And then a long and remarkable trial replete with allegations of jury tampering and public declarations of the defendants' guilt by the major New Orleans papers finally concluded with "six not guilty convictions and three mistrials." Almost immediately afterward, as many as 10,000 angry citizens, many of them young men, began congregating outside the jailhouse, where "speakers whipped the mob into a frenzy" by describing Italian migrants as thugs and gangsters who needed to be driven out of New Orleans. After a few such talks, the crowd successfully stormed first the city arsenal—taking dozens of guns and enough ammunition for the lot—and then the jail itself, overcoming defenders in both cases.

Once inside the latter building, mob members seized all of the "men who had been acquitted or given a mistrial," as well as several other Italian men who were completely unconnected to the Hennessey case, dragged them outside, and massacred them in a wild scene. Per Blakemore: "Shots rang out—hundreds of them." The bodies of eleven men, including the complete innocents, were first "riddled with bullets" and then physically ripped into pieces by the frenzied crowd. In a disgusting practice common across lynchings of African Americans, whites, and others, many crowd members took home pieces of clothing or even flesh from the mutilated bodies as mementos.

The 1891 New Orleans lynching was, at and for the time, big news. The government of Italy rapidly became aware of it and issued an official demand that the killers be brought to justice. However, the mood on this side of the pond was celebratory, Blakemore writes: "Many Americans, swept up on a tide of anti-immigrant sentiment, applauded the killings." The *New York Times*, remarkably showing worse taste than she does today, ran a page-long editorial which largely praised the mob and called Italians like those murdered—to quote—"sneaking and cowardly Sicilians, the descendants of bandits and assassins . . . a pest without mitigations."

No members of the March 14 crowd were ever punished in connection with the killings: one of them (John M. Parker) actually went on to serve as governor of the state of Louisiana, while another

(Walter Chew Flower) became one of the more notable mayors of New Orleans. Despite the obvious prominence of such men, among others holding guns and ropes that night, the one grand jury ever empaneled in the case came to the conclusion that "none of the killers could be identified." If anything, the group to suffer most following America's public debate about the lynchings was the Italian American community in the United States: the supposed "Mafia conspiracy" behind Hennessey's murder was used to justify discrimination against Italians in immigration and accommodations "for decades afterward." In all, a fascinating story about a fascinating time—today almost forgotten, perhaps for reasons of narrative.

As the overall academic data indicate, the Italian American New Orleans lynching victims (Antonio Bagnetto, James Caruso, Loretto Comitis, Rocco Geraci, Joseph Macheca, Antonio Marchesi, Pietro Monasterio, Emmanuele Polizzi, Frank Romero, Antonio Scaffidi, and Charles Traina, by the way) were hardly alone. Reviewing Robert A. Gibson's 2002 book *The Negro Holocaust: Lynching and Race Riots in the United States, 1880–1950*,[17] a 2017 opinion writer for Alabama's *Montgomery Advertiser* newspaper broke down both the overall lynching numbers across both major races and the various reasons white victims (and Blacks) met the rope and the faggot.

"Contrary to present day popular conception," author Richard Emanuel opens, "lynching was not a crime committed exclusively against Black people."[18] Citing the overall figures provided earlier in this chapter, Emanuel points out that well over a quarter of all American lynchings between 1882 and 1968 involved a white victim. Obviously and horrifically, this "posse" pattern changed following the Civil War, when mob killings of Black Americans intensified. Interestingly, although this may in some cases be an artifact of demographics, seven U.S. states had "lynch law" at one point or another but killed only whites: "Arizona, Idaho, Maine, Nevada, South Dakota, Vermont, and Wisconsin."

Gibson's and by extension Emanuel's discussions of the motives behind what we often think of as senseless killings were particularly interesting (to this writer). As Thomas Sowell has famously noted, in books like *Black Rednecks and White Liberals*, the historical white Southern crime rate was remarkably high, and quite a few whites were lynched for offenses like "murder or stealing cattle." However, the motivations behind lynch mobs were often political, and this was at least as common in white-victim cases as Black-victim cases: "The original targets of the Ku Klux Klan were Republicans, both Black and white," Emanuel writes, and lynchings were simply "by far the most effective" of various forms of political terrorism carried out by the Klan's night riders and members of similar organizations.

Looked at through this lens, the post-Reconstruction surge in lynch killings in the South can be seen as a sub-component of terrorism by white radical racists against their opponents in a racially diverse GOP. In any case, Emanuel reminds readers, the plain reality is that "more than 1,000 whites were lynched" in the United States during the recent historical past. Some were plain criminals: horse thieves and the like. However, "many of them were lynched because they were Republican, because they supported their fellow black citizens, and"—here an example of supreme irony—"because they opposed the lawless act of lynching."

At least a few major recent publications have begun to explore the complex actual picture of American lynch and posse law, "beyond Dixie." One of these, edited by Michael J. Pfeifer of my alma mater, the University of Illinois, is called simply *Lynching Beyond Dixie: American Mob Violence Outside the South*. According to reviewer Manfred Berg, American historians interested in studying lynching have, quite understandably, "long focused on racist mob violence in the Jim Crow South"—generating a plethora of case studies and other analyses focused on that region. However, current scholars conducting broader analyses are almost universally discovering that "per capita lynching rates in several Western states and territories were on a par with those in the Deep South" and that—as we have seen—Northern lynch mobs not infrequently targeted both whites and Blacks.

Interestingly, calling Sowell's *Black Rednecks* book to mind, Berg points out that both the U.S. South and "Wild" West were long characterized by similar cultures of crime and violence shared among white, Black, and Hispanic residents and involving "lynching, homicide, and inter-personal violence in general."[19] In contrast, levels of all forms of violence in New England and most of the rest of the U.S. Northeast were far lower and "never differed much" from those recorded in western European states—an independent variable that would obviously, logically, be expected to affect rates of lynching and revenge killing.*

In this context, *Lynching Beyond Dixie* argues that the classical view of lynching as a peculiarly Southern and anti-Black problem "rooted in the history of slavery and racism" is essentially inaccurate. Instead, the practice should be understood as part of a lengthy struggle between supporters of old-school vigilantism—"popular justice meted out by local communities"—and advocates of modern civilization, within which the government is perhaps more than anything else monopolist over the legitimate use of force. This struggle, Berg says after a punchy summary of his source material, "lasted for more than a century and encompassed the entire United States."

The three-fifths compromise and the steady decline of posse killings—which, as noted in passing, involved at very least hundreds of Native Americans[20] and Hispanics/Latinos[21] in addition to the white and Black totals—hardly stand alone as steps taken by Western and indeed human civilization along the rocky road up from what we would today call barbarism. Let's not forget: the passage of the American Civil Rights Act granting equal legal rights to U.S. women (1964), full adoption of the Geneva Conventions giving basic rights to all prisoners and civilians during wartime (1949), and plain rejection of the ancient Right of Conquest (1946) all occurred during the most recent eighty years of the existence of the human species. It almost

---

* To some significant extent, this is still true today and is the "dirty little secret" of American criminal justice studies. While both African Americans and many Southern rural whites still post staggeringly high crime rates, the Northern white crime rate broken out by itself seems to be below two homicides per 100,000 residents.

cannot be overemphasized here, again, that life much prior to those dates—for members of all racial and ethnic and regional groups—was unbelievably harsh by the "if it saves JUST ONE LIFE[!!!]" standards of the contemporary era.

Lynching itself, while horrid, was in one very real sense nothing more than a subcategory of unanesthetized public hanging, which was the primary form of capital punishment across the United States for centuries and was used to take tens of thousands of lives. Hanging with a knotted rope noose was a common method of legal execution from the Colonial era until the twentieth century, with the first person ever hanged in the future United States being Caucasian cattle thief Daniel Frank.[22] Not long after, following the bizarre and still famous witch trials in Salem, two men and almost twenty women were sentenced to hang by the neck until dead: academics contend that several thousand persons were hanged for witchcraft during the pre-Independence era.[23] The large majority of these executions were public and followed the lynching model, with cheery crowds in attendance.

Hanging, unlike the huge majority of those sentenced to it, survived the American Revolution, the Declaration of Independence, and the Constitutional Congress. Almost throughout the antebellum 1830s to 1850s, public executions "by rope" were extremely common. Prior to 1849, only five states (Massachusetts, New Jersey, New York, Pennsylvania, and Rhode Island) had mandated hanging in private or banned the practice. Some citizens considered these public spectacles to be barbaric, but most others treated them as we do ball games and boxing matches today: "Tens of thousands of eager viewers would show up to view hangings; local merchants would sell souvenirs and alcohol. Fighting and pushing would often break out as people jockeyed for the best view . . . of the corpse."[24]

And most of *this* took place in the relatively civilized East and upper South. As was the case with lynching and brawling, the American West was much "wilder" when it came to public executions and similar sanguinary spectacles: the Great Emancipator himself, honest Abe Lincoln, once ordered the hanging of thirty-nine Sioux warriors for the murder of white settlers during a series of raids in Minnesota and the Dakotas, though one of the men received a last-minute reprieve.[25] The death penalty was the law for multiple felony crimes in essentially every Western state, and not a few of the famously strict district judges of the West, such as Isaac Parker and Roy Bean, had so many men killed that they became specifically known as "hanging judges." Parker alone had sentenced 160 persons to death by the end of his career, 79 of whom "were executed on the gallows."[26]

During an 1881 session of the U.S. District Court of the New Mexico Territory, one such justice handed down the following eloquent sentence to a convicted thief and duelist:[27]

José Manuel Miguel Xavier Gonzales, in a few short weeks it will be spring. The snows of winter will flee away, the ice will vanish, and the air will become soft and balmy. In short, José Manuel Miguel Xavier Gonzales, the annual miracle of the years will awaken and come to pass, but you won't be there.

The rivulet will run its soaring course to the sea, the timid desert flowers will put forth their tender shoots, the glorious valleys of this imperial domain will blossom as the rose. Still, you won't be here to see.

From every treetop some wild woods songster will carol his mating song; butterflies will sport in the sunshine, the busy bee will hum happy as it pursues its accustomed vacation; the gentle breeze will tease the tassels of the wild grasses, and all nature will be glad, but you. You won't be here to enjoy it because I command the sheriff or some other officers of the country to lead you out to some remote spot, swing you by the neck from a knotting bough of some sturdy oak, and let you hang until you are dead.

And then, José Manuel Miguel Xavier Gonzales, I further command that such officer or officers retire quickly from your dangling corpse, so that vultures may descend from the heavens upon your filthy body until nothing shall remain but bare, bleached bones of a cold-blooded, bloodthirsty, throat-cutting, murdering son of a bitch.

Poetic words, those: they deserve to live. And the era of the hanging judge hardly ended with the little-mourned passing of Mr. Gonzales. The number of American hangings declined sharply following the widespread adoption of more sophisticated technologies for killing people—the gas chamber arrived on the scene in 1921, about three decades after the electric chair[28]—but this archaic punishment remained fairly frequent well into the 1940s.

The last American public hanging took place in 1936, in my adopted state of Kentucky, where a crowd of up to 30,000 assembled in Owensboro to watch the painful public execution of convicted rapist Rainey Bethea.[29] However, the last plain hanging did not take place until 1996, when Delaware murderer Billy Bailey breathed him his last.[30] For that matter, two other men—Charles Rodman Campbell and Westley Allan Dodd, both of the state of Washington—were also hanged during the early to mid-1990s. The progress of "civilization" is upward, but slow.

The trajectories of real but slow American and human abandonment of most other barbaric historical practices would virtually mirror those outlined so far for slavery, lynching, and public executions as features of street fairs. Take whipping. Like hanging, beating convicted offenders or captured enemies with a rawhide whip was an absolute commonplace, not at all racially specific, for most of U.S. history. While slaves were obviously and cruelly whipped, and history books should note this, several scholars have argued that the cruelest abuses involving "the lash" took place against sailors, military conscripts, and other troops. For decades, the U.S. Navy employed a formal procedure for whipping sailormen, that which opened with the invocation: "Men! What the law allows you, you shall have, but—by the eternal God—if any of you disobeys that law—I'll cut your back bone out. Go on with him, boatswain's mate and do your duty, or by God you'll take his place."[31]

This practice of organized flogging dates back to the very beginning of the country, if not before. The rules governing the American Colonial Navy, set down in 1775, state that a naval commander can whip a seaman up to but not beyond "twelve lashes upon his bare back with a cat-o'-nine tails." In 1799, a fully independent U.S. Congress formalized this aspect of the naval code, passing a law allowing the commander of an American ship to "apply . . . twelve lashes on the bare back of a sailor or marine" except in rare cases where even "more were ordered by a court-martial."

Even these brutal rules—twelve hits with a cat-o'-nine-tails whip would in practice involve 108 strikes with small barbed-leather whips—were often violated in practice by sadistic officers. Every source quoted so far mentions that the letter of the law "was abused in many cases," and the famous American naval history *Threescore Years* describes the fairly typical whipping of an enlisted seaman as follows:

> The shrieks of the youngster were dreadful, calling upon God and all the holy angels to save him. After the first dozen, another boat-swain's mate took up the cat, and when he had received two dozen he fainted, and hung by his wrists. The punishment was suspended for a few moments until he had revived.... [H]e then took four dozen more, making six in all, and when taken down he could not stand. The other [man] received seven dozen: he fainted, however, before he had received the first, and received the greater part of his punishment in that state. The flesh was fairly hanging in strips upon both backs; it was a sickening sight.

Remarkably, this sort of thing was far from the worst contemporary military punishment. In addition to whippings, the same source text describes sailors being forced to walk for days in teams, with each man "carry[ing] a 32 pound shot with 32 pounds of chain attached to their legs and a wooden yoke around the neck," while the similarly structured British and Dutch navies "keelhauled" miscreants—literally throwing them overboard with a rope attached and dragging them behind the ship for a period of time.[32] Most lived. Military flogging and several of these other punishments were not eliminated [in the United States] until just before Southern slaves were freed: on "17 July 1862 . . . Congress finally abolished flogging entirely."

The whip was not reserved for sailors, or even military personnel overall. The records of the Lewis and Clark cross-country trek, launched by the U.S. Army but obviously involving many civilian and Native participants, detail "a number of floggings" and whippings. On one occasion a man who had deserted from the expedition was punished with a sentence of five hundred strokes with a whip, while a different offender "was sentenced to run a gauntlet of whips."* Purely civilian whipping lasted even longer than the military variety: the *New York Times* ran a short and glad piece in 1972[!][33] noting that the last American state—Delaware, as it happens—had retired its civilian whipping post. Not long prior to that date, "the lash had been used as a punishment" for offenders of all races "for crimes ranging from robbery and larceny to wife-beating and embezzling."

No honest person would deny that this was generally *more* the case for Blacks than for whites in the premodern USA . . . but, for almost every living person within every racial and regional and "gender" group, history sucked.

---

* Native American warriors, themselves hardly soft men, were shocked by these time-consuming and brutal beatings: one Native leader who watched the first commented that it seemed kinder simply "to put the man to death."

LIE #6

"European Colonialism Was— Empirically—a No-Good, Terrible, Very Bad Thing"

What price is too high to pay for freedom? An idealistic activist would likely say there is no price too high, but this is to ignore the reality of pragmatic political and human considerations. When we talk about historical colonialism, we cannot simply assume people groups have generally confronted choices between American-style democracy and life under colonial control. In many or most cases, the alternative to colonialism was not democracy but equivalent or even worse "Native" oppression. In every transition, there are trade-offs.

So another widely accepted contemporary belief, prevalent throughout American secondary and higher education,* is that post-1800 Western colonialism was an unmitigated evil. Two major academic resources on the subject are titled simply "A Quick Reminder of Why Colonialism Was Bad"[1] and "Why Colonialism Is Wrong."[2] In reality, yet again, the truth is a bit more nuanced.

Before we explore that nuanced truth, *National Geographic*'s article "What Is Colonialism?"—one of the first resources to be found

---

* Are you noticing a pattern to how these chapters start?

during a Google search by any schoolchild researching this topic—provides a widely read summary of the conventional position on this topic. Although a bit more nuanced than "colonialism bad," the subheading reads: "The history of colonialism is one of brutal subjugation of indigenous peoples."[3] Author Erin Blakemore goes on to describe colonialism as the ill that occurs when one nation conquers or vanquishes another, "conquering its population and exploiting it" and "forcing its own language and cultural values" upon the defeated people. Colonialism of this kind is closely linked to another iffy idea: imperialism, which Blakemore argues is "the ethos of using power and influence to control another nation or people," that undergirds essentially all colonial expansion.

Blakemore's *Nat Geo* piece focuses almost totally on the colonial misbehavior of whites. A short list of ancient colonizers that is provided includes the historical Egyptians, Phoenicians, Greeks, and Romans. Their colonies are described as having been almost wholly exploitative—leeching away "the physical and population resources of the people they conquered." The article then jumps to the near-modern era, skipping over Genghis Khan and Tamerlane and their cities built of human skulls,[4] and noting that Spanish and Portuguese colonization of the New World and some African islands began during the early fifteenth century. Following another leap forward in time, "in the 1880s," European countries began the chaotic scramble for Africa, seizing large continental colonies that most states would hold until just before the beginning of World War One.

Blakemore briefly notes the beneficial side of colonialism. In a single well-written and somewhat Monty Python–esque paragraph ("But what DID the Romans ever do for us?!"), she points out that almost all European colonial governments "invested in infrastructure and trade," greatly expanded the "medical and technological knowledge" base of the countries they overran and then managed, "encouraged literacy," oversaw the adoption of modern "human rights standards," "sowed the seeds for [democracy]," and so forth. Fairly typical large colonies, such as Ghana—overseen by the

British Empire—saw improvements in "nutrition," "health," and "development gains" throughout their time under colonial administration.

But . . . lest readers take away the wrong impression, this summary is followed immediately by a longer paragraph arguing that these positive changes occurred alongside "coercion," and "forced assimilation" into Western culture. Other negative impacts of colonialism that are cited include damage to the environment, the introduction of novel diseases, and the initiation of "ethnic rivalries" and humanitarian crises that, one would logically assume, had never previously existed. The entire era of colonial expansion had a net negative impact, a typical reader would likely think.

Blakemore's piece is in fact one of the more balanced within a large literature that slants fairly hard to the left. As previously noted, a 2017 article prominently featured in the intellectual magazine *Current Affairs* was titled "A Quick Reminder of Why Colonialism Was Bad." The author here, Nathan J. Robinson, was far less subtle in his views, and his first paragraph serves as perhaps the best summary I have read of the hard anti-colonial position. To quote Robinson at some length:

> The easiest way to understand why colonialism was so horrific is to imagine it happening in your country now. It is invaded, conquered, and occupied by a foreign power. Existing governing institutions are dismantled and replaced by absolute rule of the colonizers. A strict hierarchy separates the colonized and the colonizer; you are treated as an inconvenient subhuman who can be abused at will. The colonists commit crimes with impunity against your people. Efforts at resistance are met with brutal reprisal. Sometimes massacre. The more vividly and accurately you manage to conjure what this scenario would actually look like, the more horrified you will be by the very idea of colonialism.

In response to perhaps the most obvious rebuttal to this argument—that the balance of risk and reward for subjects of a medieval-level African or Polynesian kingdom taken over by the British Empire was very different than that for modern American citizens conquered by, say, China would be—Robinson goes on to reject any cost-benefit analysis of colonialism on ethical grounds. Comparing the claim that colonial European rule was better for most of those to fall under it than anything that might have "happened in its absence" to defenses of domestic abuse used by lovers or by siblings like Pip's loathsome sister in *Great Expectations*, he contends that this may be true but that does not matter. From his apparent perspective, morality is real and likely ultimate, and constructing hospitals and one-room schoolhouses "doesn't provide one with a license to rob and murder people."

Further, Robinson argues—or seems to—the claim that colonialism was ever superior to local alternatives may not be accurate. By page six of the piece, he launches into a lengthy and fairly accurate exegesis of European colonial atrocities, noting that badly run colonial possessions, like the Belgian Congo during the era immortalized in *Heart of Darkness*, were often charnel houses at least on a par with the Confederate Old South in the United States. Mad King Leopold's Congo, Robinson argues, can fairly be described as "legalized robbery" backed up by the guns of Belgian soldiers and mercenaries—an entire nation-state turned into one gigantic work camp dedicated to rubber production. By some estimates, 10 to 11 million people were killed during the period of Belgian dominion; others were physically mutilated, with the severing of hands a common if illogical punishment for failure to harvest quickly.

The Belgian Congo was an exceptional case—and opponents of Robinson's brief are quick to point out, a sort of plantation administered directly by the king rather than a "proper" colonial possession of Belgium.[5] However, even the British Empire, often lauded as an alternative to Leopold-style brutality, was not without her sins during the colonial era. While Robinson concedes that some British military campaigns, like the suppression of the Mau Mau revolution in Kenya, were "better than the alternative," he points out that these involved "mass detention" and other practices that would be considered significant violations of human rights law today.

During the war against the Mau Mau, thousands of Kenyans were forced into labor or concentration camps. Many women credibly claimed to have been raped by British or allied Kenyan soldiers, and we know that at least two men were castrated. Other British atrocities included policies that possibly led to large-scale famines in India,[6] while French crimes were committed in colonial Algeria.[7] And so on, through a butcher's bill of some length.

The primary four or five textbooks that I reviewed for this book in fact provided a more balanced analysis of the colonial era than Mr. Robinson did, but most did scurry to describe Western colonial adventuring as uniquely bad in comparison with any previous imperial system. On occasion, this could and did reach amusing lengths. *Traditions and Encounters* (2016), for example, had some good things to say about the Mongols.

While noting that the building of the Mongol Empire brought "destruction" to Eurasia, authors Jerry H. Bentley, Herbert F. Ziegler, and Heather E. Streets-Salter (also cited briefly back in chapter one) go on to note that the Great Khans also "sponsored interaction among peoples of different societies and linked Eurasian lands more directly than ever before." In between building monuments out of human crania, they "positively encouraged travel and communication over long distances," which aided in the expansion of "trade, diplomatic travel, missionary efforts, and movements of peoples to new lands." Overall, "long distance travel and trade became much less risky," spawning a sort of new Golden Age for a group of states stretching from (conquered) Han China to Western Europe.[8]

The Bantu migration—the process of expansion during which my own assegai-wielding ancestors took over sub-Saharan Africa—also comes in for a bit of love. In *Traditions and Encounters*, migrating Bantu warriors are described in pacific terms as "absorbing" preexisting "populations of hunting, gathering, and fishing peoples" into their own more advanced farming societies. Their massive

edge in forged-iron weaponry certainly "strengthened the hand of
Bantu groups . . . against competitors" but more importantly en-
abled peaceful "cultivators" to clear new land and "expand the zone
of agriculture more effectively than before."[9] At no point is it simply
stated that the Bantu conquered or displaced almost everyone they
came across, nearly eliminating the preexisting Khoisan population.[10]

European conquerors? Well, those are treated a bit differently
(if, again, not always unfairly). In the same text, the authors say:
"The building of empires is an old story in world history. By the
19th century, however, European observers recognized that empires
of their day were different from those of earlier times." Scholars,
it is noted, "began to speak of imperialism"—defining it as harsh
and generally Western "domination over subject lands in the larger
world." While it is never coherently explained exactly how Western
imperial colonies were different from or worse than those of earlier eras, the artificial dichotomy again makes for some entertaining
moments: at one point, eighteenth-century Europeans are chided
for "*interference in the Ottoman and Quing Empires* in Southwest and
East Asia" (italics mine).[11] Shouldn't that be an oppressor-oppressor
conflict and thus no harm, no foul?

However, the presentation of the brief from one side does not
close the case against colonialism. A professor of political science
at Portland State University, Bruce Gilley (*The Case for Colonialism*),
the primary author criticized by Robinson, makes an obvious point
in reply. Moral arguments about the objective or unique evil of the
colonial era assume the existence and general acceptance—in
pre-colonial Black and Arab and Native states—of an essentially
modern ethics, where acts like aggressive war or the harsh domination of once-conquered territory were seen as not merely unfortunate in practical terms but evil, and indigenous governments did
not themselves often engage in these actions. In reality, there is
essentially no evidence that truly modern, post–right-of-conquest
moral or legal standards existed anywhere on earth before the
modern era—Iroquois or Hawaiian or Ashanti nobles were probably

no more or less ruthless than their white opponents—but there is considerable evidence of the hard material benefits of colonialism.

Gilley explains that arguments in defense of Western colonialism have "virtually disappeared" inside the left-leaning field of international relations and that claims of pro-colonial attitudes are today used to discredit public figures like rightist South African politician Helen Zille, but he contends that it is "high time to question" this negative take on a complex historical reality. Objectively speaking, he points out, there is considerable evidence that post-1800 Western colonialism "led to improvements in living conditions" for the majority of people living in the developing world, and certainly that it caused less of a "grave human toll" than subsequent post-or anti-colonial policy regimes like African socialism.[12]

To a very large extent, whether this is true is a practical and empirical rather than moral question. The many notable "minority" states without much if any history of Western colonization—Gilley provides a list that includes China, Ethiopia, Guatemala, Haiti, Liberia, Libya, Saudi Arabia, and Thailand—can simply be compared to former colonial possessions in terms of gross domestic product (GDP), income per capita, women's rights, or even professed happiness across the population. Is it in fact true that the countries just listed are richer and happier places than comparable postcolonial states like Belize, Botswana, and Singapore?

Perhaps unsurprisingly, the answer provided in "The Case for Colonialism" is no. Citing previous work by Juan and Pier-skalla, Gilley argues all data shows "significant social, economic, and political gains" under colonialism, which persisted into the postcolonial era for many former colonies. The list of these is extensive, including improvements in schooling, health care, core infrastructure, administration, rights for women and minorities, and even the hated but important category of effective tax and revenue collection.

He also notes something that has been almost forgotten—or intentionally ignored—by modern academic leftists: most Western powers, certainly including Britain and France, eventually ended slavery and peonage where trod their boot, as well as "enfran-chis[ing] untouchable and historically excluded communities." By the colonial era, the idea that some persons are so filthy, so cursed by God (or the gods), that their only role in life is to skin decaying carcasses or clean away the shit of their betters was generally *not* a Western idea but rather a "Native" idea, and those that hated and opposed it tended to be Westerners. (This was, of course, a change from the days when Aristotle's Greeks were proponents of natural slavery.)

Gilley also makes a second and (to me) more interesting point: Western colonial regimes were measurably seen as legitimate by the majority of their nonwhite subjects until very nearly the end of the colonial era. There are several common quantitative metrics of national legitimacy, and per these: "Until very late, European colonialism appears to have been highly legitimate and for good reasons." Millions of human beings moved into areas of "more intensive colonial rule" from less intensively developed areas or areas of indigenous rule, worked hard for colonial governments, utilized colonial networks services like medical centers and high schools, voted in colonial governments that were often dominated at the local level by Indigenous persons, and most notably often fought to the death in the military and police forces of the sirkars—the Western governments. Until the revolutionary beginning of the truly modern era, "the 'preservers,' 'facilitators' and [even] 'col-laborators' of colonialism . . . far outnumbered the 'resisters' . . ."

Such behavior, among the highly sophisticated "native" resi-dents of, say, West Africa or Southeast Asia, was emphatically not due to "Uncle Tom"–style subservience or awe at Western techno-logical prowess. Almost certainly, no Indonesian or Ashanti trader who saw the muskets or rifles available to outnumbered European outpost troops in the 1800s was amazed by them (although he would doubtless have started scrambling immediately to get his hands on as many as possible). Rather, the non-Western peoples of the world were as capable of pragmatically weighing their op-tions as their European friends/foes/rivals. And the alternative to occasionally brutal European rule was very often brutal indigenous rule. As Gilley points out, in the majority of areas that became colonial possessions—certainly those that did so early on, or with any degree of willingness—the residents "faced grave security threats from rival groups" and preferred being ruled by "a modernized and liberal state" than by their foemen.

Why has all of this, much of which seems obvious, become taboo to say? Once again, a big chunk of the answer may trace to the extraordinary ideological bias of modern academia. The publication of Gilley's bland scholarly article, astonishingly, resulted in multiple death threats, two separate petitions signed by roughly 2,000 academics, and the resignation of more than half the editorial board of host journal *Third World Quarterly*.[13] In this context, Gilley himself closes his piece with a fascinating third argument: much of the academic critique of colonialism was never "intended to be true" in the usual scientific sense of testing out a claim through "shared standards of inquiry . . . liable to falsification." Instead, the purpose has been using "research" to provide support for contemporary left-wing advocacy.

The prevalence of activist thinking in scholarship is evident through examples of highly controversial, trivial ideas being introduced as fact. As we have seen during recent controversies surrounding Washington, D.C.'s Smithsonian Institution, academic activists not infrequently link traits like being on time to the office or engaging in friendly competition at work to "whiteness" or "the colonial period"[14]—making it a sort of revolutionary act to refuse to engage in them. A great deal of the corpus of anti-colonial scholarship consists of this sort of thing, including a sub-genre that the author of "The Case for Colonialism" describes as "inquiry into the glories of sadomasochism among Third World women." Fascinating and timely though some of this may be, it does approximately nothing to answer the question of whether the Western colonial era was a good thing in measurable economic and political terms. On the basis of more evidence than a little bit, Bruce Gilley says it was.

In very recent years a few other scholars, mostly housed on

the political right, have dared to make similar points. Writing for the Hoover Institution in 2015, Bruce Thornton noted that the very word "colonialism" has become a synonym for oppression and a "crude epithet" used to target the West by representatives of other civilizations.[15] As a result, many Westerners—including some capable of making foreign policy decisions—have become consumed by "self-loathing," which our opponents are glad to take advantage of. However, Thornton argues, this is the result of an amoral strategic gambit: the currently popular *Traditions and Encounters*–style definition of colonialism as a uniquely Western institution considered illegitimate by the rest of the world was developed specifically by enemies of our society, and most powerful societies in fact engaged in colonialism in the past—sometimes for good and sometimes for ill.

Per Thornton and his sources, "the simplistic discrediting of colonialism and its evil twin, imperialism," began with Marxist activists during the first quarter of the twentieth century. Specifically, Communist scholars saw Western colonial activity as providing an exit door explanation for one of their beloved dialectic's greatest failures: the near-total absence of class-based revolutions in postindustrial western Europe. Vladimir Lenin himself, in 1917, "faced with the failure" of essentially all classical Marxist predictions about working-class revolution against the European bourgeoisie, wrote *Imperialism: The Highest Stage of Capitalism*, which argued essentially that colonialism made all of the world into one interlinked economic unit, with the peoples of the Third World serving as the proletariat for the globe. All of them by definition had to be oppressed, and these "Indigenous colonized peoples" might well prove the fulcrum to finally topple Evil Global Capitalism.

Zany brown- and black-skinned revolutionaries, understandably, loved these ideas even more than zany white ones did. They "influenced" virtually all of the anti-colonial campaigns that began following the Second World War, and Frantz Fanon's *The Wretched of the Earth* actually opens—albeit courtesy of the melanin-deficient Jean-Paul Sartre—with the line "All Natives of the underdeveloped countries unite!" Driven by sympathetic figures like Mr. Fanon and Mahatma Gandhi and by millions of books still in print—and widely available in our schools—this Marxist argument retains staying power today. As Thornton correctly puts it: "Leftist idealization of the colonial Third World and its demonization of the capitalist West have survived the collapse of the Soviet Union and the discrediting of Marxism, and become received wisdom both in academe and in popular culture."

However, like Gilley before him, "B Thornt" points out that a great deal of this is empirically nonsensical. He makes some of the same points about the measurable positive effects of colonialism—although this is not the focus of his article—but more importantly demonstrates that there is no mappable relationship between colonialism and modern capitalism. Historically, colonialism, or plain conquest, has been a characteristic of all societies with strength enough to engage in it.

In addition to the Communist and notoriously expansionist Union of Soviet Socialist Republics itself, a short list of famous historical colonizers might include: "the Romans in Gaul, the Arabs throughout the Mediterranean and Southern Asia, the Huns in Eastern Europe, the Mongols in China, the [Ottomans] in the Middle East and the Balkans, the Bantu in Southern Africa, the Khmer in East Asia, the Aztecs in Mexico, the Iroquois in the Northeast . . . the Sioux throughout the Great Plains." Rather clearly, colonial expansion is not a Western "thing," or a white one, or—looking across these examples—invariably a bad one.

Overseas and in communities of color Stateside, people tend to be more honest than upper-middle-class white Westerners about a whole range of issues. This one seems to be no exception. As part of a publicly visible back-and-forth conversation, a popular Indonesian website, Facts of Indonesia, recently listed a baker's dozen of often fascinating positive and negative effects of Western—in this case Dutch—colonization of that island state.[16] Balancing some bluntly stated genuine negatives ("Starvation," "A lot of disease," "Rice fields was displaced because of forced labor") was an enumerated list of at least as many positives—first among them the introduction to Indonesia of modern technology.

Per the anonymous author: "The development of science and technology was introduced by the Dutch colonial government." With perhaps a bit of dark humor, (s)he went on to note that one of the first articles of tech the Dutch and Indonesian peoples shared with one another was weaponry: each side's "light and heavy armaments," with the Dutch having a particular knack for "combat vehicles . . . transportation." However, more pacifically—albeit presumably after winning the war—the Dutch government introduced courses of modern scientific and technical education throughout the Indonesian school system. Agricultural development is listed as a particular bonus of this *cultuurstelsel* program: "As you know [Holland] is a country with the great technology in farming and agriculture . . . Indonesians became good in getting the knowledge of agriculture."

Moving on, development of national infrastructure throughout Indonesia—a near majority of which even today appears to have been built by the Dutch—is noted. Although this is described as both a positive and negative effect of colonialism, with Indonesians allegedly working on large projects without salaried pay and sometimes without rations, the website's writers concede massive builds like the Anyer–Panarukan highway (the Great Post Road) "gave totally the significant infrastructure in Indonesia." They proceed on through praise of Dutch *non*technical schooling ("Education was getting better"), improved trade and increased cosmopolitanism ("Indonesia learn[ed] foreign languages for [first] time"), and so forth. This, while hardly academic, may be one of the best and most honest takes on colonialism available: the Dutchmen were hardly perfect, but they had their good points and were certainly no worse than the local lairds who came before them.

Similarly and *very* academically, a group of Ghanaian writers recently provided nuanced but real praise for British colonial development of that country's health care system in the pages of a major journal. In their *Studies in Arts and Humanities* piece "Public

Health in Colonial and Post-Colonial Ghana: Lesson-Drawing for the Twenty-First Century," the good doctors Samuel Adu-Gyamfi, Edward Brenya, and Peter Nana Egyir contrast Ghanaian health care during British occupation with the state of affairs both beforehand and afterward . . . and conclude that the colonial health care was the best of the lot. Describing Ghanaian public health during the current century as "mired with issues ranging from the inadequacy of public health facilities, improper settlement planning, insanitary conditions . . . to the inadequacy of laws and their implementation," they argue that "this situation compared to the colonial era is a direct contradiction."[17]

In developing the Ghanaian medical system, the British first re-placed the system that had previously existed, which Adu-Gyamfi, Brenya, and Nana Egyir—educated Wa-Benzi Africans all—describe with a refreshing lack of "noble savage" nostalgia. Witch doctors were common: frontline medical care was provided by shamanic practitioners, who used herbal cocktails and "other traditional means such as the wearing of amulets" to try to prevent diseases or halt their spread. All of this was overseen by traditional rulers like tribal chiefs, who employed a range of techniques from town-wide taboos to mandatory labor on sanitary projects to promote sanitation and prevent disease. In pre-colonial Ghana, infectious disease was the primary driver for illness and death in the population.[18]

For solid amoral reasons, the British colonizers of Ghana real-ized that, unless basic health requirements were met for both Eu-ropean and African residents of Ghanaian cities and towns, healthy life in the nation would be close to impossible. As a result, multiple hospitals were built, with fully completed projects ranging at least from Cape Coast in 1868 to Korle Bu Hospital in 1923. Additional public health practices like the "provision of piped water, drainage systems, and sanitary facilities" were implemented as early as the 1880s to protect not only European settlers "but the entire Gold Coast colony as a whole." The "Public Health in Colonial and Post-Colonial Ghana" authors even argue that "preventive health care methods"—i.e., all organized screening, testing, and vaccination for disease—were pioneered by the British. In sum: "The colonial administration put measures such as health education . . . provision of health facilities, screening test, provision of incinerators, and other measures [in place] to protect not only the Europeans but the colony as a whole."

Whites and Blacks ensnared in the Atlantic World often fought one another brutally, and that legacy should not be forgotten. However, the legacy of knowledge described by Adu-Gyamfi, Brenya, and Nana Egyir was at least as real and has been at least as lasting. Well aware of facts of this kind, even the great Nigerian writer and radical Chinua Achebe has acknowledged the positive side of Western colonialism and not infrequently—he wrote in English, after all—seemed to view it as more of a good thing than a bad one.

In his last book, Achebe spoke clearly about the beneficial long-term results of Western colonialism, including "the British project of state formation and nation-building" that essentially created modern Nigeria.[19] In his There Was a Country, Achebe obviously criticizes the excesses and harmful legacies of colonialism—but also points out that it left many positive legacies behind as well. Indeed, as Bruce Gilley (again) has pointed out, Achebe contends quite explicitly that one reason for the weakness of the modern Nigerian state is that "it repudiated too much" of the institutional heritage left behind by Great Britain. In many ways, "the challenge of modernity put to Africa was a healthy one." While independence was healthy and good as well—to Achebe and most of us—the further development of African states will require "embracing, rather than spurning," many of the institutions associated with the colonial era: "educational, administrative, and social."

It is worth quoting the great African man of letters a bit more. There Was a Country certainly opens with some bog-standard anti-colonial claims—that the era of the European "scramble for Africa" and open European-African conflict (some military) "did violence to Africa's ancient societies and resulted in tension-prone modern states." To be sure! However, less conventionally,

Achebe is also full of praise for many of the Western institutions that resulted from that rough start: from the Anglican church to the grade-grouped schools to fair standardized tests and nation-wide civil service exams. At one point, even Christian missionaries come in for some love: "My father had a lot of praise for the missionaries . . . and so do I. I am a prime beneficiary of the education that the missions made a major component of their enterprise."[20]

Education, well beyond the odd mission school, is a major focus of those pages of Achebe's that praise the Sassenach. Describing the better Nigerian educational institutions of the 1930s and 1940s, the majority of them British constructed, he says: "The schools were [well] endowed financially, had excellent amenities, and were staffed with first rate teachers, custodians, cooks, and librarians." The British even established a solidly constructed and ranked university for all of West Africa, to which a young Achebe earned his first academic scholarship.

Attending institutions of this kind at the same time as "villages transform[ed] into towns" and new conveniences like reliable electricity hit the scene, Achebe recalls that the Nigerian people seemed to be "standing figuratively and literally at the dawn of a new era." Unfortunately, much of this brawny hope faded away at the end of the colonial period when an independent Nigerian government took power: the famous schools fell "into disrepair . . . and are nothing like what they were in their heyday."

Enthusiasm for at least the material improvements provided by Western colonizers—even if tempered like that of Achebe or the Facts of Indonesia writers—is not difficult to understand. At some baseline level, no one disputes that European colonial powers provided much or most of the essential infrastructure that many Third World states still rely on today. In an interesting and on-point case study, a recent Bloomberg piece ("How Overlooked Colonial Railways Could Revolutionize Transportation in Africa")[21] suggests an innovative way for modern African countries to rapidly revamp their transportation networks: simply by making use of the dozens of colonial-era transit networks that were operated and maintained for decades but are too often now simply crumbling into the landscape.

To some extent, this is already happening: this new and "somewhat surprising transportation policy is gaining steam across Africa." As author Sam Sturgis points out, the major Western powers built tens of thousands of miles of reasonably good-quality railway across the African continent, and—after decades of stagnation—functional African governments are restoring it for future use. Uganda plans to revitalize 237 miles of British-built rail, even after a deal with China to fund the project fell through.[22] While this next project is running a bit behind schedule, Ethiopia also plans to have at least 450 miles of colonial-era railroad back online in the near future. Nigeria, "Africa's most populous country," recently committed $166 million to reopening the old rail line between the national capital of Lagos and the major northern city of Kano some 700 miles away.

This "colonial reuse" policy offers dramatic hope for transportation prospects in Africa, which have been largely "beholden to road transport" for the past several decades. Per Sturgis and sources like the United Nations Economic Commission for Africa,[23] more than 80 percent of all goods transported in contemporary Africa—and 90 percent of all people—are moved by means of individually owned vehicles, on a par with America's family sedans and minivans. This leaves major African cities famously dominated by almost immobile car traffic, while more than a few rural Africans still rely on bullock carts and the like to get goods and people to market. Fortunately, an alternative is already available: redeveloping colonial railroads is beginning to seem not only like an "attractive option" but a practically achievable one. For all their flaws, the Westerners built well—and much of what they built in Africa remains.

The sub-surface implications of that fact, and of Sturgis's point about the material legacy of colonialism, are obvious. For all of their frequent follies and occasional brutalities, there exists very little evidence that most Western colonial regimes were led by more bloodthirsty or incompetent leaders than the indigenous governments that preceded (and followed) them—or that they overall did a worse job of governing. This point was made recently in a fascinating piece titled "The Other Side of Colonialism, Part I,"[24] which appeared on the consistently entertaining website How Africans Underdeveloped Africa, a resource of Black heterodox thought run by a Nigerian-Canadian writer, and which argues that any real understanding of colonialism's effects has to involve a true understanding of what Africa was like before the colonial period. Like North America, per all data, it was no earthly paradise.

Prior to colonialism, Africa could perhaps best be described as diverse and dangerous. Focusing on West Africa, the Black How Africans Underdeveloped Africa author describes the region as "a highly heterogeneous place" containing several impressive state-level societies ruled by stable hereditary kings, some intermediate societies including chiefdoms and large tribes, and "numerous small un-stratified tribal entities." Peace was an extreme rarity: the entire area, to no more or less an extent than Polynesia or inland eastern Europe, suffered "the usual problems of fractured and fractious tribal regions around the world." In the least developed tropical forest zones, warfare and raiding between tribal groups were constant, "endemic." However, even in larger societies like the Islamic and highly "civilized" Sokoto Caliphate, slavery was a key component of the local economy and thus "wars and slave raiding"—the latter often at expedition scale—took place constantly.

A few of the narratives recounted in the How Africans Underdeveloped Africa piece are worth retelling here, to shine a light onto what actual Africans—as versus later left-wing historical revisionists—thought of the pre-colonial era. The Nigerian businessman Ishiwu Ogbene, whose story endures in the text *Igbo Worlds: An Anthology of Oral Histories and Historical Descriptions*, opens by describing a lengthy period of conflict between the people of his Awaka region and the invading Eru (or Aro) tribe: "The Eru began to come to Awaka to look for slaves. . . . [T]here were many wars." Ogbene's extended family apparently fought well but eventually fled the region to escape the constant warfare. However, they did not find peace. In their new lands, Ogbene's alliance "fought many wars against Ibagwa . . . Obukpa, Iheaka, and Ihoro"—among other tribes and city-states. In a sentence that would strike most American graduate students as astonishing, the West African closes his lengthy and poignant account by saying: "Only the coming of the white man saved them."

In another region of what is now the same country, the local Indigenous rulers are described—per *A Chronicle of Abuja*, a purely indigenous history published in 1952, commissioned by the king of Abuja, and written by Mallam Hassan and Shuaibu Na'ibi—as fighting constantly against powerful invading tribes. One of these kings, Emir Ibrahim, is honored as "the warrior Emir who did his utmost to guard the land of the Abuja and prevent it from falling into the hands of the Fulani as . . . the surrounding country had long since fallen." Despite being endowed with a pleasant natural tan, the Fulani were notable and brutal conquerors—"pre-European colonizers" of the Sahel zone of western Africa—and the massive Sokoto Caliphate they established became "the second largest slave society in the world" by the mid-1900s. By opposing them, and by helping arm other opponents on enemy-of-my-enemy grounds, Ibrahim became something of a hero to nearby "pagan" Africans who still practiced traditional animist beliefs and who had been driven from their farms into nearby "forests and hills" by constant Fulani raids.

The incoming British no doubt replaced the sins of pre-colonial conquerors with their own. However, these sins—while drawing more rebuke from scholars today—were often fewer in number and less varied in kind. As Hassan and Na'ibi themselves put it: "The coming of the British was the mercy of God." After the arrival of a single stabilizing power in the region, it became possible for Abujan warriors to "rest from their strife with the Fulani, that they might live in peace with them . . . and in friendship and marriage." Perhaps most touchingly, "the Pagans came out of the forests" and were able to resume something approaching their pre-conflict lives of agriculture and barter. After a series of fort liberations and commercial exchanges, it was even the case that some—although far from all—of those who had once been taken as slaves were "restored to their homes."

As this indicates, colonialism frequently brought a *reduced* level of violence to African territories. The aims of colonizers were not, to be sure, generally noble in today's terms. In most cases, the two primary goals of colonial powers were (1) developing their post-scramble African territories using then-modern technology and (2) integrating them "into the emerging global economy." This was all done so that the new lands could be ruthlessly exploited—with products like gold and rubber shipped down proper highways to overseas markets.

However, "the first benefit therefore [was] peace": the achievement of any colonial economic goal required the near-total elimination of slave raids, highway robbery, and tribal warfare. Whatever the colonizers' motivations, the societal stability and customs that they brought along with them had many positive effects. Law arrived for utterly amoral reasons—"It is impossible to organize a colonial economy of resource extraction in a climate of personal insecurity and constant disruption"—but it usually did arrive.

And when the hated-and-loved Westerners left, it often departed. Although this has been largely forgotten today, and stable African states like Ghana and Nigeria have certainly joined the mainline global order, the retreat of the colonial powers from Africa was accompanied by an extraordinary orgy of violence. Across the continent, attempts to return to preexisting systems or to restructure governments around newer models like Marxism—often by intentionally channeling the wine-dark emotions of tribalism—resulted in brutal conflict that reached far beyond the ballot box.

The continent experienced many "revolutions," like the 1964 Zanzibar massacre of 5,000 to 20,000 Indian and Arab noncombatants by Black Africans, the Kenyan Mau Mau uprising and its aftermath, graphic ethnic violence in the Tanzanian capital of Dar es Salaam, and the first modern round of Hutu-Tutsi violence in Rwanda.

Importantly, not all or even most of the blame for this era of violence can be laid at the (pale, booted) feet of the former colonizers themselves. Obviously, as left-leaning scholars are wont to point out, some post-1960s bloodshed in Africa traces to the creation of colonial nation-states, which shoved together ill-matched groups that had not previously been in contact to the same degree. However, as a new generation of academics is beginning to note, much of it instead reflected the *return* of long-running tribal conflicts that had been suppressed or minimized for decades by colonial authorities.

In a 2019 piece for the well-regarded journal *International Organizations*, my fellow political scientist Jack Paine attempts to explain what causes "differential rates of ethnic violence in postcolonial Africa." His answer is striking in both its political incorrectness and its logical obviousness: the presence of a bunch of powerful tribes within the same area of land leads to conflict. More technically put, Paine theorizes that the presence within a postcolonial state of "ethnic groups organized as . . . precolonial state[s]" increases or exacerbates "interethnic tensions."

In other words, people groups that retain much or all of their pre-colonial identities are more likely to participate in general violence, suggesting that a significant source of contemporary conflict is the resurgence of old feuds between preexisting tribes. In fact, many weak states can be accurately said to exist as a mere thin veneer over powerful preexisting kingdoms and chiefdoms. Running some regressions and cross-tabulations, Paine finds striking evidence that this is true. From the very beginning of the postcolonial era until about 1990, thirty of the thirty-two "major civil war onsets" he analyzes (i.e., 93.8 percent) took place in countries that contained at least one pre-colonial state population.

The implications of all of this are fascinating. First, as Paine points out, the huge body of modern research focusing on postcolonial causes or even on conflicts beginning under colonialism as the sole cause of modern African political violence "overlooks longer term factors." While it might indeed be the case—and these are my words, not his—that colonizers constructed artificial states that encompass powerful pre-colonial state groups that now clash with one another, it is also the case that many such groups fought each other in the manner that *Igbo Worlds* details before any Westerners arrived. More broadly, it strikes me that it might be useful to think of many African (or eastern European, Southeast Asian, etc.) countries as "technical states" draped over collections of previously existing societies that are fighting one another as they always have.

A point that merits one final reiteration here—and that is implicitly obvious, given the presence outside the West of what are essentially premodern national feuds inside modern countries—is that colonialism and conquest are not uniquely Western endeavors. Indeed, absent contemporary academic and elite media bias, there would be no logical reason for any intelligent person to assume that this was the case. Any short list of the greatest conquerors in history would have to include the Mongols/Moghuls, the Ottoman Turks, the "Black" Moors (who conquered Spain and fought Charles Martel deep inside Europe), the Middle Eastern Muslims after the death of the Prophet Muhammad, the New World's Aztecs and Incas, and so forth. The legendary Mongol leader Genghis Khan alone killed so many people—up to 10 percent of the population of Earth at the time—that he removed 700,000,000 tons of carbon dioxide from the atmosphere and cooled the climate.[25] For most of post-Roman history, the archetypal "colonizer" was a well-mounted brown man waving a sword.

In Black Africa, as the textbook *Traditions and Encounters* (2016) noted, the great Bantu tribes have hardly dwelled on the same preserves since time immemorial. Instead, most of them migrated down from the Sahel region in the African northwest 1,000 years or less before they encountered Europeans, often conquering as they went. The series of events leading up to the legendary Zulu Wars began when Shaka's Zulu tribe—invading modern-day South Africa from the north—essentially ran into Boers and Englishmen who were invading from the south.[26] Shaka's actions, while aggressive, were hardly atypical. A standard encyclopedia article on what we call the Bantu migration notes that, prior to the unexpected arrival of iron-working Black farmers, almost all of Africa was populated by "hunter gathers and earlier pastoralists" from various Khoisan, Pygmy, and Nilo-Saharan ethnic groups.[27]

Today, suffice it to say, this is not the case: genetic and linguistic evidence suggests that Bantu dominance of the vast African continent followed not only some assimilation but also a fair amount of displacement and annihilation of preexisting peoples. And once Africa was Black, peace did not arrive. From the eleventh or twelfth century onward, multiple large and aggressive Bantu kingdoms flourished in the new lands—including not merely rough diamonds like Shaka's Zululand, but also the legendary Mali associated with warrior kings Sundiata Keita and Mansa Musa, and such places as the Mutapa Empire, which ruled over much of what is now Botswana, Zimbabwe, and Mozambique from her legendary fortress city of Great Zimbabwe and apparently traded as far afield as China.[28]

These states, some of which might seem, from an uneducated Western point of view, surprisingly sophisticated, behaved much like states anywhere else. The expansionist Kingdom of Eswatini, located in what has more recently been known as Swaziland, provides a representative example, which was selected for analysis here almost at random. Per another typical encyclopedia piece,[29] the original residents of the land that became Eswatini were Khoisan peoples who lived by hunting and gathering wild plants and produced beautiful and quite unique rock paintings, some of which survive today.

However, these relatively peaceful folk were not long to endure: the first evidence of Bantu agriculture and iron smelting in the future Eswatini dates to about 400 CE, and the region became almost entirely Black African during the migrations of the early and middle portion of the next millennium—which saw the arrival first of Nguni and Sotho tribespeople and then later of the conquering Swazi. Not terribly long after the last of these treks, legendary Swazi ruler Mswati II gave the country both its name and a substantial chunk of its lands.

Generally considered Eswatini's greatest warrior king, Mswati II roughly doubled the size of his country. He did so, as his biographers frankly concede, by launching wars against other African nations, generally without serious provocation, to seize land. He would make off with huge numbers of cattle and slaves when his campaigns to seize land were not successful. However, they generally were. Like his contemporary Shaka kaSenzangakhona ("Shaka Zulu"), the brilliant African ruler focused a great deal of energy on developing his tribal regiments—in fact, improving on an "adoption of the Zulu age-group system of military organization" implemented by his father—and wound up as Maximum Ruler of a range of peoples characterized in caste terms as "true *Swazi*," *Emakhandzambili*, *Bemdzabu*, *Emafikamuva*, and so forth.[30]

No bigot, the Eswatini king traded and fought with whites as well, making many profitable if later regretted concessions around "land and mineral rights" with European settler communities, but also sparring with foes Black and tan in "areas such as Zoutpansberg and Ohrigstad." When he died in 1865, Mswati was succeeded first by his son Ludvonga and later by King Mbandzeni—who toned down the traditional Swazi "way of conquest" but continued to interact with most of the same peoples. With sparring partners like Mswati, and certainly Shaka and Dingane of the Zulu, European conquerors were facing off against not long-settled indigenes but rather Black conquerors themselves new to most of their territory.

In an interesting footnote, while white men prevailed over these skilled opponents for a time, their moment in the African sun would be surprisingly brief in comparison to that for the post-migration Bantu lords. After a formal British declaration of Swazi independence in 1881 ("so long as the grass shall grow" and all that),[31] the region did end up as a lightly administered UK protectorate between 1906 and 1968. However, full independence came in 1968, and—while some democratic institutions certainly exist—the nation now again called Eswatini is currently ruled by Mswati III, head of the Swazi royal family and a direct lineal descendant of Mswati II the Conqueror.[32] The sun may set, as the proverb goes, but it also rises.

The entertaining Mswati Dynasty aside, the same pattern of cyclical and multicolored conquest and colony-planting obviously existed around the world—long before any Europeans arrived on the scene. In an article on the mighty Mexica—the Aztecs—cited elsewhere in the book and ominously titled "Feeding the Gods: Hundreds of Skulls Reveal Massive Scale of Human Sacrifice in Aztec Capital," Lizzie Wade points out that this indigenous American civilization was notably imperialist. The Aztecs were a fairly new imperial civilization at the time of the peak of their power and their wars with the Spanish, Wade points out, busy with the conquest of most of south-central Mexico despite "tremendous resistance from local communities."

A look at the reasons for that tremendous resistance helps put the (undoubted) imperfections of Western colonial memsahibs in some context. Simply put, a primary reason Mexica leaders wanted more lands and subject peoples was *literal* hunger: they planned to use these humans as religious sacrifice victims and a key source of meat. As Wade states, most of the people slaughtered during Tenochtitlan's legendary mass sacrifices were battle captives taken during military campaigns, like "those fought with their arch-enemy—the nearby Republic of Tlaxcala." Already-conquered peoples were in an even worse position, forced to regularly send the Aztecs large numbers of healthy young men and women as Theseus-and-the-Minotaur-style tributes.

All of this was done quite intentionally: to humiliate and break the spirit both of enemies and of restive elements among the Mexica population itself. As one source for Wade's article, the Tulane University bioarchaeologist Dr. John Verano, puts it: "The killing of captives, even in a ritual context, is a strong political statement. It's a way to demonstrate power and political influence—and . . . to control your own population." Chillingly, his sometime colleague, bioarchaeologist Ximena Chávez Balderas of Mexico's National Institute of Anthropology and History (INAH), adds a note on scale: "the more powerful" a conquering state was, the more victims it could massacre to achieve these goals. The Aztecs, recall, planned to be very powerful for a very long time.

For that matter, though both the once-mighty Mexica and the Europeans they fought are long gone, the era of colonial expansion might not be over just yet. Several recent articles on the role of China in modern Africa serve as fascinating reminders that colonialism is not a unique characteristic of white Western societies and that it arguably continues today. In a review of the book *Winner Take All: China's Rush for Resources and What It Means for the World* by the contemporary African writer Dambisa Moyo, the team at *American Outlook* points out that Communist China is "emerging as one of the preeminent market forces on the [African] continent," often by behaving in a manner that has led Western powers to label her an imperialist nation or even "neo-colonial force."[33] As Moyo herself has noted in the pages of the *New York Times*: "Since China began seriously investing in Africa in 2005, it has been routinely cast as a stealthy imperialist with a voracious appetite for commodities and no qualms about exploiting Africans to get them."

To be quite clear, Moyo describes much of this narrative, about a "POC" power well-liked by many everyday Africans, as "rubbish."* However, technical language aside, it is undoubtedly the case that China is rather openly in Africa to seek "arable land, oil, and minerals." *Winner Take All* spends dozens of pages discussing the Asian tiger's "voracious appetite for hard [metal and minerals] and soft [timber and food] commodities," and China's often-ruthless pursuit of these things inside the Motherland and elsewhere. To get them in steady supply going forward, China is investing billions of dollars in the African continent, often as part of projects that will

---

* Interestingly, and disturbingly, China appears to be better liked in much of Africa than the United States. Per the article just cited, 86 percent of survey respondents in Senegal said that China's involvement in that nation "helped make things better," versus 56 percent who said the same about the United States. Ninety-one percent of Kenyans had a favorable view of China in response to the same question, while "just" 74 percent had a favorable view of the United States.

remain under Chinese control into the foreseeable future. China also committed $153 billion in loans to African states during only the period from 2000 to 2019—usually under contracts that allow for seizure of African infrastructure if nations "struggle to meet repayments."[34]

That figure represents a relationship that is just getting started. While it slipped a bit under COVID-19 and may sometimes decline on a year-to-year basis, overall Chinese investment in Africa is projected to increase dramatically for decades to come—while virtually no serious political analysist predicts the Red Chinese getting nicer or kinder. It may well be that, as the West obsesses over the real and imagined sins of our past, other power players today are girding up for very similar behavior in the future.

Historians' blinkered obsession with Western colonialism therefore makes the lessons of history less clear. It obscures the fact that trade-offs are inevitable when swapping any system of government and that colonialism isn't necessarily going to be worse than any alternative. But also it makes it harder for us to see how common the same dynamics are today, outside the West. Once again, ideology makes us poorer historians and poorer observers of the world around us.

LIE #7

"American Use of Nukes to End World War Two Was 'Evil' and 'Unjustified'"

Another cliché which has become almost universal among Western scholars, general intellectuals, and activists is that the United States of America should feel considerable guilt about being "the only nation ever to use nuclear weapons in rage" and that we engaged in an unprecedented and probably indefensible act of evil by dropping Fat Man and Little Boy on Japanese Hiroshima and Nagasaki. Again: not so fast.

An important element in properly analyzing any historical moment is to view it in context and to truly step into the shoes of the people making difficult-to-impossible choices at that precise point in time. Historical hindsight is 20/20, but truly looking at the messy circumstances of the end of World War Two makes it impossible to justify modern armchair-generals' analyses that smugly dismiss America as uncomplicatedly evil.

The existence and nature of the conventional narrative is—as usual in this book—not particularly contested. The primary discussion of the bombings on the Perspective debate site,[1] widely accessed by high school and college students, simply assumes that they were an act of evil: it is headlined "The Bombings of Hiroshima and Nagasaki: Plain Evil or a Necessary Evil?" After a few points are made for the Necessary Evil side, author Lee Mesika goes on to argue at length that the attack was plain evil. Mesika notes that the use of atomics "completely destroyed both Hiroshima and Nagasaki," wiping out more than 90 percent of the buildings in both cities, either at once or via the firestorms that followed the initial nuclear explosions. Still more tragically, at least 250,000 people were killed by the strike—about half of them immediately and relatively humanely, but others felled months or years later by novel radiation-driven "types of illnesses and cancers."

While any human death is tragic, or so it is conventional for humans to pretend, Mesika makes the additional point that the Hiroshima and Nagasaki bombings were acts of war that primarily harmed civilians, in violation of the contemporary ethical rule that "wars should be fought between armies." In Hiroshima, at least 20,000 Japanese soldiers were killed by the dropping of Little Boy, but the usual estimate for civilian casualties is far higher and closer to 80,000. Even more remarkably, in Nagasaki, between 50,000 and 80,000 people were killed, but this toll included only "around 150 Japanese soldiers." In contrast, at least 8,200 Korean semi-slaves, who were being forced to support the Japanese war effort by laboring inside the Mitsubishi munitions plant and other factories producing military matériel, were killed in Nagasaki. "Hiroshima and Nagasaki gave new meaning to collateral damage," the Perspective article concludes: "The number of civilians killed seems unreasonably high in relation to the number of soldiers killed."

Finally, if a bit at random, Mesika goes on to argue that the Hiroshima and Nagasaki bombings did not avert the Cold War between the United States and the Union of Soviet Socialist Republics. Citing the (somewhat fringe but interesting) historical claim that the United States deployed nuclear weapons against the Japanese to demonstrate American might to the *Soviets*, he states accurately enough that this did not work. Obviously, a decades-long arms race between the USA and the USSR kicked off immediately after the conclusion of World War Two.

Stalin's government successfully completed its first nuclear weapons in 1949 and "the world . . . came close to nuclear brink-manship in 1962" during the Cuban missile crisis. In this context, Mesika contends, the World War Two nuclear bombings can be seen as a triple failure: brutal, fatal mostly to innocents, and inef-fective in terms of preventing future wars and conflicts. How, one might wonder, could such nonproductive atrocities ever be morally justified?!

Many other academic and scholastic sources argue that it can-not be. No less an entity than the *Bulletin of the Atomic Scientists* re-cently seconded the Mesika argument in print, contending as much in 2020 in an article titled "Why the Atomic Bombing of Hiroshima Would Be Illegal Today."[2] According to a roster of authors including Katherine E. McKinney, Scott D. Sagan (son of you-know-who), and Allen S. Weiner, President Harry Truman's famous justification of the dropping of the first American nuclear weapon on Hiroshima by invoking the city's status as a military base was "misleading in two important ways." First, while Hiroshima did contain both a ma-jor base for the Imperial Japanese Army and a series of factories related to the Japanese war effort, it is not accurate in contemporary legal terms to describe a "vibrant city of over a quarter of a million men, women, and children" as a sort of military installation.

Additionally, U.S. forces made little if any effort to confine their attack to military zones of the Japanese port—something that would be almost impossible to do, in any case, with nuclear bombs. In-stead, the 9,700 pound Little Boy was detonated directly above "the residential and commercial center" of Hiroshima city. The authors speculate that this was done intentionally "to magnify the shock effect on the Japanese public and leadership in Tokyo." While the brutal attack was almost certainly legal under the blasé international standards of 1945, McKinney, Sagan, and Weiner unabashedly de-scribe it as an act of evil and contend passionately that it would not meet today's tighter standards of legality.

As it happens, the same prominent team of authors has made this same case in several other highbrow academic and public in-tellectual venues. For the Lawfare legal resource, they argued in

August of 2020 that the recommendation for the Hiroshima and Nagasaki attacks from the interim committee that advised the U.S. government was "an endorsement of terror bombing with a legal veneer."[3] Here, the brief for the at least contemporary illegality of the bombings is made in a bit more detail: McKinney and her compatriots argue that similar attacks today would violate 1977 Additional Protocol I of the Modified Geneva Conventions, which bars intentional attacks on civilians ("the principle of distinction"), any harm to civilians greater than/not justified by the "direct military advantage gained" from an action ("the principle of proportionality"), and not taking all reasonable precautions to limit harm to civilians ("the precautionary principle").

Without slipping too deeply into wonkery, some of this is frankly debatable. As the authors themselves admit in passing, the United States—arguably not the world's greatest respecter of international law—is not in fact even a party to Geneva Protocol I, having repeatedly failed to send the thing along to "the Senate for its advice and consent [or] to ratification by the President."[4] However—as they also quickly point out—representatives of the United States have stated that "these core principles reflect binding customary international law" and committed at least twice to follow the modern law of war during any hypothetical future uses of American nuclear weapons. At very least, the Lawfare piece seems to support the popular claim that our attack on Japan was a barbaric one, unlikely to pass modern legal muster.

Interestingly, in the same article, McKinney, Sagan, and Weiner make a rarer claim, arguing that we should never have thought it necessary to intimidate Japan to the point of unconditional surrender, which is clearly what the back-to-back American atomic attacks were designed to do. They cite the well-known words of the Potsdam Declaration that laid out the terms for Japanese surrender ("There must be eliminated for all time the authority and influence of those who have deceived and misled the people of Japan into embarking on world conquest . . . stern justice shall be meted out to all war criminals")[5] . . . but not approvingly. Instead, these authors note an alternative suggestion that was made during the Potsdam *Con-*

ference: that the Allies promise not to try Japanese emperor Hirohito for war crimes or other offenses and to grant several additional concessions in exchange for a negotiated Japanese surrender.

The Lawfare piece is open enough about the fact that this strategy might or might not have worked: "As with all counterfactuals, we can't know with certainty whether the Japanese government would have surrendered without the . . . bomb." However, Team Weiner claim that failure to try this strategy of negotiated settlement constitutes a moral tragedy. Because total defeat of Japan could have been achieved only by the use of nuclear weapons or an invasion of the Japanese home islands, *any* version of "Truman's demand for Japan's unconditional surrender to end the war . . . was indefensible." In a truly novel take, then, at least three top contemporary scholars are arguing not merely that the historical American use of nuclear weapons was immoral but that any loss of life associated with the refusal to cut a deal with Emperor Hirohito's Japan would merit that label.

This sort of thing ("They were bad, but we, perhaps, were worse . . .") is almost unavoidable in any upper-middlebrow discussion of this issue. The *New York Times*, Gray Lady of the News, recently devoted a significant amount of ink to "The Hiroshima Pilot Who Became a Symbol of Antinuclear Protest."[6] The paper's lengthy and occasionally moving primary article focuses on Claude Eatherly, who participated in the August 6, 1945, bombing of Hiroshima and then spent decades flagellating himself for his role in a way that made him "an international celebrity" within the peace movement.

Interestingly, the *Times* women (Anne I. Harrington was the reportorial lead on this piece) note in passing that the huge majority of the ninety or more U.S. military members who participated in the attacks—"a horrific deed fit for Gods or monsters"—seem to feel little if any remorse. Many openly viewed themselves as war heroes, focusing their attention on "their fellow American servicemen, whose lives they . . . saved by obviating a need for a ground invasion of Japan." Others, such as Colonel Paul Tibbets of the

Army Air Corps unit tasked with the drops, described themselves as obeying reasonably ethical orders during a time of war. Quoth Tibbets: "The morality of dropping that bomb was not my business. . . . I have never lost a night's sleep on the deal."

Eatherly, who was not directly involved with the release of either bomb but instead piloted an advance aircraft focused on monitoring atmospheric conditions over Japan on the day in question, had a different take—and one that has landed him a place in many social studies texts. Almost immediately after the conclusion of World War Two, he reported "suffering from nightmares about the bombings" and began to claim that guilt and rage was driving him into a negative downward spiral of behavior.

In 1957 the widely read *Newsweek* article "American Hero in Handcuffs" described how Eatherly, who had been arrested in Texas after robbing the PO boxes of two Fort Worth–area post offices, had been treated for a variety of mental conditions at a Veterans Affairs hospital in Waco, forged a sizable check in New Orleans, and even "been involved in a series of stick-ups in small town grocery stores." His defense in the federal post office case, presented by a skilled team involving a lawyer and a psychiatrist, focused on the argument that Eatherly "suffered from a guilt complex stemming . . . from his role in the bombing of Hiroshima."

This strategy worked: Eatherly was found not guilty on grounds of insanity and let go. Almost immediately, he became a hero of the peace movement, and—it is no exaggeration to say—one of the most written-about figures of World War Two. Contacted by activists like the German philosopher Günther Anders and the left-leaning writer Ronnie Dugger, he argued over and over that, due to declining Japanese resistance by the late summer of 1945, "the war would have ended even without the nuclear devastation." Encouraged by his new allies, Eatherly began to engage in public acts of apology, at one point sending a written message to the population of Hiroshima: "I told them I was the major that gave the 'go ahead' to destroy Hiroshima, that I was unable to forget the act, and that the guilt of the act has caused me great suffering." The former military man asked Hiroshima survivors to forgive him and the United States, and by most accounts some did—with thirty schoolgirls injured by the atomic strike writing back to call Eatherly an innocent "victim of war . . . like us."

Not all of this activity, some scholars have argued, was fueled merely by the milk of human kindness. In late 1961, the correspondence between Eatherly and Dr. Anders was published as a for-profit book titled *Burning Conscience*. Bertrand Russell, "renowned British philosopher, mathematician, and antinuclear activist," contributed the preface and a review. Just a year later, the former bomber pilot received a Hiroshima Award in New York City for his "outstanding contributions to world peace." At one point, the National Broadcasting Corporation television network—today's NBC—filmed a multi-episode TV show based loosely on Eatherly's experiences.

In this context, more than a few critics—notably the investigative journalist William Bradford Huie—asked what might seem like an obvious question: Was Eatherly a hero or a fraud, a small-time crook cashing in on purported opposition to a necessary mission that he in fact had rather little to do with? Contemporary trends within media and education seem to provide the publicly acceptable answer to that question. One of the final articles dealing with the former pilot, who died in 1978 of throat cancer, ran in the Gray Lady and prominently contained Eatherly's take on how decent people are supposed to feel about the end of the Second World War: "The truth is that society *cannot* accept the fact of my guilt without at the same time recognizing its own far deeper guilt."

The perspective of American high school and collegiate textbooks on the end of World War Two gels well with that one, with most texts providing substantial coverage for the idea that use of atomic bombs was evil and perhaps unnecessary. After conceding that an Allied invasion of Japan involving "bitter fighting" would certainly have been possible in a scenario where nuclear weapons were not deployed, *The Unfinished Nation* goes on to argue that there were, however, "signs early in 1945 that such an invasion might not be necessary." According to author Alan Brinkley in a controversial take, "the Japanese had almost no ships or planes left with which to fight."[7]

Further, according to the textbook, previous conventional Allied attacks, like the March 1945 firebombing of Tokyo (which killed close to 85,000 people) had devastated the will of the Japanese populace to continue the conflict. Japanese moderates, who "had long since concluded the war was lost," were "looking to end the fighting." However, before these relative pacifists could prod their country toward peace, "their efforts became superfluous in August 1945, when the United States made use of a terrible new weapon it had been developing."

A People and a Nation: A History of the United States paints a similarly ambiguous if not pro-Japanese picture, framing the decision tree confronting then U.S. president Truman in terms of unanswerable questions: "Why would he not negotiate surrender terms? Was Japan on the verge of an unconditional surrender, as some argue? Or was the anti-surrender faction of Japanese military leaders strong enough to prevail? How much did [Truman's] desire to demonstrate the bomb's power to the Soviet Union . . . influence his decision? Did racism or a desire for retaliation play a role?" At very best, one might assume, after reading through all of these questions in sequence, that the morality of America's actions in 1945 will remain forever unknowable at best.

But not so fast. The general post-2000 academic presentation of nuclear deployment as the sort of thing "that can never be okay" ignores significant on-the-ground facts that would have been obvious to virtually every American in 1945. First, the use of the bombs was thought very likely to end the brutal Second World War immediately in a manner that would cost no American or Allied lives *and* not require any continued recognition of the wartime-era Imperial Japanese government. And, in fact, this is exactly what happened.

As even one of the "Evil" debaters for the Perspective—albeit the homie Justified Evil—points out in one sentence: "The bombings ended WWII." Across nearly a month of bickering during the Potsdam Conference and then after the Potsdam Declaration ("between July 17 and August 2, 1945" for the latter), the Supreme War Councillors of Japan simply "could not reach a consensus . . . regarding whether or not to surrender." Serious people expected deliberations to go on for perhaps months longer while tens of thousands of American and Japanese soldiers died in major sea battles.

Instead, the United States dropped Little Boy on Hiroshima August 6, 1945, and Fat Man on Nagasaki on August 9. The war ended almost immediately: the final papers announcing Japanese surrender were drafted and signed on August 15, 1945. As the debate site points out: "Hirohito was pushed by America's destructive bombings to break the deadlock within his War Council and agree to the terms of the declaration. The bombings of Hiroshima and Nagasaki officially ended the Second World War."

And, horrible as it is to make comparisons of this kind, that outcome doubtless saved a great many lives—perhaps millions. By this point of World War Two, Lee Mesika estimates that 41,592 U.S. Army men were dead or missing and presumed dead in the Pacific theater alone. (Another 145,706 Army soldiers were recorded as wounded.) Tolls for the Marine Corps and for Navy sailors fighting onshore were not terribly far behind, with 23,160 killed, thousands missing, and 67,199 wounded.

Other belligerents had suffered similarly: in addition to Japanese losses not reliably recorded by the Allied side, at least 9,000 "British, Indian, and British Commonwealth soldiers" were killed or disabled in the theater, while another 130,000 troops were taken as prisoners of war—with many of these latter worked to death in hellish labor camps. Obviously, continuation of the brutal Pacific War would have greatly increased all of these terrible tolls.

Although this is often forgotten or minimized today, one key reason for the staggering military—and civilian—death tolls from the Second World War was the almost totally unregulated use of powerful conventional weapons such as incendiaries and "bunker buster" bombs. While Western militaries went to great lengths to minimize collateral damage during recent conflicts like Gulf War Two, World War Two belligerents not infrequently leveled entire cities, citing what military fiction writer S. M. Stirling has referred to as the "hard cheese: there's a war on" doctrine.

As several of the sources given above point out, just one typical Allied bombing raid over Tokyo, combined with the Japanese attempt to stop the enemy B-29s via aerial combat and the use of ground-based weapons, resulted in the deaths of 120,000 to 130,000 people—many of them burned alive. Had nondeployment of Fat Man and Little Boy resulted in six to twelve more months of military conflict, "the 250,000 casualties from the atomic bombs could have easily reached millions."[8]

Celebrated right-leaning historian Victor Davis Hanson makes many of these same points at much greater length in one of the best articles I have read on this topic. Writing for *National Review*,[9] Hanson sets the stage by pointing out that "for 60 years, the United States has agonized over its unleashing of the world's first nuclear weapon." He notes, accurately, that other options were suggested to the Truman government, such as aiming the first bomb at an uninhabited peninsula or island "as a warning for the Japanese militarists to capitulate." He concedes that the bombings—while targeted at the headquarters of Japan's elite Second Army, in at least the Hiroshima case—caused "well over 100,000 fatalities, the vast majority of them civilians." The obvious question for a human to ask is asked: "Did America really want to live with [this] burden?"

However, unlike many a high school textbook or supplementary resource, Hanson goes on to provide a full and honest answer. He points out that many opponents of the use of nuclear weapons have "shied away from providing a rough estimate of how many more would have died" during conventional war fighting absent those two fateful days in August 1945: "Americans, British, Australians, Asians, Japanese, and Russians . . . through conventional bombing, continuous fighting in the Pacific, [or] amphibious invasion of the mainland." Citing contemporary supporters of U.S. president Truman, and noting that both the Russki Red Army and the American military (via Operations Coronet and Olympic) had already drawn up plans for enhanced invasion-style operations against the Japanese homeland, Hanson estimates that "a million . . . casualties and countless Japanese dead were averted by not storming the Japanese mainland over the next year."

It must be understood that these were not wildly hypothetical figures. The bombings took place shortly after a series of staggeringly bloody battles in the Pacific. Mesika's estimates of American and British losses during the pre-1945 Pacific War are bad enough, but the size and intensity of oceanic World War Two battles were actually increasing substantially as Allied forces "island-hopped" closer to Japan herself. As Hanson says, the Okinawa campaign, the last battle in the island-hopping strategic effort, which was fought between U.S. and Japanese forces from April 1 to July 2 of 1945, provides some actual basis for comparison. That struggle for the fifth-largest Japanese island, outside of the four much larger mainland islands, caused "the worst losses in the history of the U.S. Navy."

All told, Hanson estimates, there were 50,000 American casualties and 200,000 Okinawans and other Japanese killed during the Okinawa campaign. Thirty capital ships were sunk permanently (on our side), while more than 300 were badly damaged. A key factor in the battle was kamikaze attacks, involving Japanese pilots willingly flying their warplanes—often loaded with explosives—directly into Allied vessels on suicide missions "for islands and emperor." During the Okinawan fighting, just 2,000 kamikazes managed to kill 5,000 U.S. sailors and sink several battleships, and "at least 10,000 more suicide planes" were known to be waiting on the larger nearby Japanese islands of Kyushu and Honshu.

As these figures indicate, the known strategic plans that would have been followed by the Allies and opposed by the Japanese in the event of a land invasion of Japan were, quite empirically speaking, likely to take more human lives than the nuclear bombings did. Like the authors for the Perspective, Hanson points out that the single firebombing raid against Tokyo on March 9 and 10, 1945, took more lives than either atomic strike, "incinerating somewhere around 150,000 civilians, and burning out over 15 acres of the downtown." Remarkably, as that figure indicates, neither Hiroshima nor Nagasaki in fact represented "the worst single-day loss of life in military history"—or even during World War Two.

This was total war. And as Hanson explains, the dropping of Little Boy and Fat Man was understood at the time "as the continuance of that policy of unrestricted bombing" practiced by all parties—significant prior examples of which included Japan's terror bombing of Chinese Chungking as well as the near-annihilation of a sizable city (by the Western "good guys") that gave punk band the Dresden Dolls their name.

Along with the facts that the United States of 1945 simply did not have many nuclear weapons to spare, and that many of the conventional weapons allowed during World War Two could be nearly as devastating, a final factor playing into America's decision-making was something that would have seemed too obvious to need saying at the time and for decades afterward but that has been largely forgotten in our current era of frantic guilt about past conflicts with "POC." American citizens during the Second World War "hardly thought the Japanese populace," the willing allies of Nazi Germany's Adolf Hitler, "to be entirely innocent." Japan's army was itself known and widely criticized for massacres of innocent civilians, and these actions were often widely cheered back among the home islands.

The Imperial Japanese military essentially murdered 10 to 15 million Chinese noncombatants over the course of the war and engaged in similar atrocities "throughout the Pacific from the Philippines to Korea and Manchuria." Even by the very end of the conflict—late summer of 1945—Hanson notes that Japanese soldiers were actively "killing thousands of Asians each month." The Japanese not infrequently wiped out entire Indigenous populations before retreating from a particular large island or theater of battle.

The point that the Japanese were among the "bad guys" of World War Two, to an extent that greatly reduced sympathy both for Japan's soldiers and for the militaristic society that produced them, can hardly be overemphasized. Japanese fighters were not known merely for ferocity in battle—in itself hardly immoral—and for brutality toward conquered populations, but for extraordinarily ruthless treatment of both Asian and Western prisoners. In early 1944, for example, the leadership team of a major Japanese prisoner of war camp ("Taiwan POW Camp overall H.Q.") issued an order blandly titled "Kill All Prisoners Order,"[10] which specified exactly when and how recalcitrant prisoners were to be murdered.

Per the Order, issued August 1 of 1944: "At such time as the situation become urgent . . . the POWs will be concentrated and confined in their present location and, under heavy guard, the preparation for the final solution will be made."* Several acceptable methods for the large-scale execution of military prisoners were offered, including "mass bombing, poisonous smoke, poisons, drowning, decapitations." The final option is especially blasé and chilling: "or what[ever], dispose of them as the situation dictates." The overall thrust of the missive is plain: whenever mass murder might be made "necessary" by circumstances such as a planned revolt, "it is the aim not to allow the escape of a single one, to annihilate them all, and not to leave any traces." From those words, in an interesting commentary on the banality of most human evil, the order then went on to dryly discuss POW wills.

Even for those who managed to survive them, Japanese prisoner

---

* Several different situations would have provided "urgency" sufficient to justify the massacre of every captive in the camp: these included any "superior orders" mandating a slaughter, any uprising by any group of prisoners serious enough to require firearms to put down, and the perceived risk of prisoners escaping the camp and becoming "a hostile fighting force."

of war camps were horrifically and legendarily brutal—a probable legacy of the post-samurai Japanese belief that the act of surrender was inherently dishonorable. The History Collection web resource recently ran a thirty-three-page article detailing twenty "horrific details" of the Pacific War with Hitler's eastern allies, and specifically of the Japanese POW-taking process. Among the stories recounted was one tale of Allied battle captives "forced to live on a deficient diet offering as little as 600 calories per day," given only "ten ounces of rice per day . . . two ounces of rancid pork and four ounces of fish monthly" during the not-atypical White Rice Period of 1942, and subjected to sadistic medical experiments by the Mengele-like (if far less well-known) Unit 731.[11]

Allied POWs, hungry or not, were also used as slave laborers by their harsh new masters. Almost all able-bodied captives were "forced to perform labor on behalf of their captors," generally putting in "12 hour days under harsh conditions." Largely as a result of the combination of forced starvation and forced labor, at least 25 percent of all Allied prisoners of war—both Asian and Western— died during what the History Collection tactfully refers to as "their residences in Japanese encampments" during World War Two.

Per the records of the post–World War Two Tokyo Tribunal focused on Japanese atrocities, the overall rate of death for military prisoners in Japanese custody was a staggering 27.1 percent: between one in every four and one in every three men died during periods of incarceration that generally lasted less than 1.5 years. To put this in context, it was "a rate more than seven times higher than that of [Western] prisoners of war . . . under Nazi Germany." (That said, some of this death toll was due to unwitting friendly fire: the largest American POW death toll in the entire war took place when a U.S. submarine sank the *Arisan Maru*, killing 1,783 American servicemen. Also, death rates for Soviets in German prisons and Germans in eastern European countries were quite high. All of this was dwarfed by the near-total death rate of Chinese POWs held by the Japanese.)

Of course, not all Chinese, Korean, and Southeast Asian troops who were defeated in the field by the Japanese even made it to a POW camp. All participants in World War Two engaged in massacres deplorably often, but the Imperial Japanese military lapped the rest of the non-Nazi field in this category. During the not-entirely-atypical Nanjing Massacre, often known in the West as the "Rape of Nanking," Japanese troops captured the Republican Chinese capital of Nanjing, "disarm[ed] the surrendering population" of soldiers and militia defenders, and then proceeded to murder 200,000 Chinese males over the next four to six weeks.[12]

War correspondents like F. Tillman Durdin and Ralph ("Ralphie") Phillips "reported that the streets were filled with the dead" and that Chinese soldiers were subjected to atrocities that sometimes included cannibalism. Like much of the worst human evil, all this was done in accordance with formal bureaucratic orders. Not long before the conclusion of the battle for Nanjing, the Japanese Order "Riku Shi Mitsu No. 198"[13] commanded Japanese forces in the field in China to "no longer adhere to the restrictive term 'prisoner of war,'" a status carrying with it legal protections, such as the right to peacefully surrender. As a result of this terse series of commands, nearly a quarter of a million human beings died, mostly horribly.

While they were a bit more likely—for predictable reasons—to be kept alive than East Asian fighting men, women captured in arms by the Japanese also suffered horrifically: "In addition to being used alongside men for forced labor, women serving as POWs under the Japanese were routinely the victims of sexual assault"—often "every day."[14] Like Western men, these women were also more likely to be subjected to abusive scientific experiments by perversely inclined medical cadres like Unit 731. One common series of procedures sought "to explore the vertical transmission of . . . syphilis from mother to child" and involved women being both impregnated via rape and then infected with the disease. Following this initial brace of atrocities, different women "were vivisected at various stages" so that the effect of syphilis on the mother and fetus could be observed as the infection progressed.

Could anything be worse than that? Well, during a war involving

Nazi Germany and Tojo's Imperial Japanese Army (along with the British Empire and a still far-from-perfect United States), yes. Due to constant disruption of supply lines by shelling and partisan attacks, desperate troops in the field during the tail end of World War Two sometimes *ate* their opponents—and this behavior again seems to have been especially common, and often directed at Allied captives, on the part of the Japanese Army. After successful Western attacks on the primary Japanese lines of supply left Japanese soldiers without access to food, multiple Imperial units turned to the killing and cannibalism of Allied POWs. One uniquely grisly instance in New Guinea involved Japanese soldiers cruelly killing Indian captives from the British-Indian Army who'd refused to defect to the pro-Japanese Indian National Army. Per one account, from captive Hatam Ali:

> At this stage the Japanese started selecting prisoners and everyday 1 prisoner was taken out and killed and eaten by the Japanese. I personally saw this happen and about 100 prisoners were eaten at this place by the Japanese. The remainder of us were taken to another spot about 50 miles [away] where 10 prisoners died of sickness. At this place the Japanese again started selecting prisoners to eat. Those selected were taken to a hut where flesh was cut from their bodies while they were alive and they were then thrown into a ditch alive where they later died.[15]

While Ali's description of cannibalizing live prisoners bit by bit seemed to be an outlier, and many other cases of Japanese cannibalism were motivated by starvation conditions (in the usual way of war), it was also the case that cannibalism was used by Japanese soldiers as a power move even when normal food was also available—"That is to say, from choice and not of necessity."[16] Several scholars, such as the Japanese historian and researcher Yuki Tanaka, have argued that such horrific and bizarre atrocities were not even rare: "The widespread practice of cannibalism by Japanese soldiers in the Asia-Pacific War was something more than merely random incidents perpetrated by individuals or small groups subject to extreme conditions . . . [but rather] a systematic and organized military strategy," and that "cannibalism was often a systematic activity conducted by whole squads and under the command of officers."[17]

Other accounts from Allied airmen and soldiers actually describe the techniques that Japanese field cooks used with long pig. Ali's fellow Indian Havildar Changdi Ram stated for the postwar record that, on one occasion in 1944, he hid behind a tree or large shrub while Japanese Kempeitai military police slaughtered a captured American pilot and cut meat specifically from "his arms, legs, hips, and buttocks" for use in cooking. The human flesh was then chopped into small pieces and stir-fried.[18]

And so on. In the context of atrocities like these, many contemporary Western leaders were not only extremely unsympathetic to the Japanese military and the population supporting it but also very aware that ending World War Two would save perhaps millions of people from not simply death itself but many arguably worse fates. Immediately after the war, major figures discussed much of the material presented so far in this chapter quite frankly—from the reality of military atrocities on all sides to the likely devastating toll of a conventional attack on the fortified Japanese home islands.

In the December 1946 issue of the *Atlantic* magazine, in a piece to which President Harry Truman later responded in print, prominent American physicist and (secondary) atomic bomb designer Karl T. Compton quoted an "intelligent, well-informed" Japanese officer as to what would have happened absent both atomic bombings. Per that fellow, directly: "We [Japanese] would have kept fighting until all Japanese were killed, but we would have not been *defeated*." By this, the man meant something unique and culturally specific, which more than likely explains Japanese treatment of Allied captives who gave up voluntarily: in that scenario, the Japanese nation would have been broken on the horns of war but "would not have been disgraced by surrender."[19]

Compton goes on to argue—citing the testimony of several Japanese soldiers and scholars—that it is easy in retrospect "to look back and say that Japan was already a beaten nation" but that there was almost no contemporary evidence of this. Quoting an interview with one chatty and patriotic Japanese infantryman, who had actually grown up in America before volunteering for the army of his ancestral home, Compton reminds readers that most Japanese rankers believed—Baghdad Bob style—that they were winning the war until almost the day it ended. To many, even major defeats like the bloody loss of Iwo Jima "were parts of a grand strategy to lure the American forces closer and closer to the homeland, until they could be pounced on and utterly annihilated." While the specific soldier Compton relies on did not believe this, being made suspicious by "inconsistencies in official reports," he claims that "none" of his barracks mates understood the desperate nature of Japan's actual military position until "one night . . . at ten-thirty, his regiment was called to hear the reading of the surrender proclamation."

In other words, a significant Imperial Army regiment did not know that the war was over until the day it ended. In large part because of continued high Japanese morale, Compton, like several other sources cited so far, estimates that any land invasion of Japan would have involved roughly 50,000 American dead and wounded and several hundred thousand Japanese casualties during only the "operation to establish . . . initial beach-heads on Kyushu." That first mission, per both our author here and the command staff of U.S. general Douglas MacArthur, would then have been followed by a much larger and "far more costly struggle before the Japanese homeland was subdued."

And, notably, that would have been a *best*-case rather than a worst-case scenario. In a darkly plausible worst-case scenario that was war-gamed for by MacArthur, "the Japanese government lost control of its people and . . . millions of former Japanese soldiers took to guerilla warfare" within the mountain forests that cover the larger islands of the Japanese archipelago, and it might well have taken "a million American troops ten years to master the situation." Compton argues convincingly that this was fully possible, if not likely. As he points out, there was even an attempted coup d'état by militarists against the Japanese government as World War Two drew to an end, now referred to as the Kyūjō Incident. Even following the American deployment of nuclear weapons, Compton wrote, "for several days it was touch and go" as to whether the Japanese population would agree to their state's formal surrender, or whether a pro-war faction would "seize control and continue the war."

Chronologically speaking, and as noted earlier, there is little doubt the deployment of atomic weapons brought about the rapid end of World War Two and thus prevented a great deal of slaughter. As Compton and several other sources for this chapter point out, the original Potsdam ultimatum from the United States and the Allies, which called for the unconditional surrender of Japan, was given on July 26, 1945. The Japanese premier totally rejected this demand in a formal statement just a few days later, "scorning [it] as unworthy of official notice." Then, on August 6 and 9, the sun bombs were deployed on Hiroshima and Nagasaki. "On the following day, August 10, Japan declared its intention to surrender," the leadership of the island powerhouse accepting exactly the Potsdam terms on August 14, 1945. Millions lived.

A final point for this chapter is that it is very relevant that Japan's surrender was according to the specific Potsdam demands made by the Allies. The probability of this outcome is something that should have been—and was—considered before the bombs were dropped. As the end of World War Two approached, the question of what sort of victory the United States and her partners wanted—and deserved, following the losses of millions of men and hundreds of billions of dollars—began to arise. In my professional opinion as a political scientist, it actually is probable that *some* sort of negotiated semi-defeat of Japan could have been secured in the summer of

1945—or even earlier in the war—without deploying Fat Man and Little Boy. However, the terms of the Potsdam Declaration were very specific ones designed to prevent future global aggression under the Rising Sun banner.*

Clause six of the declaration, for example, focuses on limiting the power of the country's traditional elite warrior class and high military officials, saying: "There must be eliminated for all time the authority and influence of those who have deceived and misled the people of Japan into embarking on world conquest, for we insist that a new order of peace, security and justice will be impossible until irresponsible militarism is driven from the world."[20] Two sentences down the page, clause eight requires the renunciation of all Japanese claims to the Empire acquired before and during World War Two, limiting Japan's sovereignty "to the islands of Honshu, Hokkaido, Kyushu, Shikoku and such minor islands as we determine." Clause nine requires that the Japanese military forces, across all branches, be "completely disarmed" before being "permitted to return to their homes with the opportunity to lead peaceful and productive lives."

War crimes tribunals were flatly mandated. While the Allies did not quite demand that their Japanese opponents "be enslaved as a race or destroyed as a nation," clause ten of Potsdam states that "stern justice shall be meted out to all war criminals," a group very notably to include all of "those who have visited cruelties upon our prisoners." Finally, following the disarmament of her military and a full legal review of its conduct during the war, Japan was essentially commanded to become a democracy: "The Japanese government shall remove all obstacles to the revival and strength[en]ing of democratic tendencies among the Japanese people. Freedom of speech, of religion, and of thought, as well as respect for fundamental human rights shall be established."

---

* Similar terms were obviously secured from Germany, which was literally divided into several Allied-run sections following World War Two and the defeat of Nazi aggression.

This was the peace that the West wanted, deserved, and—thanks to temporary technological superiority—got. Once Hitler's proudest and strongest ally, Japan today may well fill that same role for the United States. As the writer Paul Fussell once said, controversially but accurately: "Thank God for the atom bomb."[21]

LIE #8

"Unprovoked 'White Flight,' Caused by Pure Racism, Ruined America's Cities"

A great deal of lore, reaching well beyond the popular narratives about the hippie movement and Vietnam War, surrounds "the Sixties." Another almost universal center-left, upper-middle-class narrative is that—following the social revolutions of the 1960s— white Americans ruthlessly abandoned their POC fellow city folx. Caucasians—and Caucasians alone, in many tellings of this story—"fled" American cities for racist and unethical reasons, leaving behind decaying slums, and then used harsh and unprovoked legal strictures like the Rockefeller Drug Laws to replace previous systems of racialized oppression.

As always, the truth is very different and far more complicated, but the Conventional Narrative is difficult to avoid. Princeton's Leah Boustan cites "racism" as a very primary reason for what she calls white flight, alongside a few economic motives.[1] Boustan also contends that the urban whites of the 1960s abandoned their former homes because of a biased desire to avoid "a large black migration from the rural South."[2]

A few primary sources for the major encyclopedic outlets attempt to trace the genesis of white flight—and, one suspects, of many another American pathology—back to slavery. A classic 1870 article in the *Nation* notes that thousands of whites did flee the South following the defeat of the Confederacy in the Civil War, and the *Statesman* opined about two decades later that growing Black populations were likely to "secure control of some of the Southern states" and that flight might be the best or only alternative: "Social and political equality in any Southern state must lead to one of three things: *a white exodus*, a war of races, or the destruction of representative institutions (italics mine)."[3]

Major American textbooks tend to treat the "flight" of the early modern era either as entirely the downstream result of racism or as almost incidental—an unfortunate thing that puzzlingly occurred just as Blacks migrated into major cities and the political climate happened to become heated. In an example of this latter genre, *The Unfinished Nation* notes that "Chicago, Detroit, Cleveland, New York, and other eastern and midwestern industrial cities experienced a major expansion of their black populations" at the very same time that "many whites were leaving cities."[4] More broadly, "inner cities filled up with poor minority residents" exactly when the "unskilled industrial jobs they sought diminished. Employers were moving factories and mills . . . to new locations in suburban and rural areas, smaller cities, and even abroad."

The only explanation given for such moves, in the passage just cited, is the sometimes lower cost of labor in non-urban areas (although the same book later mentions growing numbers of cars as a factor driving suburbanization). Across the texts, few extensively discuss factors like the famous big-city rioting and violence of the 1960s and 1970s—which we will dig into in depth later on—as causal for population movement, and those that do often dismiss it as somewhat understandable. Describing the 1967 Newark and Detroit riots, which killed forty-three people and injured perhaps 4,000, a different textbook source sums these up as: "Mobs attacked the shops and stores, expressing a burning grievance against a consumer society from which they were excluded by their poverty."[5]

In recent academic writings, this kind of take on racist white flight is often combined with the idea that unnecessarily harsh codes of law are today used to regulate minority populations by modern whites, especially those whites "left behind" in diverse integrated areas. One of the best-selling books in modern social science, Michelle Alexander's *The New Jim Crow*—a text assigned in probably hundreds of schools, which has its own curricular materials and study guides available online[6]—makes exactly this latter claim. To Alexander, the conventional assumption that institutional racism ended in the 1950s and 1960s (via *Brown v. Board of Education*, the Civil Rights Act, affirmative action, etc.) is incorrect. Instead, the White Man uses tools like the War on Drugs as a substitute for the Black Codes of segregation.

Alexander's claims are stunningly bold, to such an extent that it is surprising some of them are taken seriously. Early on in her book she argues that the contemporary prison system is "a stunningly comprehensive and well-disguised system of racialized social control that functions in a manner strikingly similar to Jim Crow." The goal of American policing and criminal incarceration is not keeping the streets reasonably free of sex pests and wife batterers. Rather, it is creating the racialized equivalent of a caste system, within which many or most Black and Hispanic people are legally defined as felons or other criminals and thus can be unfairly discriminated against with regard to housing, employment, and voting. Alexander explicitly feels that the development of this "system" occurred as a backlash to the Civil Rights Movement and that racist oppression is a primary goal of modern society.

If this even needs to be said, there are serious practical and logical problems with Alexander's major claims. Most Black and Hispanic citizens are *not* convicted felons, and—unlike historical serfs—most people who are felons (rapists, etc.) have diminished social status because they personally chose to do something very bad. Nonviolent drug offenders actually make up less than 10 percent of prisoners held in the state and federal hoosegows nationally, and even a left-leaning site like Felonvoting.procon.org admits that the most common single crime for which male offenders (across all races) are incarcerated is murder.[7] Despite this, however, many of these claims have become mostly undisputed conventional wisdom. In 2019, United States president Joe Biden, once a doughty crime fighter largely responsible for a major 1994 crime bill, formally apologized for his past "hard-line stance."[8]

Speaking on Martin Luther King Day to "Reverend" Al Sharpton's National Action Network MLK Jr. Breakfast, our one and only president "acknowledged the detrimental impact of his approach to crime in the late 1980s and early 1990s."* "I haven't always been right," a visibly repentant-looking Joseph Robinette Biden said: "I know we haven't always gotten things right, but I've always tried!" As Business Insider notes, Mr. Biden largely wrote what is now often considered an "infamous" mid-1990s bill, the Violent Crime Control and Law Enforcement Act of 1994—which resulted in sharply declining violent crime but is now frequently accused of having unjustly jailed tens or hundreds of thousands of people of color. And today Uncle Joe feels conventionally bad about the law. Without ever uttering the name of his bill out loud, Biden described his decisions during the crack era as having "trapped an entire generation" behind bars. Following his legal comments, he went on to argue that "white Americans overall need to work harder to address and recognize systemic racism."

Biden's positions gel fairly well with what we might call the Mainstream National Narrative—that today's racial disparities in arrests or convictions are due in large part to racist laws and more broadly that the white flight and urban collapse of the 1960s were motivated almost entirely by racism rather than other factors like increasing crime. However, as we have seen repeatedly throughout this book, reality is almost invariably far more complex than narrative. First, when examined in actual multivariate models, "white flight"—the movement of big-city Caucasians, and

---

* Biden was, at this point—in early 2019—technically speaking as a former vice president and a candidate for the presidency.

indeed of citizens of all races, to the suburbs after 1958 or so—by no means seems to be primarily the result of illogical personal bias.

In a fascinating and dead-serious academic article published in the *Journal of Urban Economics* back in 1992,[9] Robert A. Margo finds that one big factor driving American population mobility was the simple fact that, post–World War Two and post-Levittown, suburbs *existed* and many or most people suddenly had the money to move to them. Using census data from 1950 onward, Margo finds the unsurprising but rarely noted "significant positive effect of [rising] household income on the probability of a suburban residence." According to his tables and summary abstract, about half of all "population suburbanization between 1950 and 1980" can be attributed solely to the then-contemporary rise in American household income. This was true across all races, in statistical models with other major variables adjusted for.[10]

This simple quantitative conclusion is incredibly important. Simply put, around half of what is almost universally called "white flight"—and described as though it were a palefaces-only phenomenon—in conventional discourse is in reality explained simply by the facts that (1) suburbs had been built by the 1950s, (2) people had more money and could afford to move to them, and (3) there were finally jobs available way the hell out there in the *bundu*. At least in the U.S. North, these predictors often influenced behavior for citizens of all races.

This discovery that a single non-"edgy" variable in fact predicted about 50 percent of residential behavior during the 1950s to 1980s is no one-off phenomenon. The academic social sciences lean about 90 percent to the left politically and roughly 60 percent of American social scientists identify as (when these categories are combined) Communists/Marxists, radicals, or activists.[11] Likely as a result of this remarkable slant toward a single side of the political aisle, there is a near obsession within disciplines such as sociology with certain very specific phenomena: racism, anti-Semitism, sexism, class bias (sometimes), and so on. However, at least in modern America, these no doubt real factors often turn out to explain little of what scholars call a dependent variable, while intuitively obvious everyday things explain far more.

In probably my favorite example of this trend, in the field of education, the legendary John Ogbu cut through a fog of complex concepts like "stereotype threat" and "implicit assumptions" and "embedded subtle bias" to point out an obvious primary predictor of the relatively low performance of many minority students and good-time kids: they study a lot less on average than their peers.[12] Similarly, the heterodox social scientist John R. Lott Jr. has on various occasions taken the time to point out what empirically seems to actually reduce crime: respectively, more good cops on the street and taxpayers keeping legal guns at home.[13] The same sort of commonsensically obvious predictors exist here: the largest factor driving Americans to move to the suburbs was simply that, by the 1960s, they existed.

Another set of interesting articles within this whole subfield of academic research concerns the effects of highways and easily available automobiles on suburbanization. Here again we encounter the strange face of well-done but almost forgotten history: the fact that many roads were made of dirt or gravel, and the fact that most Yanks simply did not have two nice cars per household until very recently. The impact of these norms changing was significant.

Per the researcher Nathaniel Baum-Snow, writing in Oxford University Press's *Quarterly Journal of Economics*, census-style U.S. data from 1950 through 1990 indicates that "one new highway passing through a central city reduces its population by about 18 percent."[14] With the same confounders controlled for and all else held equal, "estimates imply that the aggregate central city population" in the United States would have *increased* 8 to 9 percent during the modern era "had the interstate highway system not been built."

Instead, something strikingly different happened. Between the years 1950 and 1990, the aggregate population of those U.S. central cities that had existed in 1950 "declined by 17 percent" despite large-scale population growth inside the country overall and a population surge of "72 percent *in metropolitan areas* as a whole" (italics mine). After running this calculation, Baum-Snow comes to the obvious conclusion that "the construction of new . . . highways has contributed markedly to center-city population decline." His explanation for why this happened ("changes in the amenity value of suburbs") is simplicity itself: suburbs and exurbs become pleasant places to live—rather than God-forsaken rural hinterlands—when people can easily get to them and work in them.

Overall, the economist argues that, by facilitating that livability, the construction of new highways explains "about one-third of the change in aggregate central city population" during the era that he studied. And recall that rising incomes explained about half of American suburbanization during roughly the same period. While Baum-Snow and the author who said that, Bob Margo, clearly ran different statistical models—i.e., we cannot ethically add 50 percent to 33 percent and obtain an estimate of the effect of nonracial factors on "white flight"—it is obvious that the reality of why citizens started moving out to the grasslands is complex and multivariate. Notably, also, the post–World War Two American decision to build new interstate highways does not itself seem to have been due to racism ("Let us escape *them!*"). As John McWhorter and others have pointed out, this construction happened all across the country, in regions with every imaginable kind of demographic mix.[15]

Of course, highways do not do much good for those who lack cars to drive on them. In a 2010 paper titled "A Quantitative Analysis of Suburbanization and the Diffusion of the Automobile,"[16] academics Karen Kopecky (University of Western Ontario) and Richard Suen (UC Riverside) argue that U.S. suburbanization—this time between 1910 and 1970—was also facilitated by the "diffusion" of personal vehicles throughout the population.* *These* authors construct a complex statistical regression model that includes auto prices (which fell

---

* To be fair, and as said earlier in this chapter, several classroom texts—notably including the later editions of *The Unfinished Nation*—also make this point.

during most of their period of analysis), household income (which rose), the costs of gasoline and of public alternatives like buses, and population shifts inside core cities.

They conclude that this model explains about 60 percent of suburbanization at least between 1940 and 1970—and that "falling automobile prices," along with the "rising real incomes" that were also mentioned by Dr. Margo, was the most important of the factors that they analyze. Again, Kopecky and Suen's explanation for the pattern they observe is not rocket surgery: "The adoption of the private vehicle . . . combined with rising income levels, encouraged movement to less dense areas where housing was more affordable." Interestingly, urban population growth during this same period— which obviously would have included the Black and immigrant migrations that are often described almost as the only force behind white out-migration—turned out to have fairly little impact on suburbanization when examined as a dependent variable in a multivariate academic model.

To be sure, "classic" white flight does retain some defenders. In *her* 2010 piece for the *Quarterly Journal of Economics*, the previously mentioned Leah Boustan uses the results of a solid quantitative analysis to argue that what she calls "the distinctive American pattern"—where suburbs tend to be majority-white and core cities very diverse—is in part the result of "large Black migration from the rural South" during the postwar era. Using data from a sample of large cities, and adjusting for several variables such as housing prices, Boustan concludes that Caucasians "responded to [the] Black influx by leaving central cities." Per her estimates, each arrival of a Black migrant in a major American city caused or correlated with "2.7 white departures."

The history Boustan describes—like so much in this book, for my fellow nerds—is frankly fascinating. Between 1940 and 1970, she reminds readers, at least 4 million American Blacks departed the South for the North, causing the African American share of the city-dwelling Northern/Western population to jump

"from 4% in 1940 to 16% in 1970." During the same three decades, "the median non-Southern city lost 10% of its white population."

The factors described so far clearly played a role in all of this:
many *previously* resident Blacks and Asians left the great cities as
well, and out-migration also happened where there simply weren't
many minorities at all. However, Boustan persuasively argues that
race effects played a considerable role, too. Across her data set,
"cities that received a larger flow of Black migrants" on average
lost more white previous residents than those that received fewer
migrants, and this effect was significant in statistical terms. The
typical large city in the Boustan sample took in about 20,000 new
Black residents between 1940 and 1970, and this correlated with
a not-insignificant outflow of 52,000 whites—again, with larger
numbers and percentages of whites leaving the most rapidly diver-
sifying cities.

There are some minor but relevant critiques of the original paper's thesis that can be made here. For example, as a methodologist,
it has to be noted—and Boustan does touch on this herself at one
point—that each Black arrival would be logically expected to correlate
with at least one white departure in a city where no racists existed at
all, given the usual very limited stock of urban housing.* But more
importantly, we come now to an awkward but obvious point outside
the scope of the original *Quarterly Journal of Economics* article.

Simply put, the sole reason for a white taxpayer not wanting
to move to 1990s Harlem or send their son to Compton Centen-
nial High School might not be "racism," and racism alone does
not explain urban white departure in the wake of Black (or Third
World) migration. Ethnic groups often clash with one another and
frequently boast very different crime rates. An entire academic para-
digm known as the racial proxy hypothesis centers on the argument

---

* In fact, the expected white-Black ratio here might be greater than 1:1, as white
Americans generally have larger families under one roof than do Black Americans.

that post-integration "white exodus . . . is primarily motivated by socioeconomic rather than racial concerns."[17]

While the discussion here is (again) complex, a great deal of hard empirical evidence exists that something like this is rather obviously the case. In 1999, the academic authors Julie Berry Cullen and Steven Levitt (of *Freakonomics* fame) assessed the impact of *crime* on urban, particularly white "out-migration."[18] Strikingly, across a set of good-size cities, they find a direct and measurable relationship: "Each additional reported crime is associated with a roughly one-person decline in city population." Put another way, a roughly 10% increase in crime within a typical city would "correspond to a 1% decline" in the population of the city.

Cullen and Levitt find out some other interesting things. Notably, the large majority of households driven out of cities by recent-past crime seem to have simply moved to the suburbs rather than trying out another and potentially safer city or adopting a farmer's life à la *Green Acres*. Per the authors: "Households that leave the city because of crime are much more likely to remain within [its] Standard Metropolitan Statistical Area (SMSA) than those that leave . . . for other reasons."

Perhaps most importantly, whether or not this was a starting goal, the results broken out in this "Crime, Urban Flight, and the Consequences for Cities" paper strongly challenge the canard that crime is a downstream result of poverty. If anything, the reverse seems to be the case: crime causes urban decay, which is then followed by increasing poverty. Or, more precisely put: "Causality appears to run from rising crime rates to city depopulation," and not infrequently from there to urban collapse. Detroit wept.

In the context of this finding, it is worth taking a long moment to remember how patterns of crime in the United States changed during basically the time period we are discussing: our 1960s and 1970s era of maximal political and racial conflict. Between 1963 and 1993, following a number of liberalizing changes to the criminal justice system,[19] murders jumped from a baseline of 8,640 to a peak of 24,530. Forcible rapes increased from 17,650 to 106,010.

Robberies, armed and otherwise, surged from 116,470 to 659,870. Violent aggravated assaults leapt from 174,210 to an unbelievable 1,135,610.[20] This crime was concentrated in large urban areas to a remarkable degree—Cullen and Levitt accurately note that the large-city crime rate in 1993 was four times the small-city rate and seven times the rural rate—and due heavily if not primarily to minority "perps."

This generation-long surge in general "common crime," often associated somewhat fairly with big cities and Black migrants, was accompanied for a decade or so by an upsurge in bloody urban racial and political riots. The year 1968 alone, which obviously witnessed the murder of civil rights icon Martin Luther King, saw dozens of related riots, described by multiple sources for this book as the "greatest wave of civil unrest the USA had experienced since the Civil War." No less than seven of these riots, in addition to the MLK riots overall, receive their own lengthy Wikipedia pages: Washington, D.C. (13 dead, 1,098 wounded, 6,100+ arrested); Chicago (9 dead, 300 injured, 2,000+ arrested); Baltimore (6 dead, 700 injured, 5,800+ arrested); Cincinnati (1–2 dead, 63 injured, 404 arrested); Kansas City, Missouri (6 dead, 40 injured, 1,042 arrested); Wilmington, Delaware (40 injured, 154 arrested); and Louisville, Kentucky (to be discussed later).[21]

There was even a major same-year riot—which, to be fair and clear, was also prompted by students' and workers' rights issues in that country—in Paris, France. While many of these riots were "mostly Black"—largely African American in composition—urban whites like the radical Weathermen also frequently and famously took to the streets during this period. The 1968 Democratic National Convention protests and riots in Chicago,[22] characterized by furious fighting between police and radicals and abuses by the eventually victorious police, resulted in one death as well as 650 protester arrests, more than 100 protesters hospitalized, and 192 police officers injured to some degree.[23] Almost all bloody street battles of this kind took place in the United States' major urban centers.

While this has often been minimized by social scientists,

the 1960s riots had significant negative impacts on many typical American cities where they took place—often far from the mile-spire buildings of the BosNYWash corridor or the Great Lakes metroplex. In the Kentucky metropolis of Louisville, near my hometown of Frankfort, a 1968 riot in the Parkland district developed from street fighting into a melee that eventually involved over four hundred arrests, led to the deployment of "some 2,000 national guardsmen," and caused the violent deaths of at least two young citizens.

Area civil rights leaders like Lyman Johnson are quite explicit that the extreme violence damaged the general goals of Blacks.[24] He blamed the riot for halting revitalization of the city's working-class West End, arguably for decades.

Unfortunately, in the wake of mass departures by once-burned area businesses, much of it never bounced back. In another former capital of Fly-Over Land, Detroit, the effects of mass civic violence were even more devastating. Following giant riots in 1967 *and* 1968, then mayor Coleman Young said bluntly:

> Detroit's losses went a hell of a lot deeper than the immediate toll of lives and buildings. The rebellion [his words] put Detroit on the fast track to economic desolation, mugging the city and making off with incalculable value in jobs, earnings taxes, corporate taxes, retail dollars, sales taxes, mortgages, interest, property taxes, development dollars, investment dollars, tourism dollars, and plain damn money. The money was carried out in the pockets of the businesses and the white people who fled as fast as they could. The white exodus from Detroit had been prodigiously steady prior to the riot, totaling twenty-two thousand ... but afterwards it was frantic. In 1967, with less than half the year remaining after the summer explosion, the outward population migration reached sixty-seven thousand. In 1968, the figure hit eighty thousand, followed by forty-six thousand in 1969.[25]

Sobering stuff—and all empirical data on point supports Mr. Young's claims. On almost the exact opposite side of the political spectrum, the Hoover Institute's Thomas Sowell noted that, *before* the 1967 and 1968 riots, "Detroit's black population had the highest rate of home-ownership of any black urban population in the country" and a rate of unemployment not far above 3 percent. Contra the prevailing—and academically taught—narrative that the deep-seated misery and despair of Black Detroiters caused the riots, Sowell points out that these mass disturbances themselves caused "the decline of Detroit to its current state of despair." Since 1968 (per 1970 decennial census data), the population of Detroit has fallen from 1,514,063 to just 632,464, an astonishing decline of 58 percent.[26] Those who fled the convulsing city came in all shades.

Increasing rates of crime and riot were not the only things that made the large American cities of the 1960s and 1970s unpopular places to live and raise families. A cynical wit might note that the left-leaning urban politics of the time gave whites and Blacks the chance to fight one another not only in the streets but in the classroom as well. This was the era not merely of constant civil unrest but also of practices like desegregation busing, once mocked by comic legend Chris Rock as "shipping Black and poor white kids to each other's bad schools to practice their fist-fighting skills."

Urban desegregation busing, like many another bad idea, began with legal rulings and noble intentions. Obviously, in 1954, the landmark *Brown v. Board* decision of the United States Supreme Court legally desegregated all American schools. However, because of the racially (and even ethnically) homogenous nature of many American neighborhoods during this period, the majority of American schools remained primarily ebony or alabaster institutions. In response to this "problem," SCOTUS issued a later and lesser-known decision, *Swann v. Charlotte-Mecklenburg Board of Education* (1971), which ruled that lesser federal courts could mandate busing—long-distance transshipment of students—as "a further integration tool to achieve racial balance."[27]

Busing was, almost from its inception, remarkably unpopular among both white and Black urbanites—just another damned unpleasant thing about the cities. A widely discussed large-sample Gallup poll conducted in 1973 found that only 4 percent of whites and 9 percent of Blacks supported the busing of schoolchildren beyond their immediate neighborhoods.[28] A more in-depth study conducted around the same time found that whites, in particular, opposed busing as a practice that they viewed as eroding community, attacking the concept of the neighborhood school, and causing discipline problems.[29]

Quantitative data essentially backs up these personal opinions. In the fairly typical racist but Northern city of Boston, more than 60 percent of parents (across all races) reported more fights and other serious discipline problems in their local schools following the commencement of busing, after schools like famously tough and white South Boston High School and all-Black Roxbury High School were forcibly partnered. "Even before the white flight from busing," David Frum writes, "more than half the students in the Boston public schools came from families at or below the poverty level. . . . Roxbury and South Boston were generally regarded as the two worst schools in Boston. . . . For the next three years, state troopers were stationed at South Boston High to keep order."[30]

Across the United States, non-white students generally had to travel even greater distances than white ones to get to their new bad school because of the relative sizes of the two populations and their distribution regionally. "It's abusive to our children, who need to be in their own neighborhood," one Black mother in St. Louis said poignantly. "Why uproot our babies?"[31] Despite this, however, most major cities adopted the practice and kept it around for years— albeit sometimes unwillingly, given that essentially any federal judge could order busing between two nearby districts.

Once again, more than a few weary urbanites responded by leaving for the green grass of suburbia: the adoption of unpopular "mandatory integration" policies and the resulting increase in in-school conflict led to still more white flight. Ironically, this migration, coupled with the movement of many other white children into Catholic and private schools, effectively neutralized most pro-integration effects that busing could have had. Most large urban school districts rapidly became majority non-white—and remain so to a striking extent today. In contemporary Boston, the inside-city-limits population is more than 50 percent white, but only 13 percent of Boston Public Schools students are non-Hispanic whites.[32]

The finding that, while racism *surely* played a role, economic incentives and unsuccessful left-bloc policies had much more to do with the post–World War Two collapse of many of America's great cities—and the departure of whites and successful Blacks from them—is unfortunately relevant today, because many of those same policies are being proposed again. As was noted in passing above, the 1963–1993 surge in American crime was not coincidental. It followed the *Miranda v. Arizona* case mandating that defendants be notified in full of their legal rights, the similar *Escobedo v. Illinois* matter, the adoption of the Fruit of the Poisoned Tree evidentiary doctrine (evidence obtained in any situation where "the constable blundered" is unusable in court), the idea of nonaggressive "community policing," and decades of liberal dominance of most big-city judiciaries.

Numerous excellent books, such as Mona Charen's *Do-Gooders: How Liberals Hurt Those They Claim to Help (and the Rest of Us)*, exist that make this point in detail—and discuss how a backlash in favor of "Broken Windows Policing," and increasing police and prosecutorial head-count, finally ended "the new normal for crime" in the mid-1990s. Today, however, organized movements like Black Lives Matter and the Defund the Police campaign are quite openly attempting to roll back those gains. The results of this "activism" have been utterly and unfortunately predictable.

As Jason Johnson, former deputy commissioner of police for Baltimore, recently noted in a stats-heavy piece for *USA Today*:[33] "Last year (2021), the United States tallied more than 20,000 murders—the highest total since 1995 and 4,000 more than in 2019." This represented an increase of at least 25 percent, which the FBI called out as the single biggest one-year increase in murder to occur since the agency began publishing official homicide figures. Johnson openly, and logically, attributes this astonishing jump in homicides to de-policing: "Policing is to blame, or rather the lack of it."

Following the riots after the death of George Floyd in May of 2020, a civic and even official backlash toward policing left departments "demoralized, debilitated, and in some cases, defunded." The impact of this can be measured empirically, with the key independent variable being police stops and arrests—the most basic one-on-one interactions between law enforcement officers and potentially criminal citizens. In New York City, the NYPD "logged 45,000 fewer" arrests between June and December 2020 than they had the year before—and the city saw 100+ homicides more than had previously been the case, an increase of 58 percent. In Chicago, the exact same pattern was visible: Windy City cops "made 31,000 fewer arrests—a 53% decline as murders rose 65%." In the Kentucky metroplex of Louisville, stops (vehicle) dropped 35 percent and arrests dropped 42 percent, while "homicides jumped 87%."

I myself—like Johnson, a solid hand at running the old Stata models—came to virtually identical conclusions writing for the online journal Quillette in 2021, noting that "between 2019—by no means a famously peaceful year—and 2020, homicides alone surged by 42 percent during the summer and [another] 34 percent during the fall."[34] Left-leaning magazines and journals like Vox largely attributed this trend to general chaos associated with the COVID-19 pandemic.[35] However, I noted that an alternative explanation fits the data far better: crime leapt like 1990s Mike Jordan because many large police departments had their budgets cut, and almost all of them reeled in their stops dramatically.

In Minneapolis, the city where George Floyd was killed and a city that I focus on during the piece, police reduced their routine traffic stops an astonishing 80 percent from 2019 levels beginning the week after May 25, 2020. May 25 of that year was the specific date Mr. Floyd died. In addition to the decline in routine auto stops, stops of suspicious cars, "defined as those thought to have been involved in a crime," dropped 24 percent. Stops of suspicious persons/individuals declined 39 percent. Obviously, crime surged—"And data from Chicago and other cities indicate that Minneapolis officers hardly pulled back alone." A detailed article in Bloomberg, from which I drew some of these stats, stated the obvious: the primary explanation for all this was likely "pullback—police reducing their proactive activity in the wake of public criticism of their performance."[36]

One depressing point made early on in the Quillette piece, and one that was also touched on by several of the other authors mentioned above, is that what happened in 2020 Minneapolis—and New York, and Chicago, and Louisville—was not a unique one-off phenomenon: "Similar chaos has followed such 'woke' policy moves nearly every time they have been implemented." This claim is not a "right-wing talking-point," if that even needs to be said. In the midst of what was then called the Ferguson effect, during an earlier wave of Black Lives Matter protests and riots, a popular Chicago neighborhood newspaper was forced to run the headline "Police Stops Down by 90 Percent as Gun Violence Sky-Rockets,"[37] and that header would have been similar to headlines seen during the decades-earlier "1963 Effect"—or during the George Floyd effect–linked surge in crime that followed years later.

While on this topic, that 2016 "Police Stops Down" piece, by Kelly Bauer and Mark Konkol for DNA Info, is worth analyzing in some depth. It may sum up the effects of de-policing for a non-academic audience better than any other article that I have recently read. Per the authors: "From the start of the year to last week [March 31, 2016], police made only 20,908 recorded investigative stops. . . . [O]ver the same period last year, there were 157,346 recorded stops."*

The effects of this change in policy were, as usual, predictable. Seizures of guns and other contraband declined slightly but significantly: the CPD seized 1,413 illegal firearms in spring 2015 and just 1,316 during the same period of 2016. More notably, far more criminals of all kinds simply remained on the street, committing crimes,

---

* Bear in mind: declines in police stops following the George Floyd killing represent—in many big cities—declines *from* lows reached after the Ferguson and Baltimore riots, albeit given some bounce-back toward normalcy between 2016 and 2020.

compared to the previous year: "Shootings across the city are up 80 percent. In 650 shootings so far this year, 123 people have been killed . . . and 652 wounded."

Quoted in the article, Cook County state's attorney Anita Alvarez plaintively noted that "the city is on track to have 700 murders this year," a figure that Chicago in fact surpassed by 62 illicit killings (and by 84 homicides, these being counted somewhat differently).[38] Police brass sources also appeared on the record for the piece and were remarkably open—if sometimes a bit cagey with their exact phrasing—about the relationship between outside incentives, officer morale, and stop rates and crime.

According to Dean Angelo, former Chicago cop and president of the Fraternal Order of Police: "I'll leave that up to the common sense of the citizens as to why things are not as productive, investigative stop wise . . . [but] I've never seen morale this bad in my career." Another source—probably still Angelo—who asked not to be identified for the record was even blunter. "I wouldn't accuse [officers] of being willfully irresponsible," he (or she!) said. "But, in this environment why would any officer make a stop unless they see a gun or witness a shooting? It's going to get worse before it gets better."

But, as in the past, many current residents of large blue cities probably will not be around to see it get better. Not only do the same policies that produced high crime, alongside high housing prices and frequent rioting, in the past appear to have the same results today, but the down-road impacts of those secondary results also seem to be identical. Remarkably and measurably, waves of what the *Forbes* business magazine recently called "leftugees" are currently fleeing Democratically governed cities and even states for safer and more stable "red" areas.[39]

Journalist Chris Dorsey's recent article on the leftugee phenomenon opens: "America is on the move like never before. . . . [T]he top five states seeing a mass exodus are all Democrat-controlled."[40] According to U.S. Census data, the sizable blue states of California, Illinois, Michigan, New Jersey, and New York have lost a total of

4 million residents in the recent past—just since the latest decennial census, with migration picking up speed more recently. Remarkably, the population of the state of California declined between 2010 and 2020, apparently for the first time on record. In contrast—this time according to data provided by U-Haul—"the top five states to see the greatest influx of new residents include the Republican-led states of Florida, Texas, Tennessee, Ohio, and Arizona."

As in the 1960s and 1970s, the primary drivers of today's migratory patterns seem to be bedrock quality-of-life issues. Dorsey notes that the combination of "rampant crime . . . including riots and civil unrest," a reality since the start of the Black Lives Matter movement in many large metropolitan areas, and the new complications of the "COVID-driven work-from-home phenomenon" pushed many professionals out of the cities and into more relaxed suburbs and exurbs. As was the case in the past, the large majority of these leftugees indicate that they have no plans ever to return to their former homes.

Denver, Colorado, is used as a case study throughout the *Forbes* article. Despite being less than 10 percent Black and a fairly high-income city across all racial groups,[41] the unofficial capital of the Mountain Time Zone for some reason saw surprisingly violent BLM rioting—resulting in significant injuries to seventy-three police officers.[42] Dorsey describes residents of central Denver as watching "their city burn last May, as the Democrat Mayor and Governor seemed powerless to stop the riots and subsequent property destruction . . . including to the state's capitol complex." Per his article and several others, more than a few Denverites wondered how this could be possible: Were no state troopers in their long cars—or National Guardsmen in tanks—available for a defense of the city's symbolic buildings?

Following a hushed answer of "Apparently not," many citizens fled, and population losses for Denver accrued to the benefit of nearby suburbs like Sterling Ranch. Local builder Brock Smethills, senior executive of the Sterling Ranch Development Company, summed up post-riot growth in one sentence: "People are migrating to places where they feel safe and secure and can be left alone." Throughout what sometimes sounds like an ad for the burbs—the inner Denver suburbs are described in one paragraph as "model communit[ies] of the future," combining "natural open lands . . . and . . . smart home technologies"—*Forbes* essentially approves, saying: "For Denver residents who witnessed the lawlessness of last August's riots, Sterling Ranch is not only a smart community . . . it was also a smart move."

It will likely, also, not be an uncommon one. There is no real reason to pick on Denver as riot-plagued or facing migration issues: the data-rich final pages of Dorsey's article make the point that citizens living in many post–George Floyd, post-COVID blue cities would like to GTFO. According to one recent survey, "42 percent of San Francisco Bay Area tech workers and about 40 percent of New Yorkers" would leave their cities immediately if they could find another in-person job elsewhere or permanently work on a fully remote basis. Dorsey sums up the poll's findings as "It's not that they want to live in these expensive [and violent] urban centers"; it's that they want to keep eating. "They feel they have to if they want to stay employed . . . for now."

But For Now will end: the COVID-19 pandemic did in practice two to three years ago, for most sane people—and the United States may soon see an unprecedented wave of internal migration, unless we strive hard and successfully to make big American cities more livable. As we work toward doing so, it is critical that we relearn the *actual* lessons of the past. Whites were hardly the only people to flee the cities of the 1960s and the 1970s; "racism"—as opposed to crime, rioting, and the simple reality of better opportunities elsewhere—was not the primary thing that drove them; and almost the exact same set of "push" and "pull" factors exist today.

This time around, let's discuss reality honestly.

LIE #9

"'Southern Strategy' Racism Turned the Solid South Republican"

Another thing that "everyone knows" is that, during and after the tumultuous 1960s discussed across the past few chapters, the U.S. Republican Party began to achieve popularity in the American South—and eventually Reagan-era national dominance—by appealing to racism. This approach is often referred to as the "Southern strategy."

A (literally) textbook version of this thesis can be found in *A People and a Nation*. The authors state that "Nixon pursued a highly pragmatic 'southern strategy' to attract white southerners to the Republican Party"[1] (which *American Pageant* calls "a clever but cynical plan" that involved "appointing conservative Supreme Court justices, soft pedaling civil rights, and opposing school busing").[2] Meanwhile, from Lyndon Baines Johnson—who signed the Civil Rights Act of 1964 into law—onward, the Democratic Party allegedly began to view Black civil rights as a "top legislative priority." Arrayed against the Democrats were not just "white southerners [who] resented federal intervention in what they considered local customs" but, "throughout the nation, millions of conservative Americans [who] believed that the federal government had overstepped its constitutional boundaries." All of these people(s) "wanted to reinforce local control and states' rights."[3]

The party bases "flipped" in this context, per most conventional takes on what happened, and the Republican base's anti-government and anti-Black sentiment would grow in strength from 1964 onward. So, the narrative goes, would the exploitation of it by Republican politicians, which explains modern GOP gains, particularly in the South.

A recent white paper–style posting, from the University of California, Berkeley's Othering and Belonging Institute, makes the conventional argument well. According to author John Powell,[4] after President Lyndon Johnson signed the 1964 Civil Rights Act, he flatly admitted that the Democratic Party "had 'lost the South for a generation,'" due to projected backlash from Southern whites. Per Powell, exactly this happened: Republicans began to exploit "racial resentment and antipathy," not only by criticizing the act and other civil rights legislation but more subtly by speaking out against policies like welfare and integration busing and in favor of "law and order." And this had the intended effect. At least according to the OBI's article, the South flipped from majority Democratic to solidly Republican within a decade or two, causing "the deep red now visible . . . in electoral maps."

This take, taught often in the schools, is wholly mainstream. In 2019, one of PolitiFact's featured fact checks targeted—in their words—Candace Owens's "false statement that the Southern strategy is a myth,"[5] which was rated as being a Pants-on-Fire level lie. Per journalist and researcher Amy Sherman, Owens claimed during a speaking event that Black conservatives like herself face criticism because "[we] have the audacity to think for ourselves and become educated about our history, and the myth of things, like . . . the Southern Strategy, which never happened." On social media, Owens later clarified that she was critiquing specifically the claim that elected Southern Democrats in Congress switched parties on a large scale to become Republicans. PolitiFact, however, rejected this entire argument, noting that the Southern strategy has been "documented for decades" by many different politicians and scholars, including "Republicans who were a part of it."

What exactly was the Strategy? Like Powell, Sherman describes it as involving the intentional use of vague but racialized language by late-twentieth-century GOP candidates targeting the South. Richard Nixon, allegedly, attempted to appeal to Southern whites by speaking out against interscholastic busing and by promising to appoint conservative Supreme Court justices who supported states' rights and were strict constitutional constructionists. Similarly, Reagan campaign boss man Lee Atwater—while noting that explicit appeals to racism failed in every region of the country—famously observed on tape that more subtle references to involuntary busing or slashing the taxes used to fund social programs could poll well, especially in the South.

Reagan himself, of course, referred often and famously to "welfare queens," which opponents derided as dog whistling or the use of "coded racist language." And, many would and do contend, all of this worked. The PolitiFact piece concludes with a quote from University of Arkansas historian Angie Maxwell, who argues that "the partisan shift in the South from the 1960s to George W. Bush" was the largest such shift in American history and was due in significant part to the techniques just described. The Southern strategy, to Maxwell and Sherman? A real thing, with undeniable effects.

While this is not the focus of this chapter, many prominent journalists and academics appear to feel not merely that the Southern strategy was real and successful but that the Republicans of *today* are literal white supremacists still engaged in constant low-key appeals to racist voters. A widely circulated 2020 piece in *Vanity Fair*, for example—published roughly one month before that year's Presidential election—was headlined "Donald Trump Goes Full White Supremacist at Minnesota Campaign Rally." It opened by accusing the Donald of being a racial bigot who "spent most of a . . . rally in full-on white power mode" and should use the campaign slogan "Make America White Again."

Big Orange's alleged offense, again, was "dog whistling." His use of the term "refugees," according to *Vanity Fair* scribe Bess Levin, was an obvious coded reference to non-whites. Even worse was the claim that a tide of refugees and illegal immigrants could "inundate" the United States and the state of Minnesota: this and other Trump remarks led Levin to describe him as blowing "a piercing . . . whistle to people who think there's a master race."[6] In addition to the presidential candidate, other Republicans were also condemned en bloc as racist—for not condemning Trump's alleged racism. "Trump could show up to the next debate wearing a white hood," the article dead seriously argues at one point, "and Republicans would probably still support his candidacy."

As that last line indicates, more moderate—or at least less talkative—pachyderms like Mitch McConnell and Mitt Romney aren't safe from dubious charges of subtle bigotry: such GOP mainliners are themselves frequently described as racists and slave masters when they run for office against a Democratic candidate. In 2012, then vice president Joe Biden drew headlines after telling a largely Black audience that President Barack Obama's milquetoast opponent Mitt Romney was going to "put y'all back in chains" once in the White House.

To be fair, the man now known as "Dark Brandon"[7] claims that he was referring only to the negative potential effects of Mr. Romney "unshackling Wall Street." However, that's a damned spicy financial metaphor—one that led Romney campaign spokeswoman Andrea Saul to describe *Biden* as a dog whistler, calling his comments unacceptable in the racially tense modern USA and arguing that the Biden-Obama team seemed willing to do virtually anything to win the 2020 race. Biden should apologize, Saul concluded, and Barack Obama should let the voters of America know "whether he agrees with Biden's comments." A decade and change later, neither man has ever done anything of the kind.

Remarkably, even *Black* Republicans are today sometimes referred to as white supremacists, in a social trend that evokes memories of Clayton Bigsby from the television classic *Chapelle's Show.*[8] In August of 2021, during a heated race for the California governorship, the *Los Angeles Times* went with this Chapelle-worthy title for a major article: "[Republican candidate] Larry Elder is the Black face of white supremacy. You have been warned."[9] Throughout the piece, the unambiguously African American Elder, who hails from the legendary Black neighborhood of South Central Los Angeles, is accused of using Southern strategy–style tactics himself to court white voters.

Per author Erika D. Smith and primary source Kerman Maddox, a well-known political consultant in California, Elder is famous for clashing not merely with so-called Black leaders but more importantly with common patterns of "thinking . . . in the community." He is thus "skin-folk, but not kin-folk." At its root, Elder's "white supremacy" seems to be reducible to his rejection of modern Wokeist ideology: he "just fundamentally doesn't believe" in modern critical theory or in concepts like univariate white privilege or systemic racism. This perspective, it is more than hinted, is intentionally disingenuous. Rather than treating Elder's views as the different but honorable takes of a political opponent, Smith describes them as feeling "personal—an insult to Blackness," designed to draw in white support. Not only did the Southern strategy exist, it never ended—and it is deployed today by *Blacks!*

To some extent—without ever minimizing genuinely dishonorable GOP behavior in the arena of race during the mid-twentieth century—it is cynically understandable why members of the Democratic Party might want to focus the national racial conversation on alleged misbehavior by their conservative opponents. Of the only two major political parties that exist in the United States, the Democrats were much worse, for far longer, on virtually every major racial question. As the iconic Carol Swain of Vanderbilt University notes, in an address that became a widely viewed video from Prager University, the Democratic Party opposed "virtually every major civil rights initiative" from its founding until the modern era. In a sentence worth quoting in full, Swain points out that "the Democratic Party defended slavery, started the Civil War, opposed Reconstruction, imposed segregation, perpetrated lynchings, and fought against the Civil Rights Acts of the 1950s and 1960s."[10]

Much if not all of this is simply accurate. The American Democratic Party, appropriately symbolized by the jackass, began in 1829 as a right-leaning populist party headed by Andrew Jackson, with a heavy base of support in the slave states. In contrast, the Republican Party was established in 1854 as an explicitly anti-slavery party, with a primary political goal of blocking "the spread of slavery into the new western territories of the United States." When this effort failed, and the time came for the future of the peculiar institution to be decided on the battle-field, a Republican president—Abraham Lincoln—served as supreme commander of the American/Union forces throughout the 1861–1865 Civil War, which broke the Confederacy. Barely a week after the final surrender of Confederate forces, Mr. Lincoln was assassinated by actor John Wilkes Booth—a partisan Democrat.

For many years after 1865, the two parties followed much the same trajectories. As Swain notes, influential Democrats like Andrew Johnson were almost "unified" in opposing the Thirteenth, Fourteenth, and Fifteenth Amendments to the United States Constitution—the "Civil War Amendments," which abolished chattel slavery and gave the basic rights of citizenship to Black Americans. In contrast, the three Amendments received 100 percent GOP backing, which led directly to their passage. During the Reconstruction era that followed, several hundred Black men were elected to state-level legislatures across the South, and twenty-two were elected to the United States Congress. Essentially all of these individuals ran under the elephant banner: the first elected Black Democrat in the federal Congress took office in 1935.

When the Reconstruction period ended, in 1878, "Democrats roared back into power in the South," and a near race war ensued, with the Ku Klux Klan serving basically as the military arm of Democratic landholders. Famed and hardly right-leaning historian Eric Foner, whom Swain also quotes, explicitly describes the KKK as "a military force serving the interests of the Democratic Party," and his take is the conventional one. When this time of violence ended—frankly because, for all the brave efforts of many "Negroes with guns,"[11] my race and sometime political party lost the fight—

the Jim Crow states that emerged sent heavily Democratic congressional delegations to the U.S. House and Senate for decades.

It is worth pointing out that this state of affairs prevailed well
into modern times. In the mid-1960s, when the law most Americans think of as *the* Civil Rights Act came up for a vote in Congress,
the substantial majority of organized opposition to it came from
the Democratic side of the aisle. In the end, only 61 percent of
House Democrats (152 out of 248) voted in favor of the Act, while
80 percent of Republicans (138 out of 172) did so.[12] Seventy-four
percent of all final "nay" votes came from Democrats, and the Bur-
ros at one point staged a *seventy-five-day* formal filibuster against
the bill in an attempt to disgust the GOP into abandoning it. When
President Lyndon B. Johnson famously and grudgingly signed
the act into law, he allegedly said about its upside, "I'll have them
niggers voting Democrat for 200 years"—a testament to potential
Republican backlash, but certainly also to the man's own bigotry.

Although basic etymology should tell us this, gentle reader,
it is also worth pointing out that all of the brutally racist and still-
legendary "Dixiecrats" of the era just before the Civil Rights Act
vote were Democrats. The official title of the Dixiecrat Party was the
"States' Rights Democratic Party," and the entire party began as a
breakaway faction of the Democratic Party. Even the colloquial name
of the party is a direct mix of the words "Dixie"—a common term for
the states composing the old Confederacy—and "Democrat."[13]

To a large extent, in their mostly one-party region, Dixiecrats
did not focus their attention on Republicans or third-party members at all: their initial goal was simply "to upset the election bid of
Harry Truman. By capturing the 127 electoral votes of the (historically) Solid South, they felt they could prevent either major party
candidate from winning a majority, thus throwing the election
into the House of Representatives."[14] After this strategy proved in-
sufficient to win the 1948 presidential election, and establishing
a permanent and effective third party under U.S. electoral rules
proved daunting, most leading Dixiecrats simply became standard
conservative Democrats once again. With two to three exceptions,

such as 1948 presidential candidate Strom Thurmond of South Carolina, who did not change parties for another sixteen years, almost none became Republicans.[15]

On the basis of evidence like this, some scholars and journalists, such as *National Review*'s Kevin D. Williamson, have openly argued that moderate American conservatives have historically been the true force backing improved Black civil rights in the United States and that it is remarkable that this fact is not better known. In his 2012 piece "The Party of Civil Rights," Williamson calls it amazing that, due to media bias and other factors, Democrats have been allowed to "rhetorically bury" their affiliation with public officials like Birmingham's Eugene "Bull" Connor, support for the Ku Klux Klan, and decades of unfortunately effective opposition to "practically every major piece of civil rights legislation."[16]

Dredging up almost-forgotten "tea," the same article outlines the pre-1964–1968 career of Lyndon Baines Johnson, a senator from then deeply bigoted Texas before his election as president of the United States. Williamson argues that Johnson was "practically antebellum" in his views: as a congressman, he voted repeatedly against legislation targeted not merely at enhancing civil rights and voting rights but also at preventing lynching. Johnson personally de-fanged the 1957 Civil Rights Act, leading a successful push to remove all enforcement provisions from the bill before it went up to President Eisenhower for his signature: his Senate Democrats would later stage one of the longest filibusters ever to take place against a 1960 Civil Rights Act designed specifically "to remedy the deficiencies of the 1957 Act."

So, one might wonder, what happened to cause mass changes of heart on both sides of the aisle, and the great political realignment that began in the mid- to late 1960s? Actually, the *Review* credibly contends, nothing happened and no such realignment took place for decades. Williamson makes the obvious point that Candace Owens tried to get across: if the two political parties flipped quickly and significantly on issues of civil rights, "one would expect that to show up in the electoral results" during the election years that followed in immediate sequence after 1964. In fact, this simply did not occur. As we saw with former Dixiecrats, only one of the twenty-one Democratic senators who voted against the 1964 Civil Rights Act ever changed parties to became a Republican.

Nor were these men replaced by Republicans. The remaining twenty senators continued running and getting elected as partisan Democrats for at least the next twelve years or were supplanted by other Democrats. "On average," it took twenty to twenty-five years before the seats in question swung to the GOP. As Williamson notes in a genuinely funny passage, if biased Southerners gave up on the Democratic Party because of the party's support for the 1964 Civil Rights act, "it is strange that they waited until the late 1980s and early 1990s to do so. They say things move slower in the South— but not that slow."

This historical discussion is all well and good but fails to truly answer one question: *Was* there a Southern strategy? The *National Review* article's final point might complicate this discussion, but *did* selective GOP targeting of white voters in the South occur? Did sharp-toothed consultants like Lee Atwater encourage Republicans to recruit Southerners via the use of coded racial appeals? The honest answer seems to be: Hoss, it's a lot more complicated than that.

As writer John Hinderaker has pointed out, the famous series of quotes that is often described as Atwater's admission to launching the Southern strategy is in fact mostly an empirical description of declining open and overall racism in the South. Atwater's whole premise is that, in the early 1950s, candidates *could* literally criticize "nigger[s]" in an attempt to appeal to racist voters. However, as early as 1968, this would be unthinkable ("That hurts you").[17]

Even by that point, cynical political pitches could at most focus on race-linked issues like busing. By the time of his 1981 sit-down, a few years after the publication of William Julius Wilson's epochal "The Declining Significance of Race,"[18] even that latter approach had fallen out of fashion and before long "you're talking about cutting taxes." In full context, Atwater's point seems to be that, while "dog whistles" may sometimes work, race qua race was, by a date more than forty years in the past, already a fairly insignificant driver of voter behavior.

It should also be pointed out—although it hardly ever is—that the *rest* of Atwater's interview complicates the Southern strategy question even further. The man once described by P. J. O'Rourke as "a synthesis of Huck Finn and Machiavelli" went on to drop a rarely quoted bomb that seems pretty damn noteworthy: that Ron Reagan himself "did not ... *do* a Southern strategy for two reasons," and that most of Atwater's primary clients had abandoned the technique by the time he spoke.

Reagan, per Atwater, campaigned "on the issues of economics and national defense." His entire presidential campaign "was devoid of any kind of racism." The reason for this was simply that racial issues were not of primary concern to voters near the close of the Jimmy Carter era: Atwater describes a total lack of concern among even Southern voters about then-current civil rights measures like the latest Voting Rights Act. As the right-leaning but good-faith Hinderaker sums all of this up: "So, the central point Atwater made in the interview was the exact opposite of the proposition for which liberals have endlessly quoted him."

In the same interview, Lee Atwater himself goes on to make an obvious but critical point. Whatever may have been true in 1946 or even 1964, it is absurd and unfair to label any contemporary advo-cacy for the conservative point of view as racist. Describing wide-spread American opposition to the sweeping welfare programs of the 1980s, the Mississippi Machiavelli labeled this dissatisfaction as "a mainstream thing now. It's not grounded in racism, as much as ... I'm mad as hell and I'm not going to take it anymore." While conceding that many—although by no means most—of those on welfare happen to be Black, Atwater states the obvious: clashes over U.S. fiscal and social policy are "developing into a class strug-gle issue rather than a racism issue." Unfortunately, this entire complex, and mostly accurate, position has all too often been con-densed down to one easy-to-criticize line.

A second and even deeper question about the Southern strategy follows the first banger query of "Was it tried?" The simple phrasing for this next one might be "Did it work?" *Did* the American South, while remaining basically stable in population terms, swing from the political left to the right because the Republicans made racist appeals that Democrats would no longer stoop to match and could not effectively counter? In contrast with the complex answer to the first question, the reply here basically breaks down to "No."

The argument that exactly that did happen, of course, has approached canonical status among many mossbacked pundits and academics. In his *The Emerging Republican Majority*, Kevin Phillips popularized if not coined both the term "Southern strategy" and the phrase "silent majority," and wrote about what the scholar Adolph Reed Jr. has called "a discourse of white ethnic, working- or middle-class conservatism associated with the so-called white backlash against civil rights and . . . elitist liberalism in the late 1960s and early 1970s."[19] Here we see today's mainstream narrative in full again: subtle but effective GOP pitches to this group of whites were the key element of "a liturgy of political realignment" that helped flip the South and led to the national triumph of Reagan's political movement.

But not so fast. There are major empirical problems with this argument (which, to be fair, Reed himself is critical of). As we have seen, and as Hinderaker and Atwater persuasively argue, Reagan didn't talk too terribly much—even "implicitly"—about race. And, more empirically, "the Reagan Democrat phenomenon has been greatly oversold." In reality, the sort of working-class white voters often associated with the South are more likely even today to vote for the Democratic Party than are members of the electorate as a whole. While the *single* post-1980 exception to this pattern did involve one of the elections in which Reagan campaigned, white members of trade unions and other unions broke against the Gipper even then. Almost all of the Southern racists of the 1950s and 1960s were Democrats, and poor whites *still* vote Democrat in far higher numbers than Southerners or Americans overall.

Further complicating the narrative is the simple fact that Reagan was no unique outlier. Many national-level post-1964 Republicans, like Dick Nixon, were actually pretty solid on civil rights. Nixon's favorite punching bags were hippies and other white activists rather than Black civil rights campaigners like Martin Luther King—his famously tough television ads calling Democrats the party of "acid, amnesty, and abortion"[20] primarily targeted radicals like Abbie Hoffman and the Weathermen—and Nixon supported public school integration, the 1964 Civil Rights Act, and the 1965 Voting Rights Act.[21]

Much of this was apparently rather widely acknowledged until a recent spate of revisionism, with left-leaning *New York Times* columnist Tom Wicker writing in 1970: "There's no doubt about it—the Nixon administration accomplished more in 1970 to desegregate Southern school systems than had been done in the 16 previous years. There's no doubt either that it was Richard Nixon personally who conceived and led the administration's desegregation effort."

Perhaps because of this record, Nixon in fact spent very little time campaigning in the South in 1968 and 1972. As Kevin Phillips says in *The Emerging Republican Majority*, his electoral strategy focused on the so-called Sunbelt, "that vast swath of territory stretching from Florida to Nixon's native California"—where voters were likely not to be racist at all and to be more urban and more financially stable than Southerners. And, in fact, Nixon did very well among these voters but lost the Deep South to racist Democrat George Wallace—falling to defeat in Alabama, Arkansas, Georgia, Louisiana, Mississippi, and Texas.[22]

In 1972, Nixon did take the South, but did so in the context of winning every voting region in the United States except Massachusetts and the District of Columbia. Liberal Democrat and Georgia native Jimmy Carter would win almost every one of the same states in 1976, and the South as a region would not become majority Republican until the very late 1980s or early 1990s.

The attorney and historical researcher Dan McLaughlin, along with several other modern scholars, argues that the slow political shift that resulted in the Newt Gingrich–led Republican Revolution of the 1990s actually began decades before. In an excellent analysis of Sean Trende's book *The Lost Majority: Why the Future of Government Is Up for Grabs—and Who Will Take It* for the political website RedState,[23] McLaughlin argues that the increase in support for the GOP among Southern whites was in fact "steady" if gradual between 1928 and 2010, when this support essentially peaked. He attributes this creeping growth to the simple fact that, as the Republican Party platform evolved toward what it currently is, white Southrons became substantially more compatible with "the national Republican agenda and coalition" than with the Democratic Party equivalent.

Indeed, the primary factor that slowed the regional transition from blue to red, along with plain partisan loyalties "dating back to Reconstruction," was very arguably the strategic use of racial appeals over the years by the *Democrats*. To quote the article directly: "If you take race out of the picture, it is likely that white Southerners would have switched parties earlier and in greater numbers." Very arguably, as McLaughlin claims, the first and most effective Southern strategy was pursued by the Democratic Party rather than the Republican Party.

Stripped of the hoarfrost of debatable facts That Everyone Knows, there is some obvious logic to this argument. The argument that racialist tactics were the sole or primary reason for the migration of socially conservative white Southerners into the more conservative of America's two major political parties essentially ignores the expressed positions of these voters on "economics, religion, and foreign policy/national security"—along with abortion and a host of other issues. We can obviously ask—and the article does—whether the average Georgia voter would feel more at home with Al Smith, George McGovern, Mike Dukakis, or Teddy Kennedy than with George W. Bush with regard to these issues, were the race card absent from the political deck. At some level, the clear answer is: of course not.

Voting trend-lines data, which McLaughlin and Trende himself provide in detail, supports the argument about slow-paced and ideologically driven electoral transition in the South. As far back as 1928, cracks began to appear in the monolithic façade of Democratic control of the region, with GOP candidates doing well in states like Tennessee, Texas, and West Virginia. While the Great Depression hit the impoverished "red clay" states hard, redirecting the focus of most voters toward economic issues and hampering the Republicans, this original trend picked up again as the modern era arrived.

Popular former Allied supreme commander Dwight D. Eisenhower won three Southern states in 1952 and five in 1956, "came 15,000 votes in North Carolina from carrying a majority of the Southern states" during the latter campaign. Nor did the Southern GOP base remain isolated or localized by this point in time: Ike took at least 33 percent of all ballots cast "in every state in the Old Confederacy." Similarly, Richard Nixon—running as the incumbent vice president from an administration that had stoutly defended *Brown v. Board of Education*—took three Southern states (Florida, Tennessee, and Virginia) by respectable margins in 1960, while elections in North Carolina, South Carolina, and Texas "were all decided by five points or less." All of this, unlike even the previously discussed results from the 1964 and 1968 elections, came before any partisan shift on issues of race had been alleged to have occurred.

In addition to pointing out that the South was by no means as passionately Democratic as is generally thought to have been the case before 1968, McLaughlin joins several other authors that have been reviewed so far in noting that the region did not simply shift into the GOP camp after that year. As we have seen, popular Southern Democratic candidates like Jimmy Carter (1976) and Bill Clinton (1992, 1996) were either "mak[ing] substantial inroads" into the region, or winning it outright for decades to come. Further—and this is a new point—it took many *more* years for Republican dominance at the very top of the ballot to "seep down-ticket." GOP dominance of the U.S. House, driven partly by the performance of the South, did not occur until 1994, and large states like Alabama and North Carolina did not elect GOP congressional majorities until 2010.

In addition to reviewing the growing literature that has tracked changing political attitudes among white conservative voters in the South, it is also worth noting an obvious additional point here: the politics and other characteristics of regions change when the people living in those places change. The same is in fact true for whole nations, as the endless modern debate about demographic change and issues like critical race theory reminds us. And obviously the human demographics of states like Georgia and Florida today differ greatly from the heavily agrarian, mostly working-class populations that these places boasted in 1948.

In probably the best book about this transition, *The End of Southern Exceptionalism,*[24] the political scientists Richard Johnston (University of Pennsylvania) and Byron E. Shafer (University of Wisconsin–Madison) argue that the Southern transition from Democratic to Republican control was "overwhelmingly a question not of race but of economic growth."[25] Per the two authors, in the era following World War Two, the American South semi-intentionally transitioned from a famously "backward" region to one of the "engine[s] of the national economy"—which led to the development of a large new suburban upper middle class. These citizens, many of them originally from the North, began to vote or continued to vote for Republicans.

Notably, native working-class Southern whites, "even those in areas with large Black populations," largely remained loyal to the Democrats at least until the mid-1990s. Conducting a tercile analysis, Johnston and Shafer note that, in the 1950s, 43 percent of low-income Southerners voted for Republicans at the presidential level, while 53 percent of high-income Southerners did so. By the late 1980s, the first figure had shifted slightly—to a roughly 50 percent rate of Republican voting—but the second figure had surged to 77 percent, an increase of 45 percent. Per this data, the migration of well-off voters from the rest of the United States changed the South far more than did attitude realignments among native Southerners themselves (which also occurred).

The extent of recent population shift within the United States is frankly remarkable. Per the industry-specific site NewGeography .com, throughout the post–World War One era, American population growth has taken place almost entirely in those regions of the United States that were "least populated in 1900,"[26] with this trend being most notable in the modern period from 1950 until 2010 and beyond. Simply put, the "formerly dominant East" has been completely displaced as the most populous and developed region of the United States.

The South currently contains 33 percent of the American citizenry, the West Coast and interior West 26 percent, the East Coast and New England just 22 percent, and the once "Mighty" Midwest only 19 percent. Between 1970 and 2010, the South added approximately 30 million new residents, the West 22 million, the Midwest 5.6 million, and the East just 3.2 million. Forty-nine percent of all growth during the period took place in the South, defined as the states that made up the former Confederacy.

Patterns that are significant at the level of large regions can be absolutely striking at the level of individual communities. As the New Geography piece points out, every one of the top-growth U.S. metropolitan areas during the modern era has been a Southern or Western city. Between just 1950 and 2010, Miami grew 800 percent.* Riverside–San Bernardino—"Berdoo" in California—grew 940 percent.

Phoenix increased in size 1,120 percent—as did Orlando. Most

---

* Miami grew an astonishing 111,300 percent, or 1,113 times over, between 1900 and 2010—from a sleepy fishing village into what is often considered an alpha world city.

remarkably, Las Vegas—built in the heart of the desert by the Mafia after World War Two—grew 4,070 percent. Moving the window of analysis to 1980–2010 adds Austin, Texas, and Raleigh, North Carolina, to an otherwise very similar-looking list of cities which recently became metropolises. All of this, obviously, bears directly on modern patterns of moderate GOP voting, which are very often glibly attributed to that old debbil American racism.

Ezra Klein of Vox and the *Washington Post*, well-known Twitter pugilist and devout man of the left, put a sardonic but not inaccurate spin on this pattern of population transition about a decade back, claiming in a short *WaPo* article that "Air Conditioning Created the Modern Republican Party." Making his case, Klein cites the arguments of congressional historian Nelson W. Polsby, who contends that the Dixiecrats of old vanished because of "the rise of the Republican Party in the South . . . conservatives, instead of being Dixiecrats, became Republicans." Why did that occur? Simply put, because enough Republicans moved to the South from Northern states to make the GOP a serious political alternative in the region.

This much has been said already, but Klein and Polsby have a simple and novel explanation for why it occurred: it is hot in the U.S. Deep South. Very hot. Before "the introduction . . . of residential air conditioning" in the mid-1950s, a substantial number of Yankee "snowbirds" wintered in states like Georgia and Florida, but almost none opted to live in the tropics year-round. Following technical developments in the fields of HVAC and home building, many of the same people—by definition, disproportionately successful professionals who could afford to maintain two homes—did choose to do so. Empirically speaking, increases in Republican voting track extraordinarily well with this pattern of residential migration: "the first safe Republican [congressional] seat in the South" was located in the resort community of St. Petersburg, Florida; the second was and is located in business-friendly Dallas, Texas.[27]

Commenting on what actually happened in the South, Klein makes an important point that has recurred throughout this book.

Social scientists and media members tend to favor trendy, edgy, political and racial explanations for events, "but other forces, like technological change, matter too"—and often matter more. The top economists behind the book *Freakonomics* famously attributed the mid-1990s American drop in crime to the increased availability of abortion following the 1973 *Roe v. Wade* case, although this has been contested. Klein himself, citing Gregory Koger, once pegged the historical decline in lengthy congressional filibusters to improvements in air travel, which has allowed members to head home almost at will to campaign and raise money.[28] And, it seems, we may well owe AC inventor Willis Carrier and his intellectual heirs for the heavily GOP South of today.

Life is complex and multivariate, and scholarly analysis should be as well.

#10

Bonus Lie: The Continuing Oppression Narrative

A final Big Lie often taught today in classrooms and beyond is so contemporary, widespread, and pervasive that—unlike, say, the ultimate impact of British imperial colonialism—its tenets are often not even recognized as points that can be empirically debated. This is what I have previously dubbed the "contemporary oppression narrative" (CON), the "CRT" idea that the United States of today has not progressed far beyond our bloody past: we remain a racially fraught country characterized by widespread police murder of young and especially Black men, constant back-and-forth inter-ethnic conflict (with whites generally getting the better of it), and structures of "systemic racism," "institutional bias," and "white privilege" designed to oppress minorities around every turn. According to several staggeringly popular modern thinkers, such as Robin DiAngelo and Ibram X. Kendi (né Henry Rogers), almost any gap in performance between whites and minorities can be taken as evidence of this oppression.

Of course, once again, reality turns out to be far more complex than narrative, and most of these claims are quite simply wrong. However, they are astonishingly prevalent. This book has a theme, and—worry not!—the presence of CON ideas in the classroom will be discussed in depth when we analyze the actual elementary and secondary school curricula from the 1619 Project and Zinn Education Project just a few pages down. However, the same ideas are virtually inescapable across much of day-to-day upper-middle-class life. Just a few years back, for example, Black Lives Matter leader Cherno Biko ventured onto prime-time Fox News to argue that racist police officers "murder" at least one Black citizen every day.

Per the *New York Post*, Mr. Biko informed Fox host Megyn Kelly that a totally innocent, presumably unarmed Black person is "murdered by police . . . every 28 hours" in the United States.[1] "It feels like we're in a war," Biko added. Crunching the numbers, *Post*-man Deroy Murdock—himself a human of hue—correctly concluded that murderous police officers would be "rubbing out . . . 313 innocent, law-abiding blacks annually" in Biko's scenario. As he succinctly summed up Biko's argument: "If the Black Lives Matter crowd is correct, bloodthirsty, racist cops are blasting black men like clay pigeons at a shooting range. The pace of this alleged slaughter is breathtaking."

Biko is hardly one lone nut. In what was initially one of the best-selling books of the past few years, literally called *Open Season: Legalized Genocide of Colored People*, prominent civil rights attorney Ben Crump argues that his title is no mere metaphor: police violence and white vigilantism—among other things—constitute an attempted "genocide" against American Blacks. And Crump, once the personal attorney for Trayvon Martin's mother, is no mere shyster lawyer. Per his website and Amazon biography, Crump is a member of the National Trial Lawyers' list of the top 100 American trial lawyers, *Ebony* magazine's Power 100 list of the "100 Most Influential" Black Americans, a former National Newspaper Publishers Association (NNPA) Newsmaker of the year, and an Honorary Fellow in Residence at the University of Pennsylvania Carey Law School. His book has been reviewed, online or in print, by Black Lives Matter founder Patrisse Cullors, *Kirkus Reviews*, *Publishers Weekly*, and the aptly named Book Riot.

The position of all of these power brokers, so far as I can tell, is that Crump is a good man telling the hard truth. Cullors argues that "Crump's masterful voice" and "expertise of America's corrupt power structures [sic]" have the potential to permanently change "the hierarchy by which we dangerously abide." In a starred review, *Kirkus* preachily tells potential readers: "There is much more to inequality and discrimination than we know, and Crump will open your eyes—pay attention." *Publishers Weekly* sums up the book as "alarming" in sections but calls it an entirely "credible account" of modern American race relations. Perhaps most bluntly, Book Riot says that Crump provides a "deeply disturbing account of how the justice system is used to maintain a system of inequality and justify the murder of Black Americans."

In recent years, this absolutely mainstream belief in the reality of almost genocidal levels of police and vigilante violence against Black Americans has gone hand in hand with the increasingly frequent argument that the United States of 2024 is a nation characterized by near-constant ethnic conflict. In addition to those involved in a few genuinely tragic cases of interracial violence (i.e., the Ahmaud Arbery killing), dozens of basically normal-ass white people—Sarah Braasch, Amy Cooper, "Coupon Carl," the National Basketball Association's Donte DiVincenzo, "Pool Chair" Adam Bloom, "Permit Patty," Covington Catholic High School's Nick Sandmann, "Dog Park" Emma Sarley—recently became national figures and "evidence of a disturbing trend" after simply getting into a fistfight or argument with a Black person or other minority.

Queen among these Symbols of Hate has so far probably been Oakland, California's "BBQ Becky"—actually named Jennifer Schulte ("Becky" and "Karen" are generic insults for white women)—who found herself "photoshopped into Black history" after getting into an argument with a Black family about barbecuing in a California park.[2] As I note in my book *Taboo*, nothing actually indicates that Schulte is a racist. She seems to be a politically liberal graduate of Stanford, and while both sides behaved stupidly during what became a lengthy argument, her original sin was correctly telling a Black family that they were not supposed to be using a charcoal grill in a specific pet-friendly area of Oakland's Lakeside Park.[3] However, as sources including Britain's BBC(!) have noted, she has now been edited into memes of "black history moments including Martin Luther King's I Have a Dream speech" and condemned in written pieces from London to South Africa. It's easy to see how people get a totally misleading view of reality when anecdotes are mistaken for trends.

Stories that go that viral are thought to indicate patterns. In response to this prevalent narrative of constant white-led conflict, social scientists are witnessing a fascinating and depressing phenomenon: actual citizen ratings of the quality of U.S. race relations have begun to drop, and many prominent Black public figures have started to describe themselves as exhausted by white harassment. In a genuinely poignant (if empirically nonsensical) tweet that drew roughly 1,800 likes, the journalist Elie Mystal described himself as unwilling to "put his white people armor on" to attempt potentially dangerous tasks like going to a CVS.[4] Similarly, in response to both the general American climate and one specific incident—the near-fatal police shooting of Jacob Blake—pro basketball's six-foot-seven LeBron James referred to himself and other Black Americans as constantly feeling "terrified."[5]

As the race relations data indicates, many Americans truly believe what Mystal and James are selling—and what they themselves have surely been sold. In 2021, an astonishing study from the respected Skeptic Research Center titled "How Informed Are Americans About Race and Policing?" found that "over half (53.5%) of those reporting 'very liberal' political views" believe that more than 1,000 *unarmed* Black men were killed in 2019 by American police.[6] To be more specific, 31.43 percent of "very liberal" respondents and leftists estimated that "about 1,000" unarmed Black men were killed by police officers—while 14.21 percent put the toll at "about 10,000" and 7.86 percent thought the true figure had to be higher than that.

For bog-standard liberals—literally anyone to the left of the centerline politically—the equivalent figures were 26.67 percent (for "about 1,000"), 6.67 percent, and 5.43 percent. Liberals and leftists also appear to believe that virtually all police shooting victims are Black. These two groups estimated, respectively, that 56 percent and 60 percent of all those killed by law enforcement officers are African American, with very large chunks of both populations choosing significantly higher percentages than those.* Whatever their validity, believing such things—especially as a Black person!—must be genuinely frightening indeed.

And, worse than the temporary terror of all this police and white vigilante violence, allegedly, is the "systemic racism" of virtually every modern American system. In recent years, the bizarre idea that the post–Civil Rights Act United States is intentionally structured to oppress people of color (or women, Jews, gays, the poor, etc.)—and that essentially all group gaps in performance provide evidence of this oppression—has become an inescapable part of middle-brow-on-up American life. For scholars like Boston University's well-compensated Dr. Ibram X. Kendi, racism is—to crib from myself in *Commentary* magazine—"properly thought of not as simple outgroup bias, but rather as any *system* that produces disparate outcomes between or across racial or ethnic groups."[7]

This staggeringly broad definition, of course, leads to the inescapable conclusion that racism is absolutely everywhere, something that Kendi says very openly. In books like *How to Be an Antiracist*, the scholar argues that there are only two possible explanations for a measurable difference in performance between two large groups in a given setting—for example, in response to a standardized test. These are (1) racism—some form of bias within a social "system," no matter how subtle or hidden, or (2) actual inferiority ("There is something *wrong* with Black people") on the part of the lower performing of the two groups. In an interview with the Vox podcast, Kendi summed his viewpoint up quite succinctly: "There's only two

---

* In the most recent year then on record (2019), Blacks actually made up just 24.9 percent of all people shot by U.S. police. While this is still something of an overrepresentation—the U.S. population is just 12 to 13 percent Black—it is worth noting that the Black crime rate is generally around 2.4 times the white crime rate, which obviously influences rates of Black encounters with police.

causes of, you know, racial disparities. Either certain groups are better or worse than others—and that's why they have more—or racist policy. Those are the only two options."[8]

For those accepting this framework, every group gap in, say, income that we see in modern society is due to present or past discrimination—generally racial in nature—and reverse discrimination now is required to close these gaps. Dr. Kendi himself has helpfully proposed a range of social-engineering solutions to repair the "racist" institutions of American society. Perhaps most notably, he argues that the U.S. Congress should pass an "anti-racist Constitutional amendment" that would make all "racist ideas by public officials" unconstitutional or illegal and enshrine into American law the principle that all "racial inequity is evidence of racist policy." The same amendment, incidentally, would establish a permanent federal Department of Anti-Racism composed only of "formally trained experts on racism."

Perhaps, given current trend lines, Kendi's desired future will come to pass. In the meantime, the "woke" activists of our own time are moving beyond novel but established frameworks like "systemic racism" to seek out wholly new ways to be oppressed—such as "cultural appropriation," which occurs when people from different backgrounds learn from one another. For example, according to a detailed piece ("Why Cultural Appropriation Isn't Cool") on the popular youth website ReachOut, "rocking a Native American head-dress at your next music festival may be a bigger deal than you first thought," and citizens should bone up on appropriation avoidance so as not to land in such a "sticky or offensive situation."[9]

As with many concepts on the modern left—including racism itself—the idea of cultural appropriation seems burdened with many internal pro-minority assumptions of the "It's okay for us to do this but not for you to do it" variety. For example, the ReachOut authors define appropriation as occurring only when members of "a dominant culture . . . take things from another culture that is experiencing oppression." However, the potential range of the concept remains staggeringly broad.

The authors note, accurately enough, that "racism, sexism, and homophobia" are all varieties of power-based oppression—as are classism and bias against immigrants. They describe holiday or casual imitation of Native American fashion, Japanese "geisha" culture, or the Arab style as instances of appropriation, and the same would logically apply to whites or Westerners borrowing anything from virtually any immigrant community, rich kids learning "street" styles from poor ones of whatever color, straight folx taking fads in dance or dress from the gay nightlife community, and so on. Even if a proper Department of Anti-Racism were to be established in D.C., this plague of people picking up ideas from one another seems all too likely to continue on into the foreseeable future.

All of the claims, concepts, and theories discussed so far in this chapter are very much taught in the American elementary and secondary school classroom—perhaps to a greater extent than any others discussed so far. The New York Times's 1619 Project, dedicated to the ideas that racism is "in America's DNA," almost everything unique about the United States evolved out of pre-1865 Black slavery, and our nation's true "founding date" was "the year the first enslaved Africans arrived on Virginia soil," has produced a multipronged educational curriculum that has been adopted by literally thousands of schools.[10] Like most such efforts from the activist political left, the 1619 Project curriculum is fantastically broad, extending far beyond the historical race relations issues that—whatever we might think of these authors' conclusions—are the specialty of the project's primary contributors.

The curriculum extends across grades from elementary school to law school and covers a sometimes entertaining range of topics from rhetorical analysis ("How Language Becomes Law," in which "students use rhetorical analysis skills to reflect on the media backlash to The 1619 Project . . .") to contemporary prison policy ("Examining the Legacy of Slavery in Mass Incarceration"). The scope of other closely linked lessons available through the same Pulitzer Center website is even more wide-ranging, including for instance: "Community Care Through Climate Justice," "Grabbing the Reins: The Fate of the Earth Is in OUR Hands," and "Celebrating AAPI Grassroots Action Amid the Pandemic."

Notably, 1619 and Pulitzer seem to be moving toward a more localized focus on racial conflict in *every* city from which pupils might theoretically come. Website contributor Christina Sneed— "an education and instructional coach from St. Louis"—already offers students at various grade levels curricular materials for the 1619-adjacent 1857 Project. These include lesson plans, multiple reading guides, and a variety of "extension activities," all devoted to "chronicling the history of racial injustice" specifically in St. Louis and the surrounding region of the Show-Me State. (The subproject is named after the year of the famous Lincoln-Douglas debates and the awful *Dred Scott* Supreme Court decision.) Whether or not such regionally focused content is likely to improve race relations in the United States, more of it seems certain to come from the 1619 team in the near future.

To the left of the 1619 Project and the Pulitzer Center (and how often does one get to say those words?), the Marxist Zinn Education Project also provides elementary and secondary school teaching materials. Named after Howard Zinn, the author of *A People's History of the United States*, the ZEP offers up prepared lessons and recommended books that—among other things—argue that the Second Amendment of the Constitution is racist (*Loaded: A Disarming History of the Second Amendment; The Second: Race and Guns in a Fatally Unequal America*), praise the Puerto Rican Young Lords street gang for commandeering a public hospital in the 1970s (*Takeover: How We Occupied a Hospital and Changed Public Health Care*),* provide a "learning companion" to the ruminations of

---

* The Young Lords, something of a favorite of the authors of the curriculum, are also the subject of a highly recommended nonfiction book by the author Johanna Fernández, *The Young Lords: A Radical History*. Across 480 pages, Fernandez

activist former NFL pass thrower Colin Kaepernick (*Colin in Black and White: The Kaepernick Curriculum*), detail Native American resistance to a series of proposed oil pipelines during the recent NoDAPL protests (*Our History Is the Future: Standing Rock Versus the Dakota Access Pipeline, and the Long Tradition of Indigenous Resistance; Standing with Standing Rock: Voices from the #NoDAPL Movement*), and argue against educational testing (*More Than a Score: The New Uprising Against High-Stakes Testing*).

Unsurprisingly, the goal of many citizens who believe things like those outlined above ("The United States is a genocidal white supremacist nation"), and who wish to teach children about them, is very sweeping societal change. The current list of official demands from the pro-1619 Black Lives Matter movement, accessible at www.blacklivesmatter.com, provides an illustrative example of what this might look like in practice. The very first demand, (1), is that former President Donald Trump immediately be impeached and "convicted in the United States Senate,"* charged with several serious crimes, and for good measure "banned from holding any elected office in the future." The second demand, (2), is the expulsion from Congress of all Republican lawmakers who "attempted to overturn the election and incited a white supremacist attack" on January 6. As BLM defines them, this group would include more than half of all elected House Republicans and perhaps a dozen senators; all of these persons would also be barred from ever again seeking office in the United States.[11]

And so forth. Moving down the list, Black Lives Matter wants the former president banned for life from all social media platforms; the Capitol Police, all other "law enforcement" agencies, and the U.S. military investigated in a top-to-bottom purge of

---

argues that these admittedly stylish gangbangers "redefined the character of protest, the color of politics, and the cadence of popular urban culture in the age of great dreams." Heady stuff.

* Still—or again?

suspected white supremacists; and the passage of Representative Jamaal Bowman's perhaps poorly named COUP Act.

Apparently, after they are investigated, the movement wants most police departments nationwide to be defunded ("The police were born out of slave patrols, We cannot reform an institution built upon white supremacy"), with the money saved presumably to be spent on social workers or other alternatives to the carceral system. Perhaps most sweepingly, BLM calls for an expanded version of the BREATHE legislation once proposed by President Biden, which would expend trillions of dollars on "equity screens in federal programs, investing in environmental justice at historic levels, and engaging with system-impacted communities . . . a world where Black lives matter through investments in housing, education, health, and environmental justice."

Black Lives Matter advocates and similar activists have a sweeping, aggressive agenda. This in and of itself is neither inherently immoral nor particularly surprising. If *I* believed my country was murdering tens of thousands of my kinsmen annually, or that violent ethnic conflict was one of the hallmarks of living here, or that every facially neutral system was rigged against me in some convoluted and secretive fashion, I would be up in arms—perhaps quite literally. However, there is a simple reason that I am not. Almost none of the common beliefs that underlie the arguments of these noisy, angry radicals are correct.

While the United States of America is indeed an imperfect human-founded country with a bloody history, virtually every major empirical claim made by contemporary race activists is just factually false. The Crump-Biko argument that American police officers are "murdering" or "genociding" hundreds or thousands (or tens of thousands?) of innocent Black men annually provides the clearest possible illustration of this. As I note in my book *Taboo*, well-maintained databases of police homicides, such as Killed by Police and the *Washington Post* newspaper's The Counted project have existed online for years.[12] Per the *Post*, only about 1,000 citizens total are shot and killed by on-duty police officers in a typical year: across all races, sexes, and weapons categories and out of up to 60 million annual police-citizen encounters. Nine hundred and ninety-seven such killings occurred in 2015, 963 in 2016, 987 in 2017, 983 in 2018, 999 in 2019, and 1,020 in 2020.

The very large majority of these police shooting victims and police killing victims are not Black. Across the same set of years, 258 individuals identified as Black were fatally shot by American police officers in 2015 (25.8 percent of that year's total); 238 (24.7 percent) in 2016; 224 (22.7 percent) in 2017; 228 (23.1 percent) in 2018; 252 (25.2 percent) in 2019; and 242 (23.7 percent) in 2020. Interestingly, the most recent post–George Floyd surge in Black Lives Matter activism seems to have barely impacted these annual totals: 233 Black Yanks were fatally shot by police in 2021, and 218 had been fatally shot in 2022 when I conducted a search in early December. Even more notably: while these totals could theoretically be boosted by the relatively small number of police shooting victims who remain race-unknown, there has been no recent year in which the African-American percentage of police homicides has reached even 30 percent.

The number of unarmed Black men killed annually by police is tiny even in comparison to the number of overall and African American police killings. To review the same years in order—hopefully without becoming mind-numbingly dull—the United States saw 38 shootings of unarmed Black citizens (17 by white cops) in the somewhat atypical year of 2015; 20 in 2016; 21 in 2017; 22 in 2018; 12 in 2019; and 18 in 2020.[13] Once again, Blacks made up a small minority of the *unarmed* citizens shot by police: there were 95 total unarmed victims in 2015, 64 in 2016, 71 in 2017, 58 in 2018, 54 in 2019, and 60 in 2020.

In no recent year, across all races and sexes, were even one hundred unarmed Americans shot by police: the year-by-year mean Black percentage of such shootings was just 31.8 percent. To a remarkable extent, the national mass media deals with this fact by ignoring it. Stories about killer cops murdering unarmed men ("Hands up, don't shoot!!!") have dominated national media coverage for literally the past ten years, and almost 90 percent of such coverage seems to focus on the atypical African American 20 to 30 percent of shootings. A brief cookies-deleted search for "well-known police shooting" done in 2019 for my book *Taboo* turned up two cases involving a Hispanic victim, three cases involving a white victim, and thirty-six cases featuring a Black victim within the first ten pages of results.

It might be objected that this is because the police-shootings data, if nothing else, reveal Blacks' *overrepresentation* among victims of law enforcement violence. African Americans, after all, make up less than 14 percent of the United States population but did represent more than 20 percent of cop-killing victims in every year on record—which might indicate racism.[14] However, a very simple reason for this apparent discrepancy exists: the Black crime rate (and thus police encounter rate) is currently significantly higher than the white rate. This can be easily established using uncontested data provided annually by the federal government, such as the annual Bureau of Justice Statistics abstracts from the United States DOJ.

According to that very source, in the typical pre-Floyd year of 2018, America's whites committed 2,669,900 serious violent "Index" crimes. This included 62.1 percent of 3,581,360 total such offenses against other whites (i.e., 2,224,025 total crimes); 10.6 percent of the 563,940 offenses with a Black/African American victim (59,778); 28.2 percent of the 734,410 offenses with a Hispanic or Latino victim (207,104); and 24.1 percent of all 182,230 crimes with an Asian American victim (43,917). Empirically, and unsurprisingly, most criminals in the United States are white.

In contrast, Black Americans committed 1,115,670 crimes—including 15.3 percent of all those committed against whites (547,948); an astonishing 70.3 percent of those committed against Blacks (396,450); 15.3 percent of those targeting Latinos (112,365); and 27.5 percent of offenses against Asians (50,113). All in, the U.S. white population committed 239 percent as many crimes as the Black population (let us not forget this) but did so while bulking almost exactly 500 percent as large.

Given these data points—there are roughly five times as many whites in the United States as there are Blacks—the Department of Justice itself and virtually the entire range of the statistical commentariat, from Tim Wise on the left to Maury Richards on the right, have concluded that the Black rate of serious/violent crime is 2.3 to 2.5 times the white rate. A simple adjustment for this disparity essentially closes the "police shooting gap." In fact, as Harvard University's Roland G. Fryer Jr. pointed out in a recent paper, complex "regression" models that adjust for various factors like defendant behavior find that African Americans stopped or detained by the police are about 30 percent less likely to be shot than are *equivalent* white suspects.[15]

The same Bureau of Justice Statistics tables that summarize the annual rates of crime by race put the lie to the "BBQ Becky"–inspired claim that Black Americans are constantly being harassed and attacked by white people. First and notably, given the extent to which the modern national media promotes racial tensions, it is remarkable how monochromatic serious crime in the United States is. As noted above, 62.1 percent of the 3,581,360 violent Index crimes targeting whites were committed by whites, while 37.9 percent were committed by members of all other races combined. To put these figures in context, the population of the United States is currently almost identical: 62.3 percent non-Hispanic white and 37.7 percent non-white.

Even more strikingly, 70.3 percent of all violent crimes against Black Americans, including the assault and aggravated assault offenses generally associated with harassment and hate crime, involved only a Black perpetrator. Nearly 50 percent of attacks on Hispanics were also committed by co-racialists identified only as "Hispanic/Latino" despite Hispanics being a widely dispersed population whose members can technically be part of any biological race.[16] Rather remarkably, "classic interracial crimes"—violent offenses involving either a white or a Black perpetrator and a victim of the other race—made up only 11 percent of the pool of violent Index crimes that we are discussing (607,726 offenses out of 5,479,590) and just 3 percent of the 20,828,040 crimes of all kinds reported across the United States during 2018. With complete accuracy, it can be said that the violent inter-race crime beloved of the news cameras makes up about 3 percent of all crime.

And there's more. Venturing into *Taboo* territory, it has to be noted that recent-past interracial crime in the United States has been not only very rare but almost entirely Black-on-white. Per the Bureau of Justice Statistics figures, of the 607,726 violent offenses involving Blacks and Caucasians that took place in 2018, 547,948 were Black-on-white crimes, while just 59,778 were white-on-Black crimes.

That 90 percent figure, recorded during a busy police year that obviously witnessed significant racial tensions on the ground, is somewhat atypical. However, interracial serious crime involving only Blacks and whites has been more than 70 percent Black-on-white during every recent year for which data exists. It should be noted, further, that Bureau of Justice Statistics data is based upon direct victim reports, which are compiled by trained interlocutors during an anonymous census-style annual survey, rather than on police reporting: it is considered something of a gold standard in social science, and it is highly unlikely that racial bias in any direction swayed these figures. Simply put, Black Americans assault and otherwise target white Americans far more often than the reverse happens.

At some level, this is not very surprising. While the actual math involved in predicting what rates of interracial crime "should" be gets far more complicated than this, it is hard not to notice that there are five times as many white potential targets for crimes in the United States as there are Black ones—and they have more money, something a robber might seek. However, although the Department of Justice's cold empirical figures might not run counter to logic, they certainly run counter to narrative.

Like the storyline about white policemen killing Black men for little or no reason, the widely shared belief that white rogues—à la the execrable Dylann Roof, or the "white" George Zimmerman, or the killers of Ahmaud Arbery—are an ever-present threat to Black life has been a significant part of the American zeitgeist for perhaps a decade. Stories that fit this bill very frequently receive sensationalistic coverage, while those that cut in the other direction are ignored entirely or even minimized.[17] However, as has often been the case throughout this book, a simple examination of hard data reveals that what many of our countrymen believe to be obvious reality is in fact almost the opposite of the truth.

The phenomenon of popular "woke" ideas, including formal theories widely taught throughout higher and secondary education, collapsing when confronted with empirical data extends well beyond policing and crime. Almost every time the narrative of "systemic racism" is subjected to serious quantitative analysis, it fails completely. As noted earlier, the primary argument of systemic-bias advocates such as Dr. Ibram X. Kendi and Robin DiAngelo is that pervasive contemporary racism must permeate society because this is the only possible explanation for the gaps that we see between large racial and ethnic groups in terms of variables like income, unless we wish to embrace fringe theories of "inferiority."

However, this is simply not the case. Serious social scientists, many themselves members of minority groups—Thomas Sowell, Walter E. Williams, John Ogbu, Amy Chua, Heather Mac Donald, June O'Neill, William Julius Wilson on the leftward side of the fence—have pointed out for perhaps fifty years that large human populations differ in performance because of literally dozens of factors stretching far beyond the simplistic dual options of "genes" and "racism." As a first-stage proof of case here, the range in household income between non-Hispanic American *white* groups is more than 100 percent, with Iraqi Christian migrants ($49,315) earning less than half as much on average as Australians ($100,856)—and gigantic populations like Italian Americans ($82,106), Irishmen ($76,036), and Cajuns ($68,383) falling in between.[18]

Clearly, neither significant genetic differences or race bigotry can explain these gaps among closely related Caucasian populations. And they are notable: many of the disparities just mentioned are much bigger than the household income gap between Blacks and whites—which currently sits at about $20,000, before adjustment for the smaller size of Black households. A short list of predictors that *might* explain them would have to include cultural variables (i.e., attitudes toward school and study), region of residence for each group, the structural and environmental factors that matter in each of those places—does state welfare policy influence household size?—and even things that differ between people(s) due to pure stochastic chance . . . what we used to call luck.

One very important and utterly non-controversial example of such a "stochastic independent variable" is age: the average age of each population. According to Pew Research, the (modal) average age for white Americans is fifty-eight, while the equivalent figure for Black Americans is currently just twenty-seven.[19] The modal age for Hispanics—the most common age for U.S. Latinos, across all areas of the country and among both men and women—is *eleven*. Massive differences such as these—which have a great deal to do with immigration and religion and luck, and nothing whatsoever to do with genetic inferiority—will obviously be reflected in every imaginable group outcome, from crime rate to average level of wealth.

A similarly relevant factor variable is simply geography: where people live. As of 2020, near majorities of both American Blacks and Hispanics still reside in the South or Southwest, the regions historically associated with these peoples, while a far smaller percentage of non-Hispanic whites (approximately 15 percent) does. This matters because incomes—and educational board scores—have traditionally been much lower in these "tough" agrarian regions than in the rest of the country.[20] Once again, noting these outcomes without adjusting for the regional and cultural differences that actually predict them borders on the dishonest.

Test scores themselves obviously vary widely among populations and in turn predict income and other success metrics. According to a well-done analysis by Inside Higher Ed several years back, the average SAT scores for U.S.-born test-takers are currently 941 for Blacks/African Americans, 963 for Native Americans and Alaskan "Eskimos," 986 for Native Hawaiians and other Pacific Islanders, 987 for Hispanics or Latinos, 1,118 for whites, and almost 1,200 for Asian Americans.[21]

These results once again have little if anything to do with modern racism—dark-skinned South and East Asians beat whites by more than 60 points—and seem to be predicted by the mundane variable of time spent studying. The left-leaning Brookings Institution (of all places) recently released a report showing that "white high school students study nearly twice as much as Black high-school students, with Hispanics falling in between the two"[22] and Asian Americans outperforming everybody else. Once again, these score and study differences are highly predictive of other dependent variables, including not only later-life income but also high school grades and the decision to attend college.

The most comprehensive point against the "systemic racism" argument may have been scored by the (left-leaning, if I recall correctly) economist June O' Neill, who writes on human capital. In a widely cited 1990 paper and its 2005 follow-up,[23] O'Neill—and we come to this point again—evaluates the Black-white income gap by using an actual multivariate regression analysis that adjusted for group difference in age, region of residence, standardized test scores, and a very few other variables such as number of years of education.

To quote from one quantitative review of her piece: "Overall, Black men earned 82.9 percent of the white wage." However, simply "adjusting for Black-white difference in geographic region, schooling, and age raises the ratio to 87.7 percent; adding differences in [standardized] test scores raises the ratio to 95.5 percent, and adding differences in years of work experiences raises the ratio to 99.1 percent."[24] As I note in my book *Taboo*, "At least in the modern era, less than 1 percent of the wage gap between Black and white males appears directly attributable to racism."

Other well-done studies, which look at a range of potential influences on the dependent variable—beyond simply "racism" (or genetics)—frequently, if not almost invariably, come to similar conclusions. In 2017, perhaps most notably, Harvard University's Roland Fryer found no statistically significant differences between the rates at which whites and African Americans are shot by police officers—after adding basic controls for "civilian behavior" and other "important context."[25] Indeed, white suspects proved to be 27.5 percent more likely to be shot by police officers than Black suspects, *with all else held equal.*

At some level, this "shocking" result is completely logically un-surprising. The actual and rather obvious reason that Black Americans encounter the police more often than whites, in the first place, is simply that the Black rate of violent crime is 2.4 times the white rate.[26] And, when such encounters do happen, police officers—few of whom are extreme bigots and more than a third of whom are themselves minorities[27]—tend to be what Fryer calls "utility maximizers," who certainly do not want their careers ruined by claims of involvement in a racist murder. Racism, in any real sense, exists only where otherwise identical individuals are treated differently due to the single variable of race. In this context as in many others, empirical comparison of the experiences of very similar people of different races strongly indicates that contemporary systemic racism does not exist at all.

And cultural appropriation? That's just trade. Any actually coherent definition of "appropriation"—borrowing things from other racial and social groups, for example—would render almost everything that we do socially taboo if not illegal. A typical urban Kentucky lunch for me on any given Tuesday might involve driving my German car to a Chinese American owned Mexican restaurant to meet up with two Black colleagues, and I strongly suspect that this is not unusual. Should it be verboten?

Even if we define CA to include borrowings only from groups whom one's own "team" has oppressed or warred with, this would still make perhaps *half* of everything taboo. The United States fought the nation of Japan in a bloody war characterized by brutal mutual atrocities, which is in fact discussed in this book, and beat her—while Japanese Americans were shamefully incarcerated in state-side camps. Terrible stuff, to be sure. But does this really mean that no Caucasian or Black Americans can ethically prepare Japanese-style sushi, or at least do so for sale? Fisherman's Wharf and Portland Fish Market would be hard hit indeed, should we suddenly decide on this as a societal norm.

The tough and unintentionally hilarious questions keep coming. Do anti-appropriation American *baizuo* expect any *sort of* reciprocity here, one wonders: i.e., for Japanese or Chinese businessmen to switch from their tailored Brooks Brothers suits to traditional robes to avoid offending the delicate sensibilities of butter-soft Westerners from a rival state? For that matter, here in America, how is this new rule supposed to apply in practice among members of different minority groups—who now make up some 40 percent of the population?[28] Asians and indeed Blacks have significantly higher personal incomes than Hispanics and certainly than recent immigrants.[29] Does this mean that our Latino citizens can borrow from African Americans and "Easterners," but not vice versa? And so on. At root an attempt to problematize the plain reality of citizens learning from their friendly neighbors, cultural appropriation may genuinely be one of the stupidest ideas ever dreamed up.

No race war is currently ongoing in the United States, American police shoot fewer than thirty unarmed Black men annually, interracial crime is rare indeed and largely minority-on-white, and most varieties of "systemic racism" very arguably do not exist at all. Today as in the past, reality remains complex, multivariate, and fascinating—and many of the things that "all decent people know" about it just are not actually true.

NOTES

INTRODUCTION

1. Mitchell Langbert et al, "Faculty Voter Registration in Economics, History, Journalism, Law, and Psychology," Character Issues, *Econ Journal Watch* 13, no. 3 (September 2016), 422–51, https://econjwatch.org/articles/faculty-voter-registration-in-economics-history -journalism-communications-law-and-psychology?ref=quillette.com; Jeffrey Dvorkin, "Pew Study: Journalists and Liberal Bias," NPR, June 2, 2004, https://www.npr.org /sections/publiceditor/2004/06/02/1919999/pew-study-journalists-and-liberal-bias.

2. The linking of slavery with group traits like "race" or ethnicity, although it reached new levels of intensity in the post-1700s New World, was in fact not a uniquely Western practice. As multiple scholarly sources note, including this one—John Hunwick, "Arab Views of Black Africans and Slavery," *West Africa, Islam, and the Arab World*, (Princeton, NJ: Markus Weiner Publishers, 2006), https://glc.yale.edu/sites/default/files/files /events/race/Hunwick.pdf—Arab slave masters very specifically felt themselves superior to specific groups, including the aforementioned Blacks and Slavs, and in fact were often racist to the extent of associating specific job tasks with certain groups of slaves. Religion-based slavery was even more common historically, with Christians and Muslims often seeing it as lawful to enslave both followers of the other great monotheistic faith and "infidels," but not coreligionists: David Brion Davis, "Slavery—White, Black, Muslim, Christian," *New York Review of Books*, July 5, 2001, https://www.nybooks.com /articles/2001/07/05/slavery-white-black-muslim-christian.

3. Andrew Lambert and Robert Tombs, "The Royal Navy's Campaign Against the Slave Trade," *History Reclaimed*, October 12, 2022, https://historyreclaimed.co.uk/the-royal -navys-campaign-against-the-slave-trade/.

4. "Exploitation and Abuse of Migrant Workers in Saudi Arabia," Human Rights Watch, July 2004, https://www.hrw.org/reports/2004/saudi0704/1.htm.

5. Burton Stein, *A History of India*, 2nd ed. (Chichester, West Sussex, UK: Wiley and Blackwell, 2010), 164, https://books.google.com/books?id=QY4zdTDwMAQC&pg =PA159#v=onepage&q&f=false.

6. To be ecumenical in my criticisms of man and his dark potential, the decidedly Western Confederacy held first place. "Sokoto Caliphate," Global Security, accessed January 2, 2024, https://www.globalsecurity.org/military/world/nigeria/sokoto.htm.

1: "BRUTAL 'TRUE' SLAVERY WAS VIRTUALLY UNIQUE TO AMERICA AND THE WEST"

1. Raymond Pierce, "What Is Gained By Denying America's Original Sin?," *Forbes*, February 4, 2022, https://www.forbes.com/sites/raymondpierce/2022/02/04/what-is-gained

-by-denying-americas-original-sin/; "Slavery: America's Original Sin," *UC Davis Course Catalog*, accessed October 25, 2023, https://cpe.ucdavis.edu/course/slavery-americas -original-sin-part-1.

2. Nikole Hannah-Jones, "Our Democracy's Founding Ideals Were False When They Were Written. Black Americans Have Fought to Make Them True," *New York Times Magazine*, August 14, 2019, https://www.nytimes.com/interactive/2019/08/14/magazine/black -history-american-democracy.html.

3. Alan Brinkley et al., *The Unfinished Nation: A Concise History of the American People*, 8th ed. (New York: McGraw Hill, 2016), 17, https://archive.org/details/unfinishednationooooobrin _m3s2/page/16/mode/2up?view=theater.

4. Jerry H. Bentley et al., *Traditions and Encounters*, 4th ed. (New York: McGraw Hill, 2016), 277, https://archive.org/details/traditionsencounooooobent_r2v5/page/276/mode/2up ?view=theater.

5. Diane Ravitch, "The 1619 Project: Essay by Nikole Hannah-Jones," *Diane Ravitch's Blog*, June 5, 2021, https://dianeravitch.net/2021/06/06/the-1619-project-essay-by-nikole -hannah-jones/.

6. Kay S. Hymowitz, "Uniquely Bad—but Not Uniquely American," *City Journal*, October 16, 2020, https://www.city-journal.org/slavery-failure-of-1619-project.

7. "The 1619 Project Curriculum," Pulitzer Center, https://pulitzercenter.org/lesson -plan-grouping/1619-project-curriculum.

8. Raymond Westbrook, "Slave and Master in Ancient Near Eastern Law," *Chicago-Kent Law Review* 70, no. 4 (June 1995): 1631, https://scholarship.kentlaw.iit.edu/cgi/viewcontent .cgi?article=3004&context=cklawreview.

9. I. J. Gelb, "Prisoners of War in Early Mesopotamia," *Journal of Near Eastern Studies* 32, nos. 1–2 (January–April 1973), https://doi.org/10.1086/372223, https://www.journals .uchicago.edu/doi/abs/10.1086/372223?journalCode=jnes.

10. Dan Lowe, "Aristotle's Defense of Slavery," 1000-Word Philosophy, September 10, 2019, https://1000wordphilosophy.com/2019/09/10/aristotles-defense-of-slavery/.

11. Robert Garland, "The Principles of Slavery in Ancient Greece," Wondrium Daily, August 11, 2020, https://web.archive.org/web/20230304071642/https://www.wondrium daily.com/the-principles-of-slavery-in-ancient-greece/, transcribed from "The Other Side of History: Daily Life in the Ancient World," https://www.thegreatcourses.com/courses /the-other-side-of-history-daily-life-in-the-ancient-world.

12. W. V. Harris, "Demography, Geography, and the Sources of Roman Slaves: (1999)," in *Rome's Imperial Economy: Twelve Essays* (Oxford, 2011; online edition: Oxford Academic, March 16, 2015), accessed October 25, 2023, https://doi.org/10.1093/acprof:osobl /9780199595167.003.0005, https://academic.oup.com/book/26320/chapter-abstract /194591276?redirectedFrom=fulltext.

13. "Zanj Rebellion," *Encyclopedia Britannica*, September 19, 2018, accessed October 30, 2023, https://www.britannica.com/event/Zanj-rebellion.

14. Bernard Lewis, *The Arabs in History* (London: Hutchinson, 1968), 104, https://archive .org/details/arabsinhistoryooooolewi/mode/2up?view=theater.

15. Alexandre Popovic, *The Revolt of African Slaves in Iraq in the 3rd/9th Century* (Princeton, NJ: Marcus Weiner Publishers, 1999), 154, https://archive.org/details /revoltofafricansooooopopo/mode/2up?view=theater.

16. Robert McKinney, *The Case of Rhyme Versus Reason: Ibn al-Rūmī and His Poetics in Context* (Leiden, Netherlands: Brill, 2004), 468, https://books.google.com/books?id =kfjbp_dVNYC.

17. Theodor Noldeke, *Sketches from Eastern History* (London: Adam and Charles Black, 1892), https://archive.org/details/in.ernet.dli.2015.206950.

18. Silja Fröhlich, "East Africa's Forgotten Slave Trade," Deutsche Welle, August 22, 2019, https://www.dw.com/en/east-africas-forgotten-slave-trade/a-50126759.

19. Leda Ferrant, *Tippu Tip and the East African Slave Trade* (New York: St. Martin's, 1975), https://books.google.com/books?id=McO4AAAAIAAJ.

20. "Tippu Tib," *Encyclopedia Britannica*, June 10, 2023, accessed October 25, 2023, https://www.britannica.com/biography/Tippu-Tib; Sidney Langford Hinde, *The Fall of the Congo Arabs* (Whitefish, Montana: Kessinger Publishing, 2008), https://www.amazon.com/Congo-Arabs-Sidney-Langford-Hinde/dp/1437408656.

21. Henry Morton Stanley, *Through the Dark Continent* (London: Sampson Low, 1890), https://www.loc.gov/item/2021666780.

22. D. J. Trotter, "Did Tippu Tip Lead an Army of Cannibals?," Congo Safari, October 2019. http://www.congosafari.com/cannibals/Tippu-Tip-cannibal-army.html.

23. A full PDF of Tipp's book can be found here: Michelle Decker, "The 'Autobiography' of Tippu Tip," *Interventions* 17, no. 5 (2015): 744–58, https://doi.org/10.1080/1369801X.2014.987800, https://www.academia.edu/34412584/The_Autobiography_of_Tippu_Tip_Geography_Genre_and_the_African_Indian_Ocean.

24. Abdul Sheriff, *Slaves, Spices, and Ivory in Zanzibar* (Athens: Ohio University Press, 1987), https://www.amazon.com/Slaves-Spices-Ivory-Zanzibar-Integration/dp/0821408720.

25. Robert Davis, "British Slaves on the Barbary Coast," BBC, February 17, 2011, https://www.bbc.co.uk/history/british/empire_seapower/white_slaves_01.shtml.

26. David Eltis and Stanley L. Engerman, eds., *The Cambridge World History of Slavery*, vol. 3 (Cambridge, UK: Cambridge University Press, 2011), https://www.cambridge.org/core/books/cambridge-world-history-of-slavery/893A3906E0372FFBBC596302859EDB9D.

27. Robert Davis, *Christian Slaves, Muslim Masters* (New York: Macmillan, 2004), 5.

28. Muzaffar Husain, Syed Saud Akhtar, and B. D. Usmani, *Concise History of Islam* (New Delhi: Vij Books India, 2011), 454, https://archive.org/details/statepaperspubli1ogrea/page/6/mode/2up?view=theater.

29. "Turgut Reis," *New World Encyclopedia*, accessed December 21, 2023, https://www.newworldencyclopedia.org/entry/Turgut_Reis.

30. Davis, "British Slaves on the Barbary Coast."

31. "Battle Studies, Country Studies, & Staff Rides: Barbary Wars & the Battle of Tripoli," Marine Corps University Research Library, October 24, 2023, https://grc-usmcu.libguides.com/battle-studies/barbary-wars.

32. Martina Petkova, "The Word 'Slave' Came from My People: How Slavs and Racism Go Hand-in-Hand," An Injustice!, April 6, 2021, https://aninjusticemag.com/the-word-slave-came-from-my-people-443b5ee6d53d.

33. Don Jordan and Michael Walsh, *White Cargo* (New York: NYU Press, 2008).

34. T. H. Breen and Stephen Innes, *"Myne Owne Ground": Race and Freedom on Virginia's Eastern Shore, 1640–1676* (New York: Oxford University Press, 1980), 7, https://archive.org/details/myneownegroundr00bree/mode/2up?view=theater.

35. Rosemarie McAphee, "'Black and White' in Colonial Virginia," *Footsteps* 4, no. 3 (May–June 2002), https://go.gale.com/ps/i.do?p=ITOF&id=GALE%7CA87350120&v=2.1&it=r&sid=lms&userGroupName=anon%7E824d58ff&aty=open-web-entry.

36. John Conway, *A Look at the Thirteenth and Fourteenth Amendments: Slavery Abolished, Equal Protection Established* (Berkeley Heights, NJ: MyReportLinks.com Books, 2009), 5.

37. George F. MacDonald, "The Haida: Children of Eagle and Raven: Haida Villages: War-fare," Canadian Museum of History, https://www.historymuseum.ca/cmc/exhibitions/aborig/haida/havwao1e.html.

38. Tony Seybert, "Slavery and Native Americans in British North America and the United States: 1600 to 1865," Slavery in America, 2009, https://web.archive.org/web/20120204122412/http://www.slaveryinamerica.org/history/hs_es_indians_slavery.htm.

39. "U.S. Population, 1790–2020: Always Growing," u-s history, https://www.u-s-history.com/pages/h980.html.

40. Ryan Smith, "How Native American Slaveholders Complicate the Trail of Tears Narrative," *Smithsonian*, March 6, 2018, https://www.smithsonianmag.com/smithsonian-institution/how-native-american-slaveholders-complicate-trail-tears-narrative-180968339/.

41. Philip Morgan, "Origins of American Slavery," in *America on the World Stage: A Global Approach to U.S. History*, Gary W. Reichard, Ted Dickson, and Organization of American Historians, eds. (Urbana: University of Illinois Press, 2008), 44.

42. Jennie Cohen, "Civil War Deadlier Than Previously Thought?," History, August 31, 2018, https://www.history.com/news/civil-war-deadlier-than-previously-thought.

43. "Value of $1 from 1865 to 2023," in2013dollars, accessed October 25, 2023, https://www.in2013dollars.com/us/inflation/1865?amount=1.

44. "The Blockade of Africa: How Royal Navy Ships Fought the Slave Trade," History, https://www.history.co.uk/article/the-blockade-of-africa-how-royal-naval-ships-suppressed-the-slave-trade.

45. "Anti-Slave Trade Patrols," National Museum of the U.S. Navy, February 27, 2023, https://www.history.navy.mil/content/history/museums/nmusn/explore/prior-exhibits/2020/anti-slave-trade-patrols.html.

46. "Arabs and Muslims Own Black Slaves in Five African Countries," American Anti-Slavery Group, https://www.iabolish.org/arabs-and-muslims-own-black-slaves-in-five-african-countries/.

47. Nima Elbagir et al., "People for Sale: Where Lives Are Auctioned for $400," CNN, November 15, 2017, https://www.cnn.com/2017/11/14/africa/libya-migrant-auctions/index.html.

48. "Nigeria Chibok Abductions: What We Know," BBC, May 8, 2017, https://www.bbc.com/news/world-africa-32299943.

49. United States Department of State, "U.S. Department of State Country Report on Human Rights Practices 1993—Mauritania," Refworld (United Nations High Commissioner for Refugees), January 30, 1994, https://www.refworld.org/docid/3ae6aa4d8.html.

50. John Sutter and Edythe McNamee, "Slavery's Last Stronghold," CNN, March 2023, https://www.cnn.com/interactive/2012/03/world/mauritania.slaverys.last.stronghold/index.html.

51. Dinesh D'Souza, "Two Cheers for Colonialism," SFGate, July 7, 2002, https://www.sfgate.com/opinion/article/Two-cheers-for-colonialism-2799327.php.

2: "THE 'RED SCARE' WAS A MORAL PANIC THAT CAUGHT NO COMMIES"

1. "3.2—McCarthyism and Profiling," Asian American Education Project, https://asianamericanedu.org/mccarthyism-and-racial-profiling.html.

2. Robert Divine et al., *America, Past and Present*, 8th ed., vol. 2 (New York: Pearson,

2007), 825–27, https://archive.org/details/americapastpreseooo2unse/page/826/mode/2up?view=theater.

3. Divine et al., *America, Past and Present*.

4. If one that "by the early 1950s occasionally reached the point of hysteria." Brinkley, *Unfinished Nation*, 674–75.

5. Ed Rampell, "Reckless Cruelty: The Joe McCarthy Story," *Progressive*, December 1, 2019, https://progressive.org/magazine/reckless-cruelty-the-joe-mccarthy-story-rampell/.

6. Michael Bernick, "Why the Lies of 'Trumbo' Matter," *San Francisco Chronicle*, December 31, 2015, https://www.sfchronicle.com/opinion/article/Why-the-lies-of-Trumbo-matter-6730745.php.

7. M. Stanton Evans, *Blacklisted by History* (New York: Three Rivers Press, 2007), 25.

8. Robert Novak, "McCarthy=Bad," *Weekly Standard*, November 26, 2007, https://web.archive.org/web/20181216020043/https://www.weeklystandard.com/robert-d-novak/mccarthy-bad.

9. Novak, "McCarthy=Bad."

10. Andrea Friedman, "The Strange Career of Annie Lee Moss: Rethinking Race, Gender, and McCarthyism," *Journal of American History* 94, no. 2 (2007): 445–68, https://doi.org/10.2307/25094960.

11. Godfrey Cheshire, "Trumbo," RogerEbert.com, November 6, 2015, https://www.rogerebert.com/reviews/trumbo-2015.

12. Ron Capshaw, "Film the Legend," Law and Liberty, November 30, 2015, https://lawliberty.org/film-the-legend/.

13. John Earl Haynes and Harvey Klehr, *Venona: Decoding Soviet Espionage in America* (New Haven, CT: Yale University Press, 1999), https://vdoc.pub/documents/venona-decoding-soviet-espionage-in-america-5uchvhgnbnbo, hosted at https://archive.nytimes.com/www.nytimes.com/books/first/h/haynes-venona.html?_r=1.

14. Daniel Patrick Moynihan et al., "The Experience of the Bomb," in *Report of the Commission on Protecting and Reducing Government Secrecy*, Appendix A (1987), A-36–37, https://web.archive.org/web/20110721041005/http://origin.www.gpo.gov/congress/commissions/secrecy/pdf/12hist1.pdf.

15. Moynihan et al., "The Experience of the Bomb," A-39.

16. Daniel Patrick Moynihan, *Secrecy* (New Haven, CT: Yale University Press, 1998), 146, https://archive.org/details/secrecyamericaneoomoyn.

17. Haynes and Klehr, *Venona*.

18. "People mentioned in The VENONA files," Geni, https://www.geni.com/projects/People-mentioned-in-The-VENONA-files/4490030.

19. John Elson, "Gentleman and a Spy?," *Time*, November 25, 1996, https://web.archive.org/web/20070705102235/http://www.time.com/time/magazine/article/0,9171,985571-1,00.html.

20. *How the Specter of Communism Is Ruling Our World*, Chapter Five, Part I: "Infiltrating the West," https://www.thespecterofcommunism.com/en/en-chapter-5/.

21. Al Fuller, "Whitewashing Communism," Other Half of History, January 24, 2010, https://historyhalf.com/whitewashing-communism/.

22. Alexander G. Lovelace, "Spies in the News: Soviet Espionage in the American Media During World War II and the Beginning of the Cold War," *Journal of Slavic Military Studies* 28, no. 2 (2015): 307–27, https://doi.org/10.1080/13518046.2015.1030265, https://www.tandfonline.com/doi/abs/10.1080/13518046.2015.1030265?tab=permissions&scroll=top.

23. Eric Fettmann, "Castro's Publicist and Other Communist Apologists of the Fourth Estate," *New York Post*, March 28, 2001, https://nypost.com/2001/03/28/castros -publicist-and-other-communist-apologists-of-the-fourth-estate/.

24. Kenneth Billingsley, "Hollywood's Missing Movies," *Reason*, June 2000, https://reason .com/2000/06/01/hollywoods-missing-movies/.

25. Godfrey Cheshire, "Trumbo."

26. Louis Budenz, "Invading Education," in *The Techniques of Communism* (1954). Hosted at Metropolis.cafe, https://metropolis.cafe/2020/10/27/the-techniques-of-communism -invading-education/.

27. J. B. Matthews, "Communism and the Colleges," https://www.scribd.com/document /324822226/Communism-and-the-Colleges-J-B-Mathhews.

28. Kevin Lindemann, "African American Communist: W. E. B. Du Bois (1868–1963)," Communist Party USA, February 28, 2009, https://www.cpusa.org/party_info/african -american-communist-w-e-b-du-bois-1868-1963/.

29. Bryan Caplan, "The Prevalence of Marxism in Academia," Econlib, March 31, 2015, https://www.econlib.org/archives/2015/03/the_prevalence_1.html.

30. Sean Salai, "U.S. Adults Increasingly Accept Marxist Views, Poll Shows," *Washington Times*, October 6, 2021, https://www.washingtontimes.com/news/2021/oct/6/us-adults -increasingly-accept-marxist-views-poll/.

31. Matthew Sharpe, "Is 'Cultural Marxism' Really Taking Over Universities? I Crunched Some Numbers to Find Out," Conversation, September 7, 2020, https://theconversation .com/is-cultural-marxism-really-taking-over-universities-i-crunched-some-numbers-to -find-out-139654.

32. Thurston Powers, "How Black Lives Matter Is Bringing Back Traditional Marxism," Federalist, September 28, 2016, https://thefederalist.com/2016/09/28/black-lives -matter-bringing-back-traditional-marxism/.

33. Wilfred Reilly, "Black Lives Matter's Missing Billions," Spiked Online, February 14, 2022, https://www.spiked-online.com/2022/02/14/black-lives-matters-missing -billions/.

34. Ashe Schow, "462 Financial Journalists Were Asked Their Political Leanings. Guess How Many Said They Were Conservative," Daily Wire, November 13, 2018, https://www .dailywire.com/news/462-financial-journalists-were-asked-their-ashe-schow.

35. "How Journalists View Journalists: IV. Values and the Press," Pew Research Center, May 23, 2004, https://www.people-press.org/2004/05/23/iv-values-and-the-press/.

36. Hanna Panreck, "NPR Reports Republican Candidates' 'Claims of Liberal Media Bias' Are a 'Political Tactic,'" August 8, 2022, https://www.foxnews.com/media/npr-reports -republican-candidates-claims-liberal-media-bias-political-tactic?intcmp=tw_fnc.

37. "2016 General Election Editorial Endorsements by Major Newspapers," American Presidency Project, https://www.presidency.ucsb.edu/statistics/data/2016-general -election-editorial-endorsements-major-newspapers.

38. "2016 Electoral College Results," National Archives, January 11, 2021, https://www .archives.gov/electoral-college/2016.

39. "COVID-19 Opinion Tracker," Kekst CNC, July 10, 2020, https://www.kekstcnc .com/media/2793/kekstcnc_research_covid-19_opinion_tracker_wave-4.pdf?fbclid =IwAR3HgPih2KPCdE8RUWogxBrn_yEMrNqDXdG16GYQPTj73Vkh23Jtb-tLH8U.

40. Megan Brenan, "Americans' Trust in Media Dips to Second Lowest on Record," Gallup, October 7, 2021, https://news.gallup.com/poll/355526/americans-trust-media-dips -second-lowest-record.aspx.

3: "NATIVE AMERICANS WERE 'PEACEFUL PEOPLE WHO SPENT ALL DAY DANCING'"

1. "Native American Contributions," Natural Resources Conservation Service, https://web.archive.org/web/20170119153246/https://www.nrcs.usda.gov/Internet/FSE_DOCUMENTS/nrcs141p2_024206.pdf.

2. Nancy Dieter Egloff, "'Six Nations of Ignorant Savages': Benjamin Franklin and the Iroquois League of Nations" (1987), Dissertations, Theses, and Masters Projects, William & Mary, Paper 1539625405, https://dx.doi.org/doi:10.21220/s2-bvqx-1y13.

3. "Native Americans Prior to 1492," History Central, https://www.historycentral.com/Indians/Before.html.

4. David Kennedy and Lizabeth Cohen, *The American Pageant*, 15th ed. (Boston: Cengage, 2014), 5.

5. Brinkley, *Unfinished Nation*, 431.

6. A. E. Larsen, "1492: The Conquest of Paradise: Framing the Story," An Historian Goes to the Movies, https://aelarsen.wordpress.com/category/1492-the-conquest-of-paradise/.

7. Lizzie Wade, "Feeding the Gods: Hundreds of Skulls Reveal Massive Scale of Human Sacrifice in Aztec Capital," *Science*, June 21, 2018, https://www.science.org/content/article/feeding-gods-hundreds-skulls-reveal-massive-scale-human-sacrifice-aztec-capital.

8. "Cannibalism," *Encyclopedia Britannica*, July 20, 1998, last updated December 4, 2023, https://www.britannica.com/topic/cannibalism-human-behaviour.

9. Robert Maclean, "Historia de Tlaxcala," Glasgow University Library Special Collections Department, January 2003, https://www.gla.ac.uk/myglasgow/library/files/special/exhibns/month/jan2003.html.

10. Bernard R. Ortiz de Montellano, "Aztec Cannibalism: An Ecological Necessity?," *Science* 200, no. 4342 (May 12, 1978): 611–17, https://ambergriscaye.com/pages/mayan/azteccannibalism.html.

11. Marvin Harris, *Cannibals and Kings* (New York: Random House, 1991), 235.

12. Thomas S. Abler, "Iroquois Cannibalism: Fact Not Fiction," *Ethnohistory* 27, no. 4, Special Iroquois Issue (Autumn 1980): 311, https://www.academia.edu/5099231/Iroquois_Cannibalism_Fact_Not_Fiction.

13. Barbara Alice Mann, *Iroquoian Women* (New York: Peter Lang, 2000), 36, https://archive.org/details/iroquoianwomenga0000mann/page/36/mode/2up?view=theater.

14. Donald Mitchell, "Predatory Warfare, Social Status, and the North Pacific Slave Trade," *Ethnology* 23, no. 1 (1984): 39–48, https://doi.org/10.2307/3773392, https://www.jstor.org/stable/pdf/3773392.pdf.

15. Divine et al., *America, Past and Present*, 484.

16. George F. MacDonald, "The Haida: Children of Eagle and Raven: Haida Villages: Warfare," Canadian Museum of History, https://www.historymuseum.ca/cmc/exhibitions/aborig/haida/havwao1e.html.

17. Christopher Muscato, "Dakota & Anishinaabe Peoples: Settling & Expansion of America," Study.com, https://study.com/academy/lesson/dakota-anishinaabe-peoples-settling-expansion-of-america.html.

18. "Sioux," *Encyclopedia Britannica*, July 20, 1998, last updated November 16, 2023, https://www.britannica.com/topic/Sioux.

19. Jeffrey D. Carlisle, "Apache Indian," Texas State Historical Association, September 29, 2020, https://www.tshaonline.org/handbook/entries/apache-indians#:~:text=The%20name%20Apache%20most%20probably,1000%20and%201400.

20. "Apache," *Encyclopedia Britannica*, July 20, 1998, last updated December 7, 2023, https://www.britannica.com/topic/Apache-people.

21. Laura Thompson and Elizabeth Prine Pauls, "Southwest Indian," *Encyclopedia Britannica*, July 26, 1999, last updated October 21, 2022, https://www.britannica.com/topic/Southwest-Indian.

22. Eric Sorenson, "WSU Researchers See Violent Era in Ancient Southwest," WSU Insider, Washington State University, August 4, 2014, https://news.wsu.edu/press-release/2014/08/04/wsu-researchers-see-violent-era-in-ancient-southwest/#.U9_iumNjYzJ.

23. Sorenson, "WSU Researchers See Violent Era."

24. Hampton Sides, *Blood and Thunder* (New York: Anchor Books, 2007), 266–67.

25. Paul N. Beck, *The First Sioux War: The Grattan Fight and Blue Water Creek, 1854–1856* (Lanham, MD: University Press of America, 2004), 39–41.

26. Beck, *First Sioux War*, 39–57; R. Eli Paul, *Blue Water Creek and the First Sioux War, 1854–1856* (Norman: University of Oklahoma Press, 2004), 18–24.

27. Cameron Addis, "The Whitman Massacre/Whitman Murders," *The Oregon Encyclopedia*, June 13, 2023, accessed November 14, 2023, https://www.oregonencyclopedia.org/articles/whitman_massacre/.

28. J. B. A. Brouillet, *Authentic Account of the Murder of Dr. Whitman and Other Missionaries by the Cayuse Indians of Oregon, in 1847* (Portland, Oregon: S. J. McCormack Press, 1869), https://www.loc.gov/item/03026826/.

29. Clifford Drury, *Marcus and Narcissa Whitman and the Opening of Old Oregon*, 2 vols. (Glendale, CA: Arthur H. Clark, 1973), 208.

30. Barbara Alice Mann, *The Tainted Gift: The Disease Method of Frontier Expansion* (Santa Barbara, CA: Praeger, 2009).

31. Drury, *Marcus and Narcissa Whitman*, 212–13.

32. William Mowry, *Marcus Whitman and the Early Days of Oregon* (New York: Silver, Burdett, 1901), 290, https://archive.org/details/marcuswhitmanearoomowr/page/224/mode/2up?view=theater.

33. Hampton Sides, *Blood and Thunder* (New York: Anchor Books, 2007), 301–3.

34. Sides, *Blood and Thunder*, 470.

35. Sides, *Blood and Thunder*, 159.

36. "Iroquois Wars," *The Canadian Encyclopedia*, February 7, 2006, last updated July 31, 2019, www.thecanadianencyclopedia.ca/en/article/iroquois-wars.

37. "The Beaver Wars," *Ohio History Central*, November 11, 2014, accessed December 2, 2023, https://www.ohiohistorycentral.org/w/index.php?title=Beaver_Wars.

38. R. Roy Johnson et al., eds., *Riparian Research and Management: Past, Present, Future*, vol. 1 (Fort Collins, CO: U.S. Department of Agriculture, Forest Service, Rocky Mountain Research Station, 2018), https://doi.org/10.2737/RMRS-GTR-377, https://www.fs.usda.gov/research/treesearch/57341#.

39. Kenneth Carley, *The Dakota War of 1862: Minnesota's Other Civil War* (St. Paul: Minnesota Historical Society Press, 2001), 2–6.

40. Carley, *The Dakota War of 1862*, 5.

41. "The US-Dakota War of 1862: The Acton Incident," Minnesota Historical Society, http://usdakotawar.org:80/history/acton-incident.

42. Gary Clayton Anderson, *Massacre in Minnesota: The Dakota War of 1862, the Most Violent Ethnic Conflict in American History* (Norman: University of Oklahoma Press, 2019).

43. Carrie Reber Zeman, compiler, "A Thrilling Narrative of Indian Captivity: Dispatches from the Dakota War of 1862; Camp Release List, Enumerated at Camp Release September 26, 1862," https://athrillingnarrative.com/captives-at-camp-release/list/.

44. "The US-Dakota War of 1862: Battle of Wood Lake," Minnesota Historical Society, https://www.usdakotawar.org/history/battle-wood-lake.

45. "US-Dakota War of 1862: Lower Sioux Agency," Minnesota Historical Society, https://www.mnhs.org/lowersioux/learn/us-dakota-war-1862.

46. Renae Cassimeda, "Lincoln, the Dakota 38 and the Racialist Falsification of History," World Socialist Web Site, November 9, 2020, https://www.wsws.org/en/articles/2020/11/09/dako-no9.html.

47. Stewart Huntington, "Historic Dakota Land Returns to Tribe," ICT News, March 29, 2021, https://ictnews.org/news/historic-dakota-land-returns-to-tribe.

48. Daniel Smith, "Did Settlers Commit Genocide in America?," History Is Now, May 21, 2020, www.historyisnowmagazine.com/blog/2020/5/17/did-settler-communities-commit-genocide-in-america?msclkid=93ed1ca7bdeo11ec8b399a671e3f47cf#.YoIHRFTMLIV=.

49. Sarah Laskow, "The Forgotten Black Pioneers Who Settled the Midwest," Atlas Obscura, June 14, 2018, https://www.atlasobscura.com/articles/black-pioneers-in-the-midwest?msclkid=5921bc4fbdc211eca12f899ce6b8fffd.

50. William DeLong, "The Forgotten Black Cowboys of the Wild West," All That's Interesting, March 24, 2018, https://allthatsinteresting.com/black-cowboys?msclkid=cc195eacbdc211ec952f39b47d0f197c.

51. History.com Editors, "Buffalo Soldiers," History, January 25, 2021, https://www.history.com/topics/westward-expansion/buffalo-soldiers?msclkid=5921e9a8bdc211ec8d05ec5e7ae2fd99.

4: "HIPPIES WERE THE GOOD GUYS, THE SEXUAL REVOLUTION WAS GREAT FOR WOMEN, AND THE VIETNAM WAR WAS UNPOPULAR AND POINTLESS"

1. Devin Friedman, "The Hippies Were Right After All," GQ, June 14, 2018, https://www.gq.com/story/the-hippies-won.

2. W. J. Rorabaugh, "Hippies Won the Culture War," History News Network, September 27, 2015, https://historynewsnetwork.org/article/160407.

3. Divine et al., America, Past and Present, 883, https://archive.org/details/americapastpreseooo2unse/page/882/mode/2up?view=theater.

4. Mark Atwood Lawrence, "The Disaster That Was the Vietnam War," New York Times, November 20, 2018, https://www.nytimes.com/2018/11/20/books/review/max-hastings-vietnam.html.

5. James Warren, "Vietnam: The Greatest Disaster in All of US Foreign Policy," Daily Beast, November 9, 2018, https://www.thedailybeast.com/vietnam-the-greatest-disaster-in-all-of-us-foreign-policy-2.

6. Philip Sheridan Foner, U.S. Labor and the Vietnam War (New York: International Publishers, 1989), 103, https://archive.org/details/uslaborvietnamwaoooofone/page/102/mode/2up?view=theater.

7. Rick Perlstein, "Then No One Would Be a Democrat Anymore," American Prospect, April 30, 2008, https://prospect.org/article/then-one-democrat-anymore/.

8. David Paul Kuhn, The Hardhat Riot: Nixon, New York City, and the Dawn of the White Working-Class Revolution (New York: Oxford University Press, 2020), https://www.amazon.com/Hardhat-Riot-Nixon-Working-Class-Revolution/dp/0190064714.

9. David Paul Kuhn, "The Day the Democrats Lost the White Working Class in a Hardhat Riot," Daily Beast, August 2, 2020, https://www.thedailybeast.com/the-day-the-democrats-lost-the-white-working-class-in-a-hardhat-riot.

10. Michael Lorenzini, "The Hard Hat Riots, May 8, 1970," *New York Times*, May 8, 2020, https://www.archives.nyc/blog/2020/5/8/the-hard-hat-riots.

11. Foner, *U.S. Labor and the Vietnam War*, 104.

12. By the fall of 1969, just before the Hard Hat Riot, a remarkable 84 percent of all American whites agreed with the statement that "college demonstrators were treated too leniently." Essentially the same percentage, 85 percent, believed that "black militants are treated too leniently." David Farber, "The Silent Majority and Talk About Revolution," in *The Sixties*, ed. David Farber (Chapel Hill: University of North Carolina Press, 1994), 298, https://archive.org/details/sixties0ouniv/page/298/mode2up?view=theater.

13. Frank Newport and Joseph Carroll, "Iraq Versus Vietnam: A Comparison of Public Opinion," Gallup, August 24, 2005, https://news.gallup.com/poll/18097/Iraq-Versus-Vietnam-Comparison-Public-Opinion.aspx.

14. Jennie Rothenberg Gritz, "The Death of the Hippies," *Atlantic*, July 8, 2015, https://www.theatlantic.com/entertainment/archive/2015/07/the-death-of-the-hippies/397739/.

15. Remy Melina, "Earth Day Co-Founder Killed, Composted Girlfriend," NBC, April 21, 2011. https://www.nbcnews.com/id/wbna42711922.

16. Tom Matthews, "The Tate Murders Newspaper Coverage," Historic Newspapers, October 25, 2021, https://www.historic-newspapers.com/blog/the-tate-murders-newspaper-coverage/.

17. Saul Austerlitz, "How the Hells Angels Split with Sixties Counterculture," CrimeReads, July 12, 2018, https://crimereads.com/how-the-hells-angels-split-with-sixties-counterculture/#:~:text=How%20the%20Hells%20Angels%20Split%20with%20Sixties%20Counterculture,local%20music%20scene%20and%20the%20working-class%20motorcycle%20enthusiasts.

18. Virginia Ironside, "'We Paid the Price for Free Love,'" *Daily Mail*, January 18, 2011, https://www.dailymail.co.uk/home/you/article-1346813/The-flip-1960s-sexual-revolution-We-paid-price-free-love.html.

19. Naomi Schaefer Riley, "'Free Love' Attitude of 1970s Sexualized Underage Girls," *New York Post*, March 6, 2016, https://nypost.com/2016/03/06/sick-legacy-of-70s-free-love-attitudes/.

20. Samuel Blumenfeld, "Liberal Parents, Radical Children," Libertarianism.org, February 1, 1976, https://www.libertarianism.org/publications/essays/liberal-parents-radical-children.

21. History.com Editors, "Communism Timeline," History, May 22, 2023, https://www.history.com/topics/russia/communism-timeline.

22. History.com Editors, "Domino Theory," History, November 9, 2022, https://www.history.com/topics/cold-war/domino-theory.

23. Prak Chan Thul, "Four Decades on, Cambodia Reflects on Its 'Killing Fields' Nightmare," Reuters, January 7, 2019, https://www.reuters.com/article/us-cambodia-rouge-idUSKCN1P10IT.

5: "THE FOUNDERS COUNTED SLAVES AS 'THREE-FIFTHS OF A PERSON' AND 'THE ONLY VICTIMS OF LYNCHINGS' WERE BLACK"

1. Kate Masur, "Lawmaker's Ridiculous Explanation for the Three-Fifths Compromise on Slavery," CNN, May 7, 2021, https://www.cnn.com/2021/05/07/opinions/tennessee-lawmaker-lafferty-bogus-interpretation-on-slavery-masur/index.html.

2. Alex Bollinger, "Tennessee Republican Defends Counting Black People as 3/5 of Human Beings," LGBTQ Nation, May 5, 2021, https://www.lgbtqnation.com/2021/05/tennessee-republican-defends-counting-black-people-3-5-human-beings/.

3. Theodore R. Johnson, "We Used to Count Black Americans as 3/5 of a Person. For Reparations, Give Them 5/3 of a Vote," *Washington Post*, August 21, 2015, https://www.washingtonpost.com/posteverything/wp/2015/08/21/we-used-to-count-black-americans-as-35-of-a-person-instead-of-reparations-give-them-53-of-a-vote/.

4. Carol Swain, "Why the 3/5ths Compromise Was Anti-Slavery," PragerU, July 22, 2018, https://www.prageru.com/video/why-the-threefifths-compromise-was-anti-slavery.

5. Sanford Levinson, "Three-Fifths Compromise Was an Understandable Deal on Slavery," *New York Times*, July 1, 2015, https://www.nytimes.com/roomfordebate/2013/02/26/the-constitutions-immoral-compromise/three-fifths-compromise-was-an-understandable-deal-on-slavery. This is one of five pieces published to debate the issue. Others argued the compromise was "understandable, if no less immoral" and "inevitable," and another posed a series of counterfactuals and then wishy-washily lamented the compromise. The fifth is the only one brave enough to outright say the Union wasn't worth the compromise and poses a relatively rosy counterfactual future where the South's slavery collapsed like that in Haiti. But even that writer asked elsewhere: "Could the Framers have ended slavery while creating a unified, 'more perfect Union'?" before admitting, "Certainly not. No one at the Convention envisioned a national government with the power to regulate social institutions at the local level. Moreover, any suggestion that the national government might end slavery in the states where it existed would have been promptly voted down." But he argues that way too much ground was given. Paul Finkelman, "The Founders and Slavery: Little Ventured, Little Gained," *Yale Journal of Law and the Humanities* 13, no. 2 (2001), https://ssrn.com/abstract=1432083.

6. Allen C. Guelzo, "The Constitution Was Never Pro-Slavery," *National Review*, April 18, 2019, https://www.nationalreview.com/magazine/2019/05/06/the-constitution-was-never-pro-slavery.

7. Rachel Sharp, "Ahmaud Arbery's Murderers Sentenced to Life in Prison for Federal Hate Crime," *Independent*, August 8, 2022, https://www.independent.co.uk/news/world/americas/crime/ahmaud-arbery-trial-gregory-mcmichaels-b1952385.html.

8. *Guardian* Staff, "Ahmaud Arbery's Murderers Sentenced to Life in Prison for Federal Hate Crime," *Guardian*, August 8, 2022, https://www.theguardian.com/us-news/2022/aug/08/travis-mcmichael-murderer-ahmaud-arbery-sentenced-life-federal-hate-crime.

9. Yahoo! News Video, "Harris: 'Lynching Is Not a Relic of the Past,'" Yahoo!, March 29, 2022, https:/ news.yahoo.com/harris-lynching-not-relic-past-213425219.html.

10. Divine et al., *America, Past and Present*, 477, https://archive.org/details/americapast preseo0002unse/page/476/mode/2up?view=theater.

11. The later editions of this text, in particular, go into heartrendingly gory detail about the actual process of lynching—again, almost entirely in the context of Black victims. One passage that can be viewed online reads: "A mob captured a black man and woman, their guilt or innocence unknown. They were tied to trees, and their fingers and ears were cut off as souvenirs. The most excruciating form of punishment consisted of a large corkscrew in the hands of some of the mob. This instrument was bored into the flesh of the man and woman, in the arms, legs, and body, and then pulled out—the spirals tearing out big pieces of raw, quivering flesh every time it was withdrawn. Finally, both

people were thrown on a fire and burned to death. "A relief," a witness said. Divine et al., *America, Past and Present*, 638, https://archive.org/details/americapastpreseooo2unse /page/638/mode/2up?view=theater.

12. Brinkley, *Unfinished Nation*, 375.

13. Douglas Linder, "Famous American Trials: Lynching," University of Missouri–Kansas City (UMKC) School of Law, accessed October 25, 2023, http://law2.umkc.edu/faculty /projects/ftrials/shipp/lynchingsstate.html.

14. Jason Johnson, "Why Violent Crime Surged After Police Across America Retreated," *USA Today*, April 9, 2021, https://www.usatoday.com/story/opinion/policing/2021/04 /09/violent-crime-surged-across-america-after-police-retreated-column/7137565002/.

15. Though, notably, extremely disparate racial violence was centralized in the Deep South: Virginia 17:83, Texas 141:352, Tennessee 47:204, South Carolina 4:156, North Carolina 15:86, Mississippi 42:539, Louisiana 56:335, Kentucky 63:142, Georgia 38:492, Florida 25:257, Arkansas 58:226, Alabama 48:299. Linder, "Famous American Trials."

16. Erin Blakemore, "The Grisly Story of One of America's Largest Lynching[s]," History, October 25, 2017, https://www.history.com/news/the-grisly-story-of-americas-largest -lynching.

17. Robert Gibson, *The Negro Holocaust: Lynching and Race Riots in the United States, 1880– 1950* (Yale–New Haven Teachers Institute, 2002), https://teachersinstitute.yale.edu /curriculum/units/1979/2/79.02.04.x.html.

18. Richard Emanuel, "Many Whites Were Lynched for Fighting Racism," *Montgomery Advertiser*, September 28, 2017, https://www.montgomeryadvertiser.com/story/opinion /2017/09/25/many-whites-were-lynched-fighting-racism-opinion/700690001/.

19. Comparable European rates can be compared at "Homicide Rate—Country Rankings," Global Economy, https://www.theglobaleconomy.com/rankings/homicide_rate/Europe.

20. Tariq Tahir, "Lynched and Driven from Their Land: Native Americans Are Pictured in Haunting Photos on the 100th Anniversary of Their Last Battle Against Settlers," *Daily Mail*, January 9, 2018, https://www.dailymail.co.uk/news/article-5250487/Photos -Native-Americans-100-years-battle.html.

21. Richard Delgado, "The Law of the Noose: A History of Latino Lynching," *Harvard Civil Rights–Civil Liberties Law Review* 44 (2009), University of Alabama Legal Studies Research Paper no. 2533521, available at https://ssrn.com/abstract=2533521.

22. "1623: Daniel Frank, the First Hanging in the USA," Executed Today, August 5, 2012, http://www.executedtoday.com/2012/08/05/1623-daniel-frank-the-first-hanging-in -the-usa/.

23. Richard Stack, *Dead Wrong: Violence, Vengeance, and the Victims of Capital Punishment* (New York: Bloomsbury, 2006).

24. Laura E. Randa, ed., *Society's Final Solution: A History and Discussion of the Death Penalty* (Lanham, MD: University Press of America, 1997), https://www.ojp.gov/ncjrs/virtual -library/abstracts/societys-final-solution-history-and-discussion-death-penalty.

25. Vincent Schilling, "The Traumatic True History and Name List of the Dakota 38," ICT News, December 26, 2020, https://indiancountrytoday.com/news/traumatic-true -history-full-list-dakota-38.

26. "Isaac Charles Parker (1838–1896)," *Encyclopedia of Arkansas*, July 26, 2023, https:// encyclopediaofarkansas.net/entries/isaac-charles-parker-1732/.

27. Jack Smith, "Page out of the Old West and a Poetic, Hanging Judge," *Los Angeles Times*, October 18, 1990, https://www.latimes.com/archives/la-xpm-1990-10-18-vw-3280-story .html.

28. History.com Editors, "First Execution by Lethal Gas," History, February 5, 2021, https://www.history.com/this-day-in-history/first-execution-by-lethal-gas.

29. "Kentucky," Death Penalty Info, April 14, 2022, https://deathpenaltyinfo.org/state-and-federal-info/state-by-state/kentucky.

30. Karl Vick, "An Execution in the Old Way," Washington Post, January 26, 1996, https://www.washingtonpost.com/archive/local/1996/01/26/an-execution-in-the-old-way/0fbf3f86-9ecd-4457-bb37-87ffd74018e6/.

31. This description of naval flogging sources to Gene Oleson, "Naval Discipline: Flogging," Dear Surprise, December 16, 2013, https://thedearsurprise.com/naval-discipline-flogging/?msclkid=9216e53bb5bc11ec9efa7593417f2ac3, which quotes the book Three-score Years by former U.S. sailor and naval carpenter Samuel F. Holbrook. From my reading, the boatswain's mate was the specific sailor generally designated as flogger.

32. Kara Goldfarb, "Keelhauling: Inside the Deranged Torture Method Used to Keep Sailors in Line," All That's Interesting, November 7, 2022, https://allthatsinteresting.com/keelhauling.

33. "Whipping Post Banned by New Delaware Law," New York Times, July 9, 1972, https://www.nytimes.com/1972/07/09/archives/whipping-post-banned-by-new-delaware-law.html?msclkid=38fe0e1bb5bd11ecb009bdda2e295924.

6: "EUROPEAN COLONIALISM WAS—EMPIRICALLY—A NO-GOOD, TERRIBLE, VERY BAD THING"

1. Nathan J. Robinson, "A Quick Reminder of Why Colonialism Was Bad," Current Affairs, September 14, 2017, https://www.currentaffairs.org/2017/09/a-quick-reminder-of-why-colonialism-was-bad.

2. Massimo Renzo, "Why Colonialism Is Wrong," Current Legal Problems 72, no. 1 (2019): 347–73, https://doi.org/10.1093/clp/cuz011https://academic.oup.com/clp/article-abstract/72/1/347/5610175?redirectedFrom=fulltext.

3. Erin Blakemore, "What Is Colonialism?," National Geographic, October 6, 2023, https://www.nationalgeographic.com/culture/article/colonialism.

4. Jon Henley, "Why Genghis Khan Was Good for the Planet," Guardian, January 26, 2011, https://www.theguardian.com/theguardian/2011/jan/26/genghis-khan-eco-warrior.

5. Bruce Gilley, "The Case for Colonialism: A Response to My Critics," Academic Questions 35, no. 1 (Spring 2022), https://doi.org/10.51845/35.1.14, https://www.nas.org/academic-questions/35/1/the-case-for-colonialism-a-response-to-my-critics.

6. Benjamin Robert Siegel, Hungry Nation: Food, Famine, and the Making of Modern India (Cambridge, UK: Cambridge University Press, 2016), 6.

7. Manu Saadia, "France Should Apologize for Colonialism in Algeria," Washington Post, February 2, 2017, https://www.washingtonpost.com/news/global-opinions/wp/2017/02/23/france-should-apologize-for-colonialism-in-algeria/.

8. Bentley et al., Traditions and Encounters, 264, https://archive.org/details/traditionsencounooobent_r2v5/page/264/mode/2up?view=theater.

9. Bentley et al., Traditions and Encounters, 42.

10. Gemma Berniell-Lee et al., Molecular Biology and Evolution 26, no. 7 (July 2009): 1581–89, https://doi.org/10.1093/molbev/msp069, https://academic.oup.com/mbe/article/26/7/1581/1123707.

11. Bentley et al., Traditions and Encounters, 534 and 537, https://archive.org/details/traditionsencounooobent_r2v5/page/534/mode/2up?view=theater.

12. Bruce Gilley, "The Case for Colonialism," *Third World Quarterly* (September 8, 2017), https://doi.org/10.1080/01436597.2017.1369037, https://web.pdx.edu/~gilleyb/2_The%20case%20for%20colonialism_at2Oct2017.pdf.

13. Gilley, "The Case for Colonialism," https://www.nas.org/academic-questions/35/1/the-case-for-colonialism-a-response-to-my-critics.

14. Chacour Koop, "Smithsonian Museum Apologizes for Saying Hard Work, Rational Thought Is 'White Culture,'" *Miami Herald*, July 17, 2020, https://www.miamiherald.com/news/nation-world/national/article244309587.html.

15. Bruce Thornton, "The Truth About Western 'Colonialism,'" Hoover Institution, July 21, 2015, https://www.hoover.org/research/truth-about-western-colonialism.

16. Tri Setiya, "13 Effects of Dutch Colonialism in Indonesia," Facts of Indonesia, https://web.archive.org/web/20210307081632/https://factsofindonesia.com/effects-of-dutch-colonialism-in-indonesia.

17. Samuel Adu-Gyamfi et al., "Public Heath in Colonial and Post-Colonial Ghana: Lesson-Drawing for the Twenty-First Century," *Studies in Arts and Humanities* 3, no. 1 (2017): 34–54, https://doi.org/10.18193/sah.v3i1.89.

18. Samuel Agyei-Mensah and Ama de-Graft Aikins, "Epidemiological Transition and the Double Burden of Disease in Accra, Ghana," *Journal of Urban Health* 87, no. 5 (September 1, 2019): 879–9, https://doi.org/10.1007/s11524-010-9492-y.

19. Bruce Gilley, "Chinua Achebe on the Positive Legacies of Colonialism," *African Affairs* 115, no. 461, (October 2016): 646–63, https://doi.org/10.1093/afraf/adw030, https://web.pdx.edu/~gilleyb/Achebe_Final_AsPublished.pdf.

20. Chinua Achebe, *There Was a Country: A Memoir* (New York: Penguin Books, 2013), 1, 14, https://archive.org/details/therewascountrymoooochin/page/336/mode/2up-?q=%22tension-prone+modern+states%22.

21. Sam Sturgis, "How Overlooked Colonial Railways Could Revolutionize Transportation in Africa," Bloomberg, February 2, 2015, https://www.bloomberg.com/news/articles/2015-02-02/how-overlooked-colonial-railways-could-revolutionize-transportation-in-africa.

22. Elias Biryabarema, "Uganda to Reopen Century-Old Rail Link After China Fails to Fund New Line," Reuters, August 4, 2023, https://www.reuters.com/world/africa/uganda-reopen-century-old-rail-link-after-china-fails-fund-new-line-2023-08-04/.

23. *Africa Review Report on Transport: A Summary*, United Nations Department of Economic and Social Council, September 29, 2009, https://sustainabledevelopment.un.org/content/documents/AfricanReviewReport-on-TransportSummary.pdf.

24. OChigbo, "The Other Side of Colonialism, Part 1," How Africans Underdeveloped Africa, July 21, 2020, https://hauda.org/2020/07/21/the-other-side-of-colonialism-part-1/.

25. Henley, "Why Genghis Khan Was Good for the Planet."

26. Donald Morris, *The Washing of the Spears: A History of the Rise of the Zulu Nation Under Shaka and Its Fall in the Zulu War of 1879* (New York: Da Capo Press, 1998).

27. "The Bantu Migration," History Guild, https://historyguild.org/early-africa/.

28. Evan Andrews, "7 Influential African Empires," History, January 11, 2017, updated July 19, 2020, https://www.history.com/news/7-influential-african-empires.

29. "Eswatini: Finance and Trade," *Encyclopedia Britannica*, accessed October 30, 2023, https://www.britannica.com/place/Eswatini/Finance-and-trade.

30. Hilda Kuper, *The Swazi: A South African Kingdom* (Fort Worth, TX: Harcourt Brace College Publishers, 1997).

31. "Country Facts," Permanent Mission of the Kingdom of Eswatini to the United Nations, https://www.un.int/eswatini/swaziland/country-facts.

32. "Mswati III," *Encyclopedia Britannica*, September 29, 2023, https://www.britannica.com/biography/Mswati-III.

33. "Dambisa Moyo on China in Africa," *American Outlook, Africa Rising*, Spring 2015, 49–50, https://www.sagamoreinstitute.org/wp-content/uploads/2020/08/China-in-Africa-articles-from-American-Outlook-Africa-Rising-Edition.pdf.

34. Ralph Jennings, "Charting the Future of China's Infrastructure Projects in Africa After a Decade of Lending," VOA News, December 15, 2021, https://www.voanews.com/a/charting-the-future-of-china-s-infrastructure-projects-in-africa-after-a-decade-of-lending-/6355784.html.

7: "AMERICAN USE OF NUKES TO END WORLD WAR TWO WAS 'EVIL' AND 'UNJUSTIFIED'"

1. Lee Mesika, "The Bombings of Hiroshima and Nagasaki: Plain Evil or a Necessary Evil?," Perspective, 2023, https://www.theperspective.com/debates/politics/bombings-hiroshima-nagasaki-necessary-evil-just-evil/.

2. Katherine E. McKinney, Scott D. Sagan, and Allen S. Weiner, "Why the Atomic Bombing of Hiroshima Would Be Illegal Today," *Bulletin of the Atomic Scientists*, July 1, 2020, https://thebulletin.org/premium/2020-07/why-the-atomic-bombing-of-hiroshima-would-be-illegal-today/.

3. Katie McKinney, Scott D. Sagan, and Allen S. Weiner, "Hiroshima and the Myths of Military Targets and Unconditional Surrender," *Lawfare Blog*, August 21, 2020, https://www.lawfareblog.com/hiroshima-and-myths-military-targets-and-unconditional-surrender.

4. Howard Levie, "The 1977 Protocol I and the United States," *Saint Louis University Law Journal* 38, no. 2 (Winter 1993–1994): 469–84, https://digital-commons.usnwc.edu/cgi/viewcontent.cgi?article=1483&context=ils.

5. "Potsdam Declaration," Atomic Archive, https://www.atomicarchive.com/resources/documents/hiroshima-nagasaki/potsdam.html.

6. Anne I. Harrington, "The Hiroshima Pilot Who Became a Symbol of Antinuclear Protest," *New York Times*, August 6, 2020, https://www.nytimes.com/2020/08/06/magazine/hiroshima-claude-eatherly-antinuclear.html.

7. Brinkley, *Unfinished Nation*, 694.

8. Mesika, "The Bombings of Hiroshima and Nagasaki."

9. Victor Davis Hanson, "60 Years Later," *National Review*, August 5, 2005, https://www.nationalreview.com/2005/08/60-years-later-victor-davis-hanson/.

10. "Kill All Prisoners Order," Wikisource, July 2, 2022, https://en.wikisource.org/wiki/Kill_All_Prisoners_Order.

11. Steve, "20 Horrific Details About Japanese POW Camps During World War II," History Collection, December 30, 2018, https://historycollection.com/20-horrific-details-about-japanese-pow-camps-during-world-war-ii/3/?msclkid=efa28f23b5d811eca2110639f96b5faf.

12. History.com Editors, "The Rape of Nanking," *History*, September 26, 2023, https://www.history.com/this-day-in-history/the-rape-of-nanking.

13. Ikuhiko Hata, *Nanking jiken: Gyakusatsu no kōzō* (Tōkyō: Chūō Kōron Shinsha, 2007), 197.

14. Steve, "20 Horrific Details."

15. Yuki Tanaka, *Hidden Horrors* (Boulder, CO: Westview Press, 1996), 121, https://archive.org/details/hiddenhorrorsjapooootana/page/126/mode/2up?q=systematic&view=theater.

16. Edward Russell, *The Knights of Bushido* (New York: Dutton, 1958), 240, https://archive.org/details/knightsofbushidoooooruss_i6w8/page/236/mode/2up?q=ram.

17. Tanaka, *Hidden Horrors*, 126–27.

18. Russell, *The Knights of Bushido*, 235–36.
19. Karl Compton, "If the Atomic Bomb Had Not Been Used," *Atlantic*, December 1946, https://www.theatlantic.com/magazine/archive/1946/12/if-the-atomic-bomb-had-not-been-used/376238/.
20. *Foreign Relations of the United States*, Diplomatic Papers, Volume II, the Conference of Berlin (the Potsdam Conference), 1945, ed. Richardson Dougall (Washington: Government Printing Office, 1960), Document 1382, https://history.state.gov/historicaldocuments/frus1945Berlinv02/d1382.
21. Paul Fussell, "Paul Fussell—'Thank God for the Atom Bomb,'" David Labaree on Schooling, History, and Writing, August 9, 2021, https://davidlabaree.com/2021/08/09/paul-fussell-thank-god-for-the-atom-bomb/.

8: "UNPROVOKED 'WHITE FLIGHT,' CAUSED BY PURE RACISM, RUINED AMERICA'S CITIES"

1. Leah Boustan, "The Culprits Behind White Flight," *New York Times*, May 15, 2017, https://www.nytimes.com/2017/05/15/opinion/white-flight.html.
2. Leah Platt Boustan, "Was Postwar Suburbanization 'White Flight'? Evidence from the Black Migration," *Quarterly Journal of Economics* 125, no. 1 (February 2010): 417–43, https://doi.org/10.1162/qjec.2010.125.1.417.
3. George C. Ohren, "The Coming Struggle," in *The Statesman*, vol. 5, Walter Thomas Mills and Andrew J. Jutkins, eds. (Chicago: Statesman Publishing), 147, https://books.google.com/books?id=oSQxAQAAMAAJ&printsec=frontcover&source=gbs_ge_summary_r&cad=0#v=onepage&q&f=false.
4. Brinkley, *Unfinished Nation*, 695.
5. Divine et al., *America, Past and Present*, 884.
6. Michelle Alexander, *The New Jim Crow: Mass Incarceration in the Age of Colorblindness* (New York: New Press, 2012), Study & Organizing Guides, https://newjimcrow.com/study-guides.
7. "Incarcerated Population by Type of Crime Committed," Britannica Pro Con, March 23, 2023, https://felonvoting.procon.org/incarcerated-felon-population-by-type-of-crime-committed/.
8. John Haltiwanger, "Biden Played Key Role in Pushing US to Take Hardline Stances on Crime in 1990s, and Now He's Apologizing as 2020 Looms," Business Insider, January 22, 2019, https://www.businessinsider.com/biden-apologizes-for-pushing-hardline-laws-on-crime-immigration-in-1990s-2019-1.
9. Robert A. Margo, "Explaining the Postwar Suburbanization of Population in the United States: The Role of Income," *Journal of Urban Economics* 31, no. 3 (May 1992): 301–10, https://www.sciencedirect.com/science/article/abs/pii/009411909290058S.
10. For interested wonks, Lawrence Thurston and Anthony M. J. Yezer come to similar conclusions in the same journal in 1994: "Causality in the Suburbanization of Population and Employment," *Journal of Urban Economics* 35, no. 1 (January 1994): 105–18.
11. Caplan, "The Prevalence of Marxism in Academia."
12. John U. Ogbu, *Black American Students in an Affluent Suburb: A Study of Academic Disengagement* (New York: Routledge, 2009).
13. John Lott Jr., *More Guns, Less Crime* (Chicago: University of Chicago Press, 2010).
14. Nathaniel Baum-Snow, "Did Highways Cause Suburbanization?," *Quarterly Journal of Economics* 122, no. 2 (May 2007): 775–805, https://doi.org/10.1162/qjec.122.2.775, https://academic.oup.com/qje/article/122/2/775/1942140.

15. John H. McWhorter, *Winning the Race Beyond the Crisis in Black America* (New York: Gotham Books, 2005).

16. Karen A. Kopecky and Richard M. H. Suen, "A Quantitative Analysis of Suburbanization and the Diffusion of the Automobile," *International Economic Review* 51, no. 4 (2010): 1003–37, http://www.jstor.org/stable/40929500.

17. See Samuel H. Kye, "The Persistence of White Flight in Middle-Cass Suburbia," *Social Science Research* 72 (2018): 38–52, https://www.sciencedirect.com/science/article /abs/pii/S0049089X17305422, both for an excellent page-long overview of the "racial proxy" idea and a critique of it. Interestingly, the author, sociologist Sam Kye, then of the University of Indiana at Bloomington, does find some evidence of continuing white flight today. However, this is apparently *more* prevalent in middle-class or well-off—and presumably conventionally liberal—suburban areas than in poorer ones, and seems to be at least as much a response to Latino and Asian migration as to Black migration. We will see, I suppose, if his results replicate.

18. Julie Berry Cullen and Steven D. Levitt, "Crime, Urban Flight, and the Consequences for Cities," *Review of Economics and Statistics* 81, no. 2 (May 1999): 159–69, https://doi .org/10.1162/003465399558030.

19. Mona Charen, *Do-Gooders: How Liberals Hurt Those They Claim to Help (and the Rest of Us)* (New York: Penguin, 2004).

20. "United States Population and Number of Crimes, 1960–2019," Disaster Center, accessed November 1, 2023, https://www.disastercenter.com/crime/uscrime.htm.

21. Kaitlyn Crain Enriquez, "April 1968 Washington, D.C. Riots," National Archives, April 5, 2023, https://unwritten-record.blogs.archives.gov/2023/04/05/april-1968 -washington-dc-riots/; Tony Briscoe and Ese Olumhense, "Rage, Riots, Ruin," *Chicago Tribune*, August 16, 2018, https://graphics.chicagotribune.com/riots-chicago-1968 -mlk/index.html; Margery Harriss, "Recalling Baltimore's 1968 Riots," *Baltimore Sun*, April 3, 1998, https://www.baltimoresun.com/news/bs-xpm-1998-04-03-1998093147 -story.html; Walter C. Rucker and James N. Upton, *Encyclopedia of American Race Riots* (Westport, CT: Greenwood, 2007), 107; "Final Report," Mayor's Commission on Civil Disorders, Kansas City, MO, August 15, 1968, https://mediaassets.kshb.com /pdf/Final%20Report%20Mayor's%20Commission%20on%20Civil%20Disorde .pdf?_ga=2.31884286.1100263164.1536088211-464552632.1531840984; Raymond Wolters, *The Burden of Brown: Thirty Years of School Desegregation* (Knoxville: University of Tennessee Press, 1984), 190.

22. Neil Steinberg, "The Whole World Watched: 50 Years After the 1968 Chicago Convention," *Chicago Sun-Times*, August 17, 2018, https://chicago.suntimes.com/2018/8 /17/18439080/the-whole-world-watched-50-years-after-the-1968-chicago-convention.

23. History.com Editors, "1968 Democratic Convention," History, March 16, 2018, https:// www.history.com/topics/1960s/1968-democratic-convention.

24. Bruce M. Tyler, "The 1968 Black Power Riot in Louisville, Kentucky," University of Louisville, November 20, 2008, https://web.archive.org/web/20060910011628 /http://www.louisville.edu/a-s/history/tyler/kentuckyriots.html.

25. Coleman Young, *Hard Stuff: The Autobiography of Mayor Coleman Young* (New York: Viking, 1994), 179.

26. In contrast, the increasing pre-riot integration appears to have reduced the population of the "D" only slightly. Between 1960 and 1970, the population of the city fell from 1,670,144 to 1,514,063—and bear in mind that the three post-riot years referenced by Mayor Young could seem to explain essentially all of this decline. The relevant numbers can be found here: Intergovernmental and Regional Affairs,

"Transit History of the Detroit Region," Michigan Legislature, https://legislature
.mi.gov/documents/2009-2010/CommitteeDocuments/House/Intergovernmental
%20and%20Regional%20Affairs/Testimony/Committee13-3-31-2009.pdf.

27. "*Swann v. Charlotte-Mecklenburg Board of Education*," Oyez, accessed October 30, 2023,
www.oyez.org/cases/1970/281.

28. "Gallup Finds Few Favor Busing for Integration," *New York Times*, September 9, 1973,
https://www.nytimes.com/1973/09/09/archives/gallup-finds-few-favor-busing-for
-integration.html.

29. David Frum, *How We Got Here: The 70's, the Decade That Brought You Modern—for
Better or Worse* (New York: Basic Books, 2000), 255.

30. Frum, *How We Got Here*, 257–58.

31. Frum, *How We Got Here*, 263.

32. "Busing, Segregation, and Education Reform in Boston," Poverty USA, https://www
.povertyusa.org/stories/busing-segregation-and-education-reform-boston. Boston is
by no means some low-performing outlier in terms of racial diversity and comity. The
equivalent figure for the Chicago Public Schools—the famous "CPS" in my original
hometown—stands at 11 percent. That data, as well as a range of other striking income
and aptitude figures, can be accessed: "Demographics: Racial/Ethnic Report, 2023–
2024," Chicago Public Schools, October 4, 2023, https://www.cps.edu/about/district
-data/demographics/#a_racial-ethnic-report.

33. Johnson, "Why Violent Crime Surged After Police Across America Retreated."

34. Wilfred Reilly, "Did the BLM Protests Against the Police Lead to the 2020 Spike in
Homicides?," Quillette, January 27, 2021, https://quillette.com/2021/01/27/did-the
-blm-protests-against-the-police-lead-to-the-2020-spike-in-homicides/.

35. German Lopez, "The Rise in Murders in the US, Explained," Vox, December 2, 2020,
https://www.vox.com/2020/8/3/21334149/murders-crime-shootings-protests-riots
-trump-biden.

36. Sarah Holder et al., "The Precipitous Drop of Police Traffic Stops in Minneapolis,"
Bloomberg, September 14, 2020, https://www.bloomberg.com/graphics/2020
-minneapolis-police-stops/.

37. Kelly Bauer and Mark Konkol, "Chicago Police Stops Down by 90 Percent as Gun
Violence Skyrockets," DNA Info, March 31, 2016, https://www.dnainfo.com/chicago
/20160331/bronzeville/chicago-police-stops-down-by-90-percent-as-gun-violence
-skyrockets/.

38. Azadeh Ansari and Rosa Flores, "Chicago's 762 Homicides in 2016 Is Highest in
19 Years," CNN, January 2, 2017, https://www.cnn.com/2017/01/01/us/chicago-murders
-2016/index.html.

39. Chris Dorsey, "America's Mass Migration Intensifies as 'Leftugees' Flee Blue States and
Counties for Red," *Forbes*, March 17, 2021, https://www.forbes.com/sites/chrisdorsey
/2021/03/17/americas-mass-migration-intensifies-as-leftugees-flee-blue-states-and
-counties-for-red/.

40. While Dorsey's piece stands out, it is worth noting that several authors have made
this point for publications across the ideological spectrum—and even across the pond.
James Gordon is also worth a quick read: James Gordon, "The Blue Exodus," *Daily
Mail*, January 14, 2021, https://www.dailymail.co.uk/news/article-9686593/Americans
-flee-liberal-coastal-cities-New-York-California-favor-red-states-Arizona-Idaho.html.

41. "QuickFacts: Denver County, Colorado," Census, https://www.census.gov/quickfacts
/denvercountycolorado.

42. "75 Denver Police Officers Injured During Black Lives Matter Protests and Riots," Fox 31, June 21, 2020, https://kdvr.com/news/local/75-denver-police-officers-injured-during-george-floyd-protests-and-riots/.

9: " 'SOUTHERN STRATEGY' RACISM TURNED THE SOLID SOUTH REPUBLICAN"

1. Mary Beth Norton et al., *A People and a Nation*, vol. 2: *Since 1865*, Brief Tenth Edition (Boston: Cengage, 2015), 806.

2. Kennedy, *American Pageant*, 880.

3. Norton et al., *A People and a Nation*, 770–71.

4. John A. Powell, "The New Southern Strategy," *Othering and Belonging Institute* (blog), https://belonging.berkeley.edu/new-southern-strategy.

5. Amy Sherman, "Candace Owens' False Statement That the Southern Strategy Is a Myth," Politifact, April 10, 2019, https://www.politifact.com/factchecks/2019/apr/10/candace-owens/candace-owens-pants-fire-statement-southern-strate/.

6. Entertainingly, illegal immigration did in fact hit all-time highs just two years later under President Joe Biden, who beat Trump to win the 2020 election. Nick Miroff, "Border Arrests Have Soared to All-Time High, New CBP Data Shows," *Washington Post*, October 20, 2021, https://www.washingtonpost.com/national/border-arrests-record-levels-2021/2021/10/19/289dce64-3115-11ec-a880-a9d8c009a0b1_story.html.

7. Sarakshi Rai, "What Is the 'Dark Brandon' Meme That Has Taken the White House by Storm?," *Hill*, August 9, 2022, https://thehill.com/homenews/3594308-what-is-the-dark-brandon-meme-that-has-taken-the-white-house-by-storm/.

8. "Clayton Bigsby, the World's Only Black White Supremacist—Chappelle's Show," Comedy Central, November 11, 2019, https://www.youtube.com/watch?v=BLNDqxrUUwQ.

9. Erika D. Smith, "Column: Larry Elder Is the Black Face of White Supremacy. You've Been Warned," *LA Times*, August 20, 2021, https://www.latimes.com/california/story/2021-08-20/recall-candidate-larry-elder-is-a-threat-to-black-californians.

10. Carol Swain, "The Inconvenient Truth About the Democratic Party," PragerU, May 22, 2017, https://www.prageru.com/video/the-inconvenient-truth-about-the-democratic-party.

11. That phrase is a reference to this book, which describes similar heroic efforts a bit further down the United States' historical time line: Robert F. Williams, *Negroes with Guns* (Detroit: Wayne State University Press, 1998).

12. Clark L. Maxam and MaryCarol B. Maxam, "Democrat/GOP Vote Tally on 1964 Civil Rights Act," *Wall Street Journal*, December 31, 2002, https://www.wsj.com/articles/SB1041302509432817073.

13. "Dixiecrat," *Encyclopedia Britannica*, October 25, 2023, https://www.britannica.com/topic/Dixiecrat; Evan Andrews, "Why Is the South Known as 'Dixie'?," History, November 28, 2018, https://www.history.com/news/why-is-the-south-known-as-dixie.

14. Kari Fredrickson, *The Dixiecrat Revolt and the End of the Solid South, 1932–1968* (Chapel Hill, NC: The University of North Carolina Press, 2001), 3–7, https://archive.org/details/dixiecratrevolte0000fred_z5d7/mode/2up?view=theater.

15. "Strom Thurmond," *Encyclopedia Britannica*, June 22, 2023, https://www.britannica.com/biography/Strom-Thurmond.

16. Kevin D. Williamson, "The Party of Civil Rights," *National Review*, May 21, 2012, https://www.nationalreview.com/2012/05/party-civil-rights-kevin-d-williamson/.

17. John Hinderaker, "What Did Lee Atwater Really Say?," *Powerline Blog*, June 9, 2013, https://www.powerlineblog.com/archives/2013/06/what-did-lee-atwater-really-say.php.

18. Justin Steinhauer, "William Julius Wilson Discusses 'The Declining Significance of Race' on Voice of America's Press Conference USA," *Library of Congress Blogs*, July 2, 2015, https://blogs.loc.gov/kluge/2015/07/william-julius-wilson-discusses-the-declining-significance-of-race-on-voice-of-americas-press-conference-usa/.

19. Adolph Reed Jr. "The 2004 Election in Perspective: The Myth of 'Cultural Divide' and the Triumph of Neoliberal Ideology," *American Quarterly* 57, no. 1 (March 2005): 1–15, https://www.jstor.org/stable/40068247.

20. Timothy Noah, "'Acid, Amnesty, and Abortion': The Unlikely Source of a Legendary Smear," *New Republic*, October 22, 2012, https://newrepublic.com/article/108977/acid-amnesty-and-abortion-unlikely-source-legendary-smear.

21. Henry Griffin, "Nixon's Record on Civil Rights," Richard Nixon Foundation, August 4, 2017, https://www.nixonfoundation.org/2017/08/nixons-record-civil-rights-2/.

22. Wallace Garneau, "The Myth of the 'Southern Strategy,'" Daily Libertarian, February 6, 2019, http://thedailylibertarian.com/the-myth-of-the-southern-strategy/.

23. Dan McLaughlin, "The Southern Strategy Myth and the Lost Majority," RedState, July 11, 2012, https://redstate.com/dan_mclaughlin/2012/07/11/the-southern-strategy-myth-and-the-lost-majority-n43726.

24. Byron E. Shafer and Richard Johnston, *The End of Southern Exceptionalism: Class, Race, and Partisan Change in the Postwar South* (Cambridge, MA: Harvard University Press, 2009).

25. Clay Risen, "The Myth of 'the Southern Strategy,'" *New York Times*, December 10, 2006, https://www.nytimes.com/2006/12/10/magazine/the-myth-of-the-southern-strategy.html.

26. Wendell Cox, "Measuring Current Metropolitan Area Growth from 1900," New-Geography, November 11, 2014, https://www.newgeography.com/content/004767-measuring-current-metropolitan-area-growth-1900.

27. Nelson Polsby, "Institutional Change in the U.S. Congress," Berkeley Institute of International Studies, September 3, 2002, https://iis.berkeley.edu/publications/nelson-polsby-institutional-change-uscongress.

28. Ezra Klein, "Did the Invention of the Airplane End the Filibuster?," *Washington Post Voices*, November 13, 2009, https://web.archive.org/web/20210515025042/http://voices.washingtonpost.com/ezra-klein/2009/11/did_the_invention_of_the_airpl.html.

10: BONUS LIE: THE CONTINUING OPPRESSION NARRATIVE

1. Deroy Murdock, "Black Lives Matter's Numbers Are Bogus," *New York Post*, November 6, 2015, https://nypost.com/2015/11/06/black-lives-matters-numbers-are-bogus/.

2. "BBQ Becky: Woman Photoshopped into Black History After Barbecue Complaint," BBC, May 18, 2018, https://www.bbc.com/news/newsbeat-44167760.

3. Tom Cleary, "Jennifer Schulte, 'BBQ Becky': 5 Fast Facts You Need to Know," Heavy, May 17, 2018, https://heavy.com/news/2018/05/jennifer-schulte-bbq-becky/.

4. https://twitter.com/ElieNYC/status/1374385601504440331.

5. Dave McMenamin, "LeBron James Says Black Community 'Terrified' of Police Conduct," ABC News, August 25, 2020, https://abcnews.go.com/Sports/lebron-james-black-community-terrified-police-conduct/story?id=72590427.

6. The SRC's remarkable and sometimes hilarious report can be accessed here: https://www.skeptic.com/research-center/reports/Research-Report-CUPES-007.pdf. As will be discussed later in this chapter, the actual number of specifically Black, specifically unarmed men killed in the United States during a typical year varies between 10 and 30.

7. Wilfred Reilly, "The New Definition of Racism," *Commentary*, May 2022, https://www .commentary.org/articles/wilfred-reilly/racism-ibram-x-kendi/.

8. Sean Rameswaram and Lauren Katz, "Professor Ibram X. Kendi on Why It's Not Enough to Admit When You're Being Racist: 'Challenge Those Racist Ideas,'" Vox, June 1, 2020, https://www.vox.com/2020/6/1/21277220/george-floyd-protests-ibram-x -kendi-today-explained.

9. "Why Cultural Appropriation Isn't Cool," ReachOut, https://au.reachout.com/articles /why-cultural-appropriation-isnt-cool.

10. I will note that two organizations with which I am involved, the center-right Black-led 1776 Unites initiative and the Foundation Against Intolerance and Racism, have produced alternative curricula—both well received by scholars and parents, if less effusively praised by the national media: "1776 Unites Educates," 1776 Unites, https://1776unites.org/our-work/curriculum/; "Fairness, Understanding & Humanity in the Field of K–12 and Higher Education," Foundation Against Intolerance and Racism, https://www.fairforall.org/fair-in-education.

11. "BLM's 7 Demands," Black Lives Matter, accessed October 13, 2023, https://blacklivesmatter .com/blm-demands/.

12. "902 People Have Been Shot and Killed by Police in the Past 12 Months," *Washington Post*, updated October 23, 2023, accessed October 31, 2023, https://www.washingtonpost .com/graphics/investigations/police-shootings-database/.

13. Here, we may indeed have seen a small "BLM" effect: there were only eleven police shootings of unarmed Black citizens in 2021, and just seven had taken place by the late fall/early winter of 2022, according to the above *Washington Post* source. However, it is worth again pointing out that the police pull-back likely responsible for this resulted in the United States reaching a post-1995 high of more than 20,000 murders. Johnson, "Why Violent Crime Surged After Police Across America Retreated."

14. Mohamad Moslimani et al., "Facts About the U.S. Black Population," Pew Research Center, March 2, 2023, https://www.pewresearch.org/social-trends/fact-sheet/facts-about -the-us-black-population/.

15. Roland G. Fryer Jr. "An Empirical Analysis of Racial Differences in Police Use of Force," *Journal of Political Economy* 127, no. 3 (2019): 1210–61, https://scholar.harvard .edu/fryer/publications/empirical-analysis-racial-differences-police-use-force.

16. Only Asian Americans broke this pattern, and this group did so to a fairly remarkable extent. In 2018–2019, almost 25 percent of attacks on U.S. Asians were committed by whites, 27.5 percent were committed by Blacks, 21.4 percent were committed by Hispanics and by "other" groups such as Native Americans . . . and just 24 percent were committed by Asians! While "white supremacy" by no means seems to be the driving force here—to put it mildly—the phenomenon of thugs of all ethnic backgrounds seeking out Asian American targets in U.S. cities is a real one: Wilfred Reilly, "Crime Against Asians Isn't Due to White Supremacy," *Commentary*, May 2021, https://www.commentary.org/articles/wilfred-reilly/crime-against-asians-isnt -due-to-white-supremacy/.

17. Some of the "race cuts in the wrong direction" stories that linger ignored on the AP wire are fairly remarkable. In June of 2022, popular Caucasian high school athlete Ethan Liming was beaten to death by three older African American males *in the parking lot of LeBron James's I Promise High School* after shooting one of them with a "Splatrball Water Bead Blaster" toy: Leah Barkoukis, "LeBron James Silent After Arrests Made in Murder of Teen at His Akron School," Townhall, June 14, 2022, https://townhall.com /tipsheet/leahbarkoukis/2022/06/14/lebron-james-school-murder-n2608653. While

nothing indicates that race was the primary factor at work in this case—a brawl followed the Super Soaking—the victim's father has mentioned it as a factor, and it is all too easy to imagine the national reaction were the races reversed.

18. U.S. Census Bureau, "Selected Population Profile in the United States," American Community Survey, ACS 1-Year Estimates Selected Population Profiles, Table S0201, 2022, accessed on October 30, 2023, https://data.census.gov/table/ACSSPP1Y2022 .S0201?q=American+Community+Survey&t=-A0.

19. Katherine Schaeffer, "The Most Common Age Among Whites in U.S. Is 58—More Than Double That of Racial and Ethnic Minorities," Pew Research Center, July 30, 2019, https://www.pewresearch.org/fact-tank/2019/07/30/most-common-age-among -us-racial-ethnic-groups/.

20. "State Performance Compared to the Nation," Nation's Report Card, https://www .nationsreportcard.gov/profiles/stateprofile?chort=2&sub=MAT&sj=AL&sfj=NP &st=MN&year=2022R3.

21. Scott Jaschik, "New SAT, Old Gaps on Race," Inside Higher Ed, September 26, 2017, https://www.insidehighered.com/news/2017/09/27/scores-new-sat-show-large-gaps -race-and-ethnicity.

22. Wilfred Reilly, "The New Definition of Racism," *Commentary*, May 2022, https://www .commentary.org/articles/wilfred-reilly/racism-ibram-x-kendi/.

23. June O'Neill, "The Role of Human Capital in Earnings Differences between Black and White Men," *Journal of Economic Perspectives* 4, no. 4 (Fall 1990): 25–45, https://www .aeaweb.org/articles?id=10.1257/jep.4.4.25; June O'Neill and Dave M. O'Neill, "What Do Wage Differentials Tell Us About Labor Market Discrimination?," National Bureau of Economic Research Professional Working Papers - #w11240, https://www.nber.org /system/files/working_papers/w11240/w11240.pdf.

24. Dinesh D'Souza, *The End of Racism: Principles for a Multi-Racial Society* (New York: Free Press, 1995).

25. Roland Fryer, "An Empirical Analysis of Racial Differences in Police Use of Force," National Bureau of Economic Research Professional Working Paper 22399, https:// scholar.harvard.edu/files/fryer/files/empirical_analysis_tables_figures.pdf.

26. U.S. Department of Justice: Office of Justice Programs, Bureau of Justice Statistics, "Criminal Victimization, 2018," National Crime Victimization Survey, Tables 1, 14, 15, https://bjs.ojp.gov/content/pub/pdf/cv18.pdf.

27. "Police Officer Demographics and Statistics in the USA," Zippia Statistics, accessed December 15, 2023, https://www.zippia.com/police-officer-jobs/demographics/.

28. Mike Schneider, "The Census Bureau Sees an Older, More Diverse America in 2100, in Three Immigration Scenarios," Associated Press, November 9, 2023, https://apnews .com/article/growth-population-demographics-race-hispanic-f563ebc4537f83792f3f91 ba5d7cdade.

29. "Earnings of Men Aged 20–59, by Age Group and Race/Ethnicity, 2020–2021," Research, Statistics, and Policy Analysis Office—Social Security Administration, accessed December 12, 2023, https://www.ssa.gov/policy/docs/factsheets/at-a-glance/earnings -men-age-race-ethnicity.html.

INDEX

ABOUT THE AUTHOR

Wilfred Reilly is an associate professor of political science at Kentucky State University. He has written for and contributed to *Newsweek*, *Commentary*, *Tablet*, Spiked, Quillette, *National Review*, and *Academic Questions*, among other outlets.